The **MAILBOX**®

W9-BGI-605

**Grades 4–5**

# Building Math Basics

**The core math skills fourth and fifth graders need!**

- **Number Sense**

- **Addition and Subtraction of Larger Numbers**

- **Basic Multiplication and Division Facts**

- **Multiplication and Division of Larger Numbers**

- **Fractions**

- **Decimals**

- **Geometry**

- **Measurement**

- **Data Analysis and Graphing**

**And much, much more!**

Peaches
$0.99 lb.

Manufactured in the United States
10  9  8  7  6  5  4  3  2  1

**www.themailbox.com**

# Table of Contents

## Number and Operations

## Geometry

# Measurement

# Data Analysis and Probability

# Algebra

# Building Math Basics

**Managing Editor:** Debra Liverman

**Editorial Team:** Becky S. Andrews, Kimberley Bruck, Karen P. Shelton, Diane Badden, Thad H. McLaurin, Lauren E. Cox, Peggy W. Hambright, Sherry McGregor, Karen A. Brudnak, Sarah Hamblet, Hope Rodgers, Dorothy C. McKinney, Marcia Barton, Jacqueline Beaudry, Melissa Bryan, Ann E. Fisher, David A. Green, Liz Harrell, Terry Healy, Ann Hefflin, Kim A. Howe, Elizabeth H. Lindsay, Kim Minafo, Cindy Mondello, Jennifer Otter, Lauren Zavisca, Tammie Babbitt, Jenny Barrington, Brooke Beverly, Kim Bostick, Sara Burnett, Francine Camino, Chris Christensen, Lydia Conard, Colleen Dabney, Jill Davis, Drew Deapo, Margo Dill, Judy Edwards, Michelle Ehrich, Sharon M. Fisher, Linda Gosnell, Trease Gould, Shawna Graham, Melody Hazelton, Lindsay Hennarichs, Carey Hightower, Jim Hutcheson, Judy Kaegi, Julie Kaiser, Elaine Kaplan, Karen Kovalcik-Schiffel, Shannon Long, Lisa M. Mellon, Sandy Norton, Rebecca O'Bryon, Lisa Odom, Clara O'Sullivan, Kirsten Perry, Barbara Peters, Leah Reeve, Marsha Schmus, Patty Slagel, Jan Smith, Christy Stortz, Kristi Titus, Dianne Wade, Jennifer Wood

**Production Team:** Lisa K. Pitts, Pam Crane, Rebecca Saunders, Jennifer Tipton Cappoen, Chris Curry, Sarah Foreman, Theresa Lewis Goode, Ivy L. Koonce, Clint Moore, Greg D. Rieves, Barry Slate, Donna K. Teal, Tazmen Carlisle, Amy Kirtley-Hill, Kristy Parton, Debbie Shoffner, Cathy Edwards Simrell, Lynette Dickerson, Mark Rainey, Clevell Harris

# Number Sense

## Go Fish!

This variation of Go Fish will reel student pairs into reinforcing number forms! In advance, make four copies of page 8 on tagboard and cut apart the cards. For each game card, program each round with a different number in written or expanded form. (Repeat a digit no more than twice in one round.) Store the cards along with the directions below in a resealable plastic bag and then place the bag at a center. Guide pairs of students through the directions to play the game. For additional practice with number forms, see the reproducible on page 9.

**Object of the game:** to make the standard form of the number for that round

### To play:

1. Each player selects a game card.
2. One player shuffles the numeral cards and stacks them facedown on the playing surface.
3. Each player draws seven numeral cards.
4. Player 1 asks Player 2 for a numeral that he needs to form his Round 1 number.
5. If Player 2 has this numeral, he gives it to Player 1 and Player 1 takes another turn. If not, he says, "Go Fish!" and Player 1 draws a card from the pile.
6. If Player 1 has all the numeral cards needed to make his number, he lays down the cards for Player 2 to check. If not, Player 2 takes a turn.
7. Play continues in this manner until one player forms his number. Then both players return their numeral cards to the pile.
8. Players repeat Steps 2–7 for each remaining round of play.

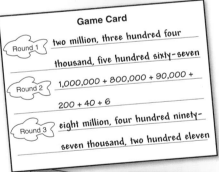

**Game Card**

| | |
|---|---|
| Round 1 | two million, three hundred four thousand, five hundred sixty-seven |
| Round 2 | 1,000,000 + 800,000 + 90,000 + 200 + 40 + 6 |
| Round 3 | eight million, four hundred ninety-seven thousand, two hundred eleven |

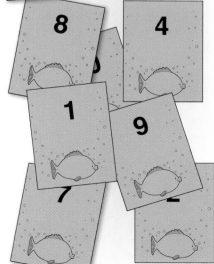

# Mystery Numbers

Clue students in to number sense with this whole-class game. Think of a number between 1,000 and 1,000,000 and secretly write it on a sheet of paper. Then write a series of clues (see the example) to help students determine the mystery number. After reading aloud all the clues, have a student volunteer identify the number by writing it in standard form on the board. As a class, use the clues to verify the written number. Then pair your students and ask each pair to think of its own mystery number and clues. Next, have each pair, in turn, read aloud its clues and challenge the class to identify the mystery number.

---

Mystery Number: 24,689

Clues:
- When rounded to the nearest thousand, my number is 25,000.
- The hundreds digit is 6.
- The ones digit is 9.
- The value of the tens digit is 80.

---

# Rounding Reminder

Students can sing their way to remembering the rule of estimation using rounding with this simple song. Introduce the song by singing it as you model how to estimate using rounding. Then have students softly sing the song as they practice rounding a few numbers themselves.

Estimation
(sung to the tune of "Alouette")

Estimation, we know estimation.
Rounding numbers, that's the way to go!

Underline the place value.
Then you see the one next door.
One next door—five or more?
Round it up or else ignore!
Estimation!

Estimation, we know estimation.
Rounding numbers, that's the way to go!

# Bringing Numbers to Order

Review both rounding and ordering numbers with this fast-paced game. Divide students into groups of four and give each student a blank card. To begin, direct each child to write a six-digit number near the top left-hand corner of his card. Then call out a place value, such as thousands. Have the student circle that place value in his number, round his number to that place, and write his rounded number beside it. Next, call out, "Bring your numbers to order!" Give the members in each group one minute to arrange their cards in order from least to greatest according to the rounded numbers. Check each group's arrangement, awarding one point for each correctly rounded number and three points if its cards are arranged correctly. To play additional rounds, have students cross out the numbers from the previous round. Continue play in a similar manner, varying the requested number of digits and the place value. The group with the most points at the end of the game is the winner.

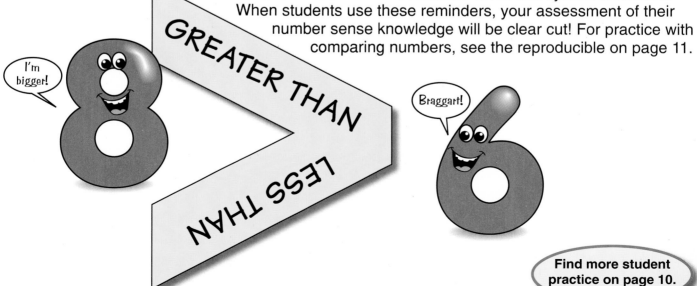

# Symbol Solution

Do your students mix up inequality symbols when comparing numbers? This easy-to-make reminder clears up any confusion! Die-cut a letter *V* for each student in your class. Distribute the letters and have each student label one as shown. Model how to position the symbol so that "GREATER THAN" is readable when that symbol is needed and "LESS THAN" is readable when that symbol is needed. When students use these reminders, your assessment of their number sense knowledge will be clear cut! For practice with comparing numbers, see the reproducible on page 11.

Find more student practice on page 10.

# Numeral and Game Cards
Use with "Go Fish!" on page 5.

**Game Card**

Round 1 _____

_____

Round 2 _____

Round 3 _____

_____

Name_____  Date _____

# Unlucky Ladybug

Lana got her friends' tickets for the Ladybug Raffle all mixed up!
Read the written form of the raffle number for each of her friends.
Find its matching standard form on a ticket and write the name on
the line. The first one has been done for you.

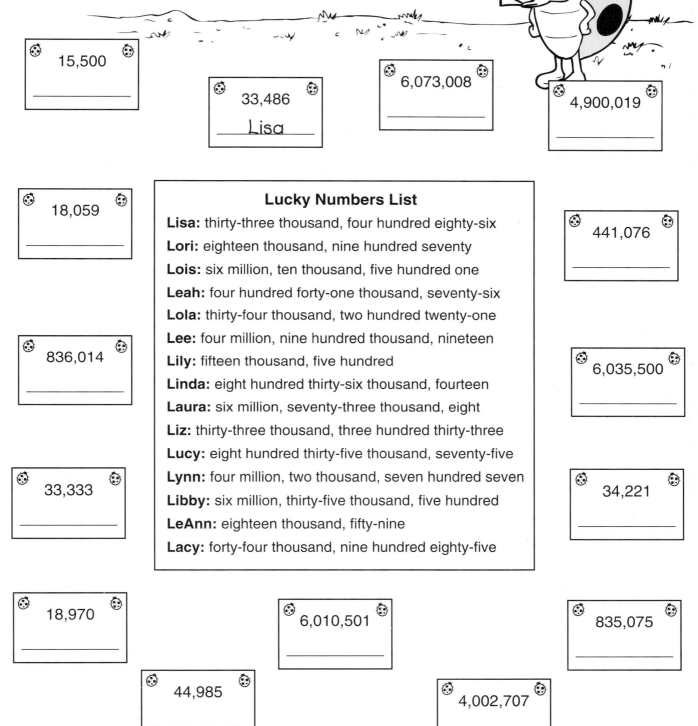

15,500

_____

33,486

_Lisa_

6,073,008

_____

4,900,019

_____

18,059

_____

441,076

_____

### Lucky Numbers List

**Lisa:** thirty-three thousand, four hundred eighty-six

**Lori:** eighteen thousand, nine hundred seventy

**Lois:** six million, ten thousand, five hundred one

**Leah:** four hundred forty-one thousand, seventy-six

**Lola:** thirty-four thousand, two hundred twenty-one

**Lee:** four million, nine hundred thousand, nineteen

**Lily:** fifteen thousand, five hundred

**Linda:** eight hundred thirty-six thousand, fourteen

**Laura:** six million, seventy-three thousand, eight

**Liz:** thirty-three thousand, three hundred thirty-three

**Lucy:** eight hundred thirty-five thousand, seventy-five

**Lynn:** four million, two thousand, seven hundred seven

**Libby:** six million, thirty-five thousand, five hundred

**LeAnn:** eighteen thousand, fifty-nine

**Lacy:** forty-four thousand, nine hundred eighty-five

836,014

_____

6,035,500

_____

33,333

_____

34,221

_____

18,970

_____

6,010,501

_____

835,075

_____

44,985

_____

4,002,707

_____

Name_____ Date _____

# Peg's Patchwork Pattern

Peg is working on a new quilt pattern. Follow the directions below
to color the pieces to show the pattern.

**If a number has**
    a 1 in the tens place, color it green
    a 2 in the hundred thousands place, color it purple
    a 4 in the hundreds place, color it yellow
    a 5 in the ten thousands place, color it brown
    a 9 in the thousands place, color it blue
    a 3 in the ten thousands place, color it red
    a 6 in the ones place, color it orange
    an 8 in the millions place, color it black

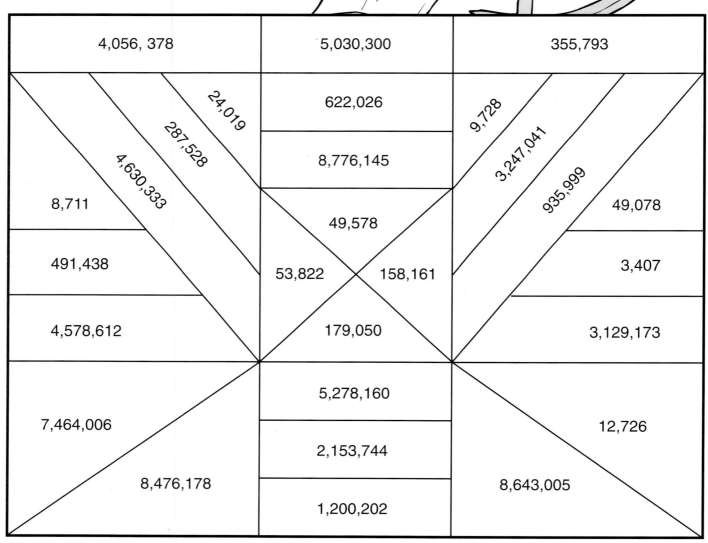

| 4,056, 378 | 5,030,300 | 355,793 |

24,019
287,528
4,630,333
622,026
8,776,145
9,728
3,247,041
8,711
935,999
49,078
491,438
49,578
3,407
53,822   158,161
4,578,612
179,050
3,129,173
7,464,006
5,278,160
12,726
2,153,744
8,476,178
8,643,005
1,200,202

Name_____    Date _____

# Dare to Compare

Compare each pair of numbers. Write < or > in the circle and color a matching strawberry below.

1. 4,785 ◯ 4,875

2. 1,021 ◯ 1,012

3. 26,345 ◯ 25,345

4. 69,096 ◯ 69,906

5. 80,430 ◯ 80,420

6. 47,942 ◯ 47,944

7. 101,558 ◯ 100,585

8. 266,732 ◯ 256,739

9. 380,460 ◯ 308,640

10. 874,215 ◯ 874,218

11. 670,472 ◯ 679,471

12. 534,000 ◯ 533,900

13. 2,040,200 ◯ 1,040,200

14. 3,577,557 ◯ 3,757,557

15. 8,063,216 ◯ 8,036,210

16. 1,111,001 ◯ 1,111,010

17. 5,564,218 ◯ 5,654,228

18. 3,795,090 ◯ 3,759,070

19. 6,600,060 ◯ 6,660,060

20. 9,758,216 ◯ 9,658,220

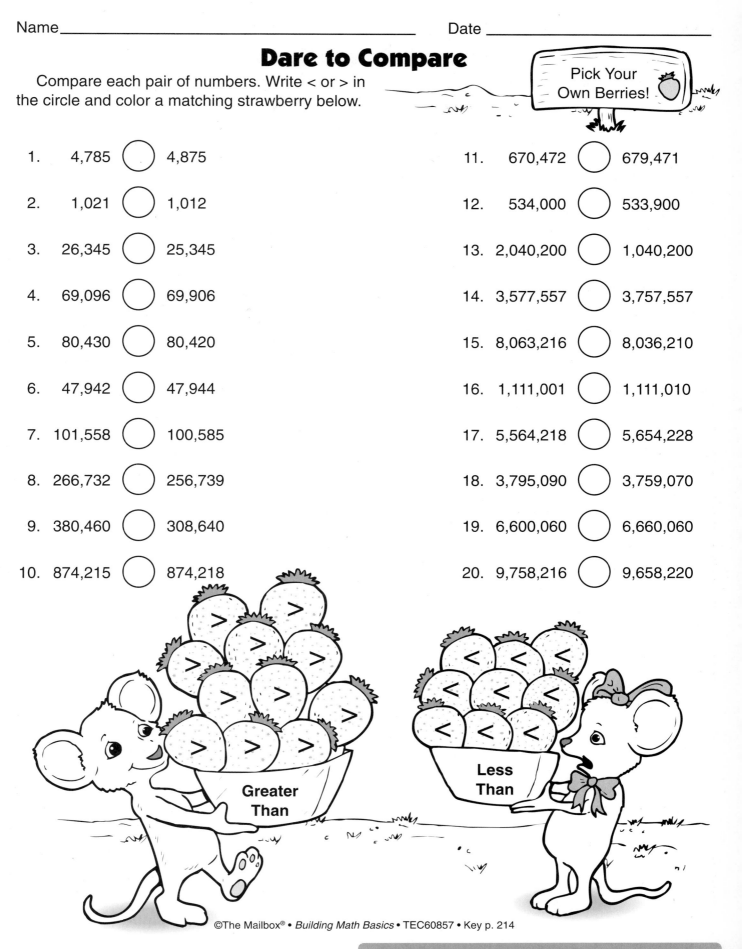

Greater Than

Less Than

# Equivalent Forms

## Easy-to-See Equivalents

Students will see the relationship between fractions and decimals with this small-group activity. Divide students into groups, giving each group four coffee filters, a ruler, and scissors. Guide the groups through the steps below to prepare their filters. Next, model how to identify equivalent fractions and decimals by placing one or more cutout decimal sections atop the fraction-labeled circles. For example, have each group name the fractions that equal 0.25 by placing one decimal section (0.25) on each appropriate fraction circle. Point out that 0.25 covers one section labeled "$\frac{1}{4}$" and two sections labeled "$\frac{1}{8}$." Therefore, 0.25 is equal to $\frac{1}{4}$ and $\frac{2}{8}$. Repeat, using two decimal sections to model 0.50, three sections for 0.75, and all four sections for 1.00. If desired, have each group divide another filter into fourths, label each section "25%," and cut the sections apart. Students can use the cutouts to identify equivalent fractions, decimals, and percents.

**To prepare filters:**
Filter 1: Fold it in half. Draw a dividing line and label each section "$\frac{1}{2}$."
Filter 2: Fold it into fourths. Draw dividing lines and label each section "$\frac{1}{4}$."
Filter 3: Fold it into eighths. Draw dividing lines and label each section "$\frac{1}{8}$."
Filter 4: Fold it into fourths and cut apart on fold lines. Label each section "0.25."

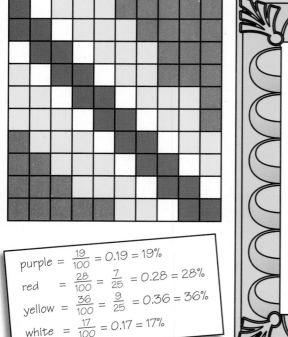

purple $= \frac{19}{100} = 0.19 = 19\%$

red $= \frac{28}{100} = \frac{7}{25} = 0.28 = 28\%$

yellow $= \frac{36}{100} = \frac{9}{25} = 0.36 = 36\%$

white $= \frac{17}{100} = 0.17 = 17\%$

## Picture This

This kid-pleasing activity lets students color their way to practicing equivalent forms. Give each student a 10 x 10 grid cut from ½-inch graph paper, a small index card, and glue. Instruct each child to make a design by coloring squares on the grid, using at least three colors and leaving fewer than 20 squares white. On the index card, have him write the number of squares for each color as a fraction of 100. Then guide the child to write each fraction in simplest terms, as a decimal, and as a percent. Post the grids and cards on a bulletin board titled "Picture This: Equivalent Forms."

# Flowering Fractions

Watch students' knowledge of equivalent forms grow with this partner activity. In advance, program one three-inch construction paper circle with a fraction in simplest form for every two students. Then divide students into pairs and give each duo a programmed circle, construction paper, scissors, markers or crayons, and glue. Explain that the circle will be the center of a flower. Next, have each pair cut out five to eight flower petals and label each with a decimal, percent, or fraction that is equivalent to the fraction on the circle. Direct each pair to glue its petals to the circle to complete its flower. If desired, prepare extra circles for early finishers. Display the completed flowers below the title "Equivalencies in Bloom."

$\frac{15}{40}$

0.25

$\frac{1}{4}$

25%

0.250

$\frac{6}{16}$

# Recipe for Success

This mouthwatering activity helps students write equivalent fractions, mixed numbers, and decimals. In advance, ask each student to bring in a copy of her favorite recipe. (Provide several extra recipes for students who forget.) Then display a recipe's ingredients list on an overhead transparency. Model how to rewrite the ingredients list, replacing each fraction and whole number with an equivalent decimal. Next, give each student an index card on which to copy her recipe's ingredients list using equivalent decimals. Finally, have students switch cards with a classmate and convert the amounts back to fraction form on another sheet of paper. After students check their answers against the original recipes, have them switch cards with additional classmates.

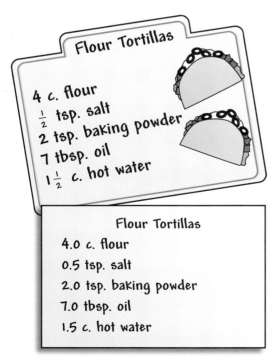

**Flour Tortillas**

4 c. flour
$\frac{1}{2}$ tsp. salt
2 tsp. baking powder
7 tbsp. oil
$1\frac{1}{2}$ c. hot water

### Flour Tortillas

4.0 c. flour

0.5 tsp. salt

2.0 tsp. baking powder

7.0 tbsp. oil

1.5 c. hot water

**Find more student practice on pages 14–17.**

Name_____  Date _____

# Dessert Dilemma

Help Baker Bill fill each bakery order. For each dessert on an order, list the equivalent fraction and how many pieces Bill needs. Use the sample desserts at the top of the page to help you.

Cookies

Cake    Pie

### ①

| dessert | fraction | pieces |
|---|---|---|
| 50% of a cake | | |
| 50% of a pie | | |
| 50% of a dozen cookies | | |

### ②

| dessert | fraction | pieces |
|---|---|---|
| 0.40 of a cake | | |
| 0.75 of a pie | | |
| 0.75 of a dozen cookies | | |

### ③

| dessert | fraction | pieces |
|---|---|---|
| 100% of a cake | | |
| 25% of a pie | | |
| 75% of a dozen cookies | | |

### ④

| dessert | fraction | pieces |
|---|---|---|
| 0.1 of a cake | | |
| 1.0 of a pie | | |
| 0.25 of a dozen cookies | | |

Name_____ Date_____

# Celebrate!

Color by the code.

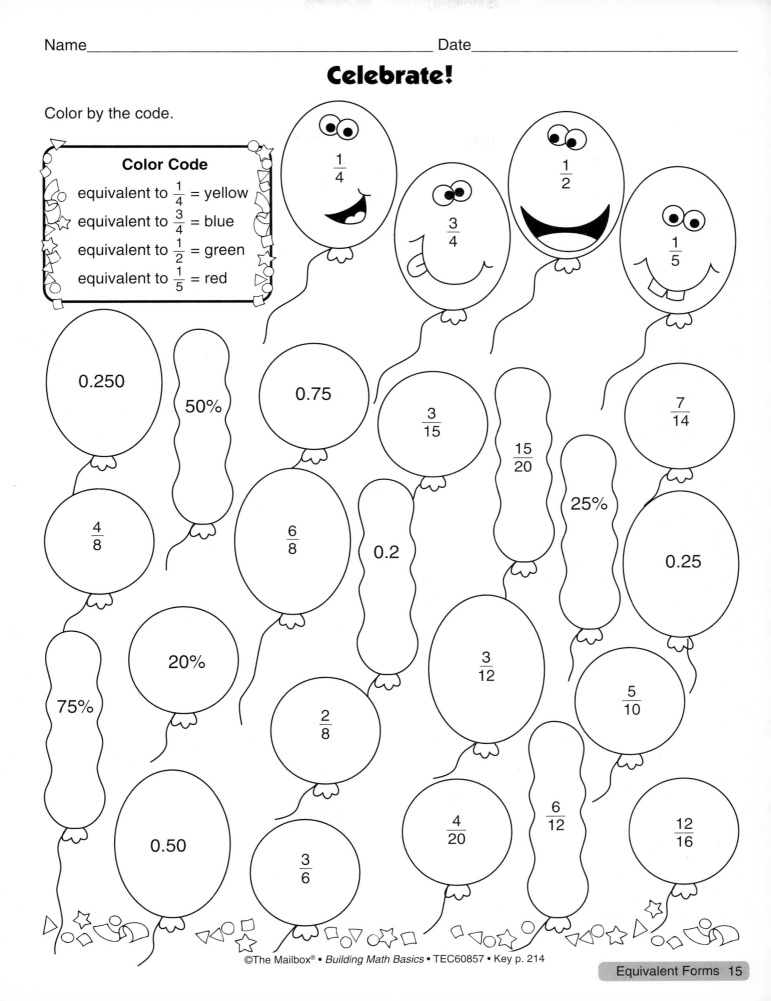

$\frac{1}{4}$

$\frac{3}{4}$

$\frac{1}{2}$

$\frac{1}{5}$

0.250

50%

0.75

$\frac{3}{15}$

$\frac{15}{20}$

$\frac{7}{14}$

$\frac{4}{8}$

$\frac{6}{8}$

0.2

25%

0.25

75%

20%

$\frac{3}{12}$

$\frac{5}{10}$

$\frac{2}{8}$

0.50

$\frac{3}{6}$

$\frac{4}{20}$

$\frac{6}{12}$

$\frac{12}{16}$

Name_____    Date_____

# "Eggs-tra" Special Equivalents

Complete the chart below.
Then use the chart to answer the questions.

**Fraction  Decimal  Percent**

| Fraction | Decimal | Percent |
|---|---|---|
|  |  | 20% |
|  | 0.5 |  |
| $\frac{1}{4}$ |  |  |
|  | 0.75 |  |

E. Clara used $\frac{1}{4}$ of a dozen eggs to make cookie dough. What percent of the eggs did she use? _____

O. Hanna dropped 0.75 of a dozen eggs. What percent of a dozen eggs did she drop? _____

T. Roger scrambled 0.25 of the eggs. What fraction of the eggs are left? _____

K. Roger boiled $\frac{2}{4}$ of a dozen eggs. What percent of the eggs did he have left? _____

A. Clara and Hanna are making potato salad with 50% of a dozen eggs. What decimal shows the amount of eggs that will not be used? _____

L. Roger and Hanna tried tossing eggs to each other. They broke $\frac{1}{5}$ of the eggs they used. What percent of the eggs broke? _____

Y. Clara played catch by herself and caught 0.75 of a dozen eggs she tossed. What fraction of the eggs did she drop? _____

## Why shouldn't you tease egg whites?
To find out, write the letter in the matching blank.

They can't ____ ____ ____ ____    ____    " ____ ____ ____ ____!"
           $\frac{3}{4}$   0.5  50%  25%    0.5    $\frac{1}{4}$  75%  20%  50%

Name_____ Date _____

# Plenty of Pizza

Pepper's pizza party was a big hit! Shade each pizza to show what part of a pizza each person ate. Then write the equivalent fraction on the line.

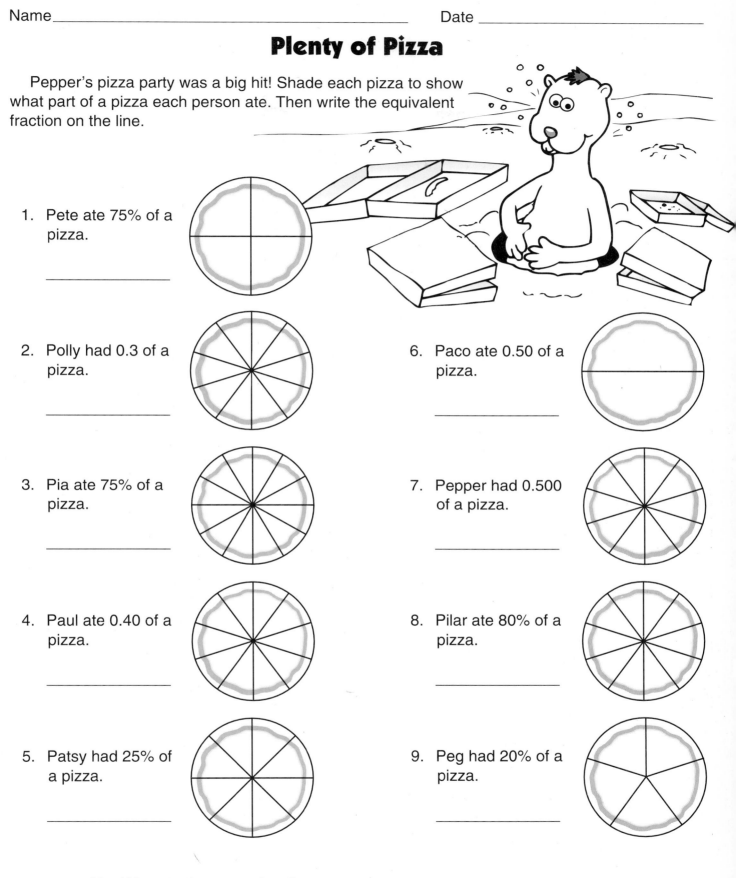

1. Pete ate 75% of a pizza.

_____

2. Polly had 0.3 of a pizza.

_____

3. Pia ate 75% of a pizza.

_____

4. Paul ate 0.40 of a pizza.

_____

5. Patsy had 25% of a pizza.

_____

6. Paco ate 0.50 of a pizza.

_____

7. Pepper had 0.500 of a pizza.

_____

8. Pilar ate 80% of a pizza.

_____

9. Peg had 20% of a pizza.

_____

10. Who ate the most pizza? _____

# Adding Larger Numbers

$$321$$
$$+ 527$$

## Correct or Incorrect?

This independent learning center is a bushel of fun! First, gather two baskets and a supply of laminated apple cutouts. Label one basket "Correct" and the other basket "Incorrect." Next, use an overhead marker to write an addition problem on each cutout, varying the skills to match your students' needs. Divide the cutouts in half and solve one half of the problems correctly. On the other half, write incorrect solutions. Then place the cutouts and the baskets in a center. To use the center, a student chooses an apple, checks the addition problem, and places the cutout in the appropriate basket. Throughout the year, wipe the apples clean and reprogram them with a fresh set of problems.

# Four in a Row

This variation on a popular game adds up to fun! Draw a 6 x 6 grid on the board as shown. Next, divide the class into four teams: A, B, C, and D. Have one student from each team come to the board and close her eyes. On the board, write four identical addition problems. Then direct each child to open her eyes and solve one of the problems. The first student to correctly solve the problem writes her team's letter anywhere on the grid. Continue playing in this manner until one team connects four of its symbols in a vertical, horizontal, or diagonal row.

# Puzzling Pieces

Here's a small-group activity that will easily fit into your lesson plans! Divide your class into groups of three students. Give each group 15 small index cards and a resealable bag or envelope. On a scrap sheet of paper, have each group make up and solve five addition problems containing three-, four-, or five-digit numbers. Next, instruct one student from each group to copy each addend and each solution from the problems onto a separate index card as shown. Have the group label the addend cards "A" and the solution cards "S." Then direct the group to shuffle its cards and place them in the bag. On your signal, have each group switch bags with another group and try to piece the addition problems back together correctly. Remind students that two "A" cards should add up to an "S" card. Allow group members to check each other's work before switching puzzles with a different group.

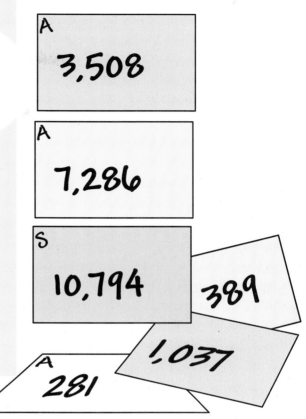

## Fun With Birthdays

Use students' birthdays to reinforce adding larger numbers. Divide students into groups of three or four, and give each student a sticky note. Have each student write his birthday in number form on the note and place it in the center of the group's workspace. For example, July 29 would be 729 and December 3 would be 1203. Then direct each student to find the sum of all the birthdays in his group, showing his work on a sheet of paper. Instruct each group to verify that all its members arrived at the same solution. Next, challenge groups with a variety of questions such as the following: Which two birthdays result in the smallest sum? The largest? Can you add any three birthdays together to get a sum greater than 2,000? Finally, reconfigure the groups by having some players switch groups or by combining two groups and repeat the activity.

**Find more student practice on pages 20–25.**

Name_____  Date _____

# Marathon Maze

Add. Show your work on another sheet of paper. Color each correct problem. Connect the colored boxes to show the path to the cheese.

23 + 69 = 92

94 + 37 = 121

62 + 27 = 79

45 + 27 = 72

56 + 73 = 129

62 + 43 = 95

73 + 49 = 132

86 + 35 = 121

**Finish**

22 + 97 = 118

75 + 40 = 105

29 + 66 = 95

99 + 88 = 188

39 + 17 = 56

85 + 13 = 97

59 + 46 = 105

47 + 78 = 135

81 + 22 = 103

30 + 95 = 125

# Beautiful Blooms

Add. Write the missing number in each box. Each time you use a number, color a matching flower.

1.  639
   + 23□
   ‾‾‾‾‾
    871

2.  1□7
   + 951
   ‾‾‾‾‾
   1,108

3.   47□
   + 642
   ‾‾‾‾‾
   □,□18

4.  532
   + 18□
   ‾‾‾‾‾
   □19

5.  420
   +□□□
   ‾‾‾‾‾
   845

6.  □04
   + 3□6
   ‾‾‾‾‾
   1,01□

7.  3□5
   + □4□
   ‾‾‾‾‾
   918

8.  41□
   + 4□5
   ‾‾‾‾‾
   903

9.  □88
   + 5□6
   ‾‾‾‾‾
   1,40□

10. 5□7
   + □6□
   ‾‾‾‾‾
   1,217

11.  29□
   + □26
   ‾‾‾‾‾
   1,2□4

12.  876
   + 5□3
   ‾‾‾‾‾
   1,□1□

13.  251
   + □8□
   ‾‾‾‾‾
   4□0

14.  17□
   + □27
   ‾‾‾‾‾
   9□3

15.  5□□
   + □58
   ‾‾‾‾‾
   1,313

Name_____     Date _____

# Piles and Piles

Add the numbers on each pile of leaves to find the sum.
Show your work on another sheet of paper.

341  117  214  209  121  119

Sum _____ (E)

256  197  948  398  796  595

Sum _____ (B)

507  170  159  192  115  186

Sum _____ (M)

993  909  103  441  291  136

Sum _____ (E)

146  157  220  508  149  155

Sum _____ (Y)

401  177  338  219  188  506

Sum _____ (F)

230  182  251  425  117  205

Sum _____ (E)

711  624  408  572  194  312

Sum _____ (A)

305  983  712  233  624  141

Sum _____ (E)

**What did the caterpillar say when it saw the huge pile of leaves?**

To answer the question, match each letter to a numbered line below.

I can't "  ___  ___  –  L  ___  ___  ___  "
           3,190  2,998      1,410  2,821  1,829

___  ___  Y                ___  ___  ___  S  !
1,329              1,121  1,135  2,873

©The Mailbox® • *Building Math Basics* • TEC60857 • Key p. 214

# Wheel of Wonder

Add. Write each answer in the corresponding boxes on the Ferris wheel. The first one has been done for you. (Hint: The first digit in each answer is the same as the last digit of the previous problem's answer.)

1.  214
    741
  + 107
    1,062

2.  791
    332
  + 980

3.  608
    815
    724
  + 901

4.  266
    48
    463
  + 99

5.  316
    21
    225
  + 79

6.  124
    376
    502
  + 180

7.  21
    65
    88
  + 43

8.  2,315
    806
  + 4,790

9.  33
    24
    13
  + 56

10. 1,742
    1,407
    2,856
  + 172

11. 218
    305
    93
    54
  + 61

12. 512
    372
  + 407

13. 756
    120
    46
  + 81

14. 723
    999
    711
  + 601

15. 251
    36
    93
  + 41

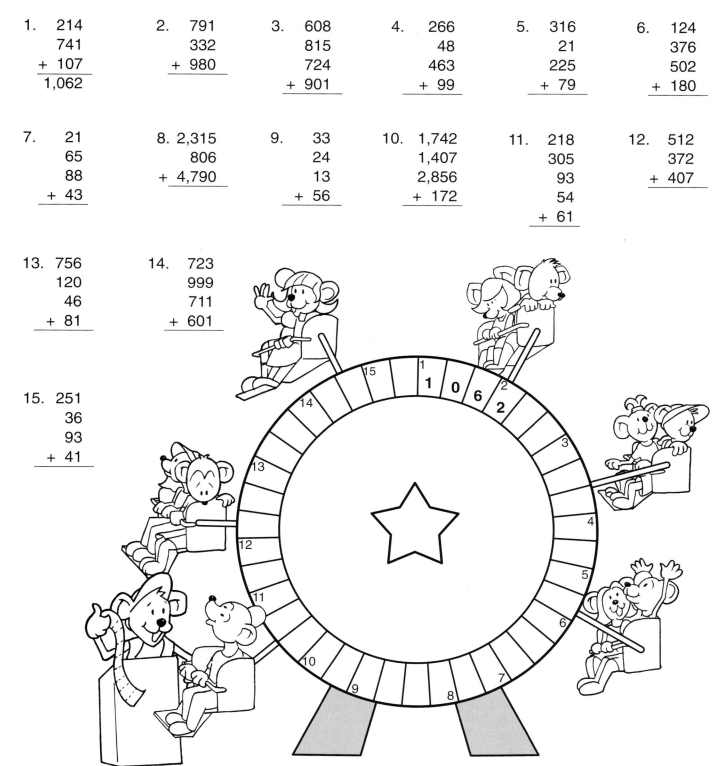

# Wheels of Your Own

You have $30,000 to create your own dream car! Choose a body, a set of wheels, a motor, and a paint color from the choices below. Keep track of the money you spend on the invoice below.

| Choices | | | |
|---|---|---|---|
| **Body** | **Wheels** | **Motor** | **Color** |
| truck $21,000 | chrome: 4 for $3,000 | racing motor fast $5,000 | black $3,000 |
| SUV $20,000 | silver: 4 for $2,000 | V-8 motor  powerful $4,000 | silver $2,500 |
| sports car $19,000 | silver: 4 for $2,000 | V-6 motor  average $3,500 | red $2,400 |
| sedan $16,000 | basic: 4 for $1,600 | 4-cylinder motor slow but great on gas $3,000 | dark blue $1,500 |

| Invoice | | |
|---|---|---|
| | Choice | Price |
| Body | | |
| Wheels | | |
| Motor | | |
| Color | | |
| Must be under $30,000. | **Total** | |

# Imagine This

Solve.
Show your work on another sheet of paper.

1. Your hardest subject is math, and you made an A. Your parents gave you $50 for your hard work. You go shopping and choose sneakers for $23 and a CD for $15. You also want to buy a gift that costs $10 for a friend.

   Do you have enough money to buy all three items?

   _____

2. You're hosting a party for your best friend. You want to buy decorations for $12 and a cake for $9. You also want chips for $4, soda for $3, and ice cream for $5.

   If you have $35, can you buy these items?

   _____

3. You invite your friends over one afternoon. You order a pizza for $11 and rent your favorite movie for $5. Then you go to an arcade to play video games and spend $6.

   How much total money did you spend?

   _____

4. Your family goes on vacation. You buy $6 T-shirts for five friends. You also buy two mugs for $4 each and you buy a book, which costs $8, for your grandparents.

   How much total money did you spend?

   _____

5. You buy a new coat for $48 and a video game for $13. You also buy a magazine for $5 and school supplies for $8. Your final purchase is something you've wanted for a long time, which costs $25.

   How much total money did you spend? _____

Adding Larger Numbers: story problems 25

# Subtracting Larger Numbers

## Subtraction Jar

Give the estimation jar a brand-new purpose with this weekly challenge! First, fill a jar with a unique item—such as toothpicks, cotton balls, or rubber bands—being sure to count the items. Next, instruct each student to set up an estimation log as shown. Then have each student estimate the number of items in the jar. Explain that the jar will remain on display for one week, during which time the student can revise his estimate. At the end of the week, announce the actual count. Instruct the student to find the difference between this number and his estimate and record it in his log. Fill the jar with a new item each week and repeat this process. After a predetermined number of weeks, have each student add up the numbers in his difference column. Name the student with the lowest total the best estimator!

| Date | Item | Estimate | Actual Count | Difference |
|------|------|----------|--------------|------------|
| 11-4 | cotton balls | 327 | 412 | 85 |
| | | | | |
| | | | | |
| | | | | |
| | | | | |
| | | | | |
| | | | | |

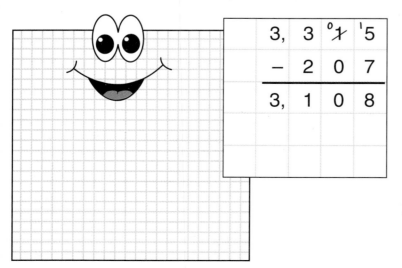

$$\begin{array}{r} 3,3\overset{0}{\cancel{4}}\,{}^{1}5 \\ -\ 2\ 0\ 7 \\ \hline 3,1\ 0\ 8 \end{array}$$

## Grid Guidance

Keep grids or graph paper on hand to help the student who has a hard time keeping her numbers lined up when subtracting. Show the student how to set up her subtraction problem by writing one digit in each box and lining up the digits in the ones, tens, hundreds, and thousands places. Then, as she solves the problem, she can focus on subtracting, not on lining up the numbers.

# Road Trip

27

Map out great subtraction skills with a fun road trip! In advance, collect a road atlas or map of the United States for every four students in your class. Also program a strip of paper with a number between 700 and 900 for each group. Then divide students into small groups and have each group draw a strip. Explain that the group will take an imaginary journey and that the number drawn determines how many miles it can travel on a round trip. Instruct each group to write an itinerary, listing each city on its route, the approximate number of miles to the city, and a subtraction equation that shows the round-trip mileage less the miles traveled between cities. If desired, have each group switch itineraries with another group and check its subtraction. Congratulate the team whose round trip came closest to its original number of miles.

**825**

Group 1
leave Peoria, IL
arrive Bloomington, IL

$$825 \text{ miles} - 37 \text{ miles} = 788 \text{ miles}$$

leave Bloomington, IL
arrive Springfield, IL

$$788 \text{ miles} - 65 \text{ miles} = 723 \text{ miles}$$

## Destination: Zero

All your students need to play this high-rolling subtraction game is dice, paper, and pencils! Pair students and then guide them through the steps below.

**Steps:**

1. Player 1 rolls the die four times, recording each digit rolled. She then arranges the digits to make the largest number possible and subtracts that number from 70,000.
2. Player 2 checks Player 1's answer and then takes a turn in the same manner.
3. Play continues for ten rounds.
4. The player whose final difference is closer to zero at the end of the game is the winner.

**Sylvia**

**Round 1**
5, 6, 4, 3
$$70,000 - 6,543 = 63,457$$

**Round 2**
3, 4, 2, 3
$$- 4,332 = 59,125$$

**Round 3**

**Deion**

**Round 1**
5, 1, 1, 6
$$70,000 - 6,511 = 63,489$$

**Round 2**
3, 2, 6, 1
$$- 6,321 = 57,168$$

**Round 3**

**Find more student practice on pages 28–33.**

# How Many?

Subtract.

How many times can you subtract 10 from 95?

(T) 89 – 22 = _____

(N) 73 – 31 = _____

(J) 96 – 66 = _____

(A) 94 – 13 = _____

(H) 55 – 41 = _____

(G) 75 – 55 = _____

(O) 35 – 23 = _____

(U) 19 – 13 = _____

(I) 55 – 40 = _____

(C) 48 – 37 = _____

(R) 99 – 17 = _____

(D) 21 – 11 = _____

(S) 88 – 67 = _____

(M) 53 – 30 = _____

(W) 78 – 56 = _____

(E) 37 – 35 = _____

(P) 58 – 45 = _____

(Q) 79 – 27 = _____

(B) 27 – 11 = _____

(L) 66 – 21 = _____

Help Ally Gator solve the riddle by matching the circled letters to the numbered lines below.

— BECAUSE

___ ___ ___ ___ , ___ ___ ___ ___ ___ ___ ___ ___ ___ ___ ___ ___ ___ ___ ___
12  42  11  2     67  21     81     22  14  12  15  67  14  2   45  12  42

___ ___ ___ ___ ___ ___ ___ !
15  67     2  52  6  81  67

___ ___ ___ ___ ___ ___ ___ ___
2  45  12  42     42  2  22

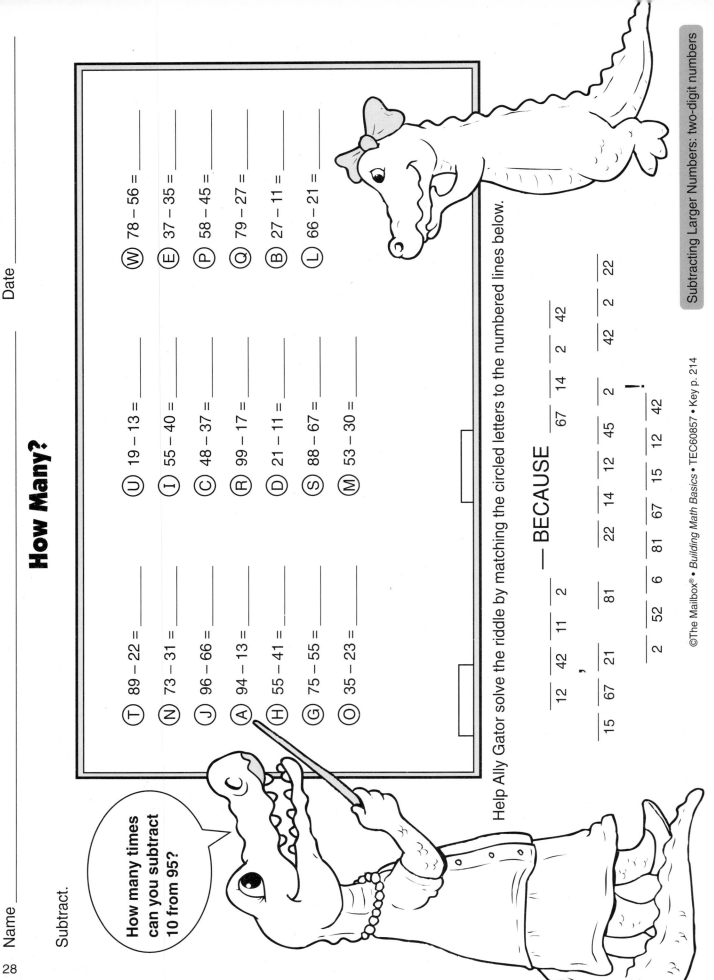

Name _____   Date _____

# Snorkel Time!

Round each number to its highest place value. Then subtract. Cross out the matching answer in the answer bank. The first one has been done for you.

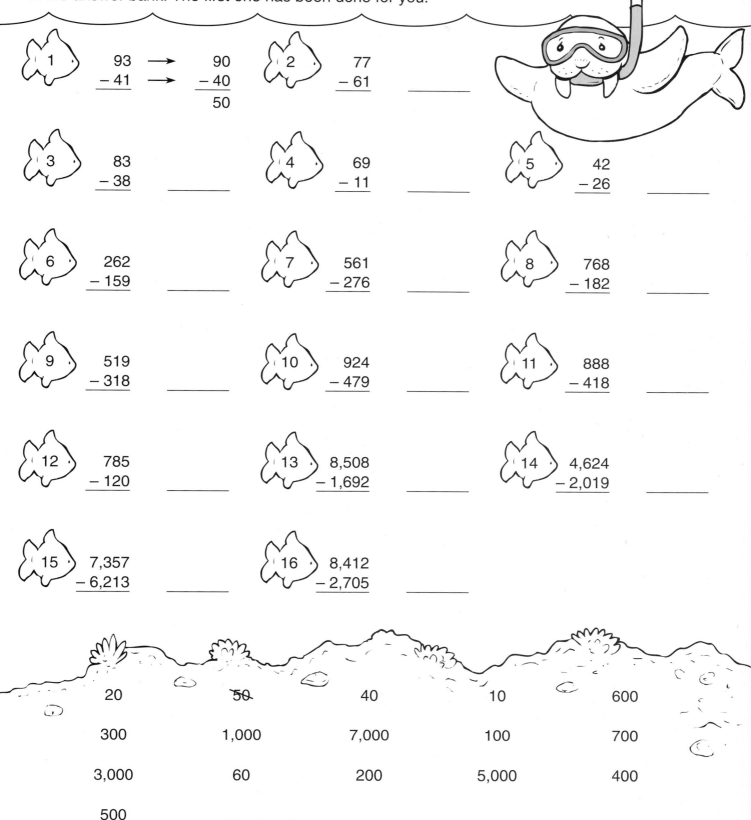

1.  $93 \rightarrow 90$
    $-41 \rightarrow -40$
    $50$

2.  $77$
    $-61$
    _____

3.  $83$
    $-38$
    _____

4.  $69$
    $-11$
    _____

5.  $42$
    $-26$
    _____

6.  $262$
    $-159$
    _____

7.  $561$
    $-276$
    _____

8.  $768$
    $-182$
    _____

9.  $519$
    $-318$
    _____

10. $924$
    $-479$
    _____

11. $888$
    $-418$
    _____

12. $785$
    $-120$
    _____

13. $8,508$
    $-1,692$
    _____

14. $4,624$
    $-2,019$
    _____

15. $7,357$
    $-6,213$
    _____

16. $8,412$
    $-2,705$
    _____

Answer bank:

| 20 | 50 | 40 | 10 | 600 |
| 300 | 1,000 | 7,000 | 100 | 700 |
| 3,000 | 60 | 200 | 5,000 | 400 |
| 500 | | | | |

# Where Did They Go?

Eight worms are hiding in the boxes below. Solve each problem. Circle the problems that have matching answers. (Hint: You should have eight circled areas to represent the eight hiding worms.) The first worm has been found for you.

| | | | | | |
|---|---|---|---|---|---|
| 59<br>− 33<br>26 | 178<br>− 152<br>26 | 57<br>− 12 | 365<br>− 320 | 89<br>− 44 | 575<br>− 503 |
| 47<br>− 21<br>26 | 263<br>− 232 | 44<br>− 13 | 79<br>− 48 | 148<br>− 103 | 393<br>− 321 |
| 338<br>− 312<br>26 | 93<br>− 32 | 375<br>− 314 | 86<br>− 25 | 96<br>− 24 | 189<br>− 117 |
| 182<br>− 121 | 79<br>− 18 | 369<br>− 313 | 29<br>− 21 | 84<br>− 72 | 429<br>− 417 |
| 288<br>− 232 | 157<br>− 101 | 98<br>− 42 | 568<br>− 560 | 109<br>− 101 | 25<br>− 13 |

# Melba's Masterpiece

Melba Squeaker is finishing her masterpiece. Help her figure out which tile to put in each empty square. Write the missing number in each square. Then color a matching tile below.

©The Mailbox® • *Building Math Basics* • TEC60857 • Key p. 215

Name _____   Date _____

# Spaniel in Space

Subtract. Write each answer in the top boxes of the next problem. The first one has been done for you.

Dog Star Space Station

1.
$$\begin{array}{r} 9,000 \\ -\phantom{0}259 \\ \hline 8,741 \end{array}$$

2.
$$\begin{array}{r} 8,741 \\ -1,024 \\ \hline \end{array}$$

3.
$$\begin{array}{r} \square\square\square\square \\ -\phantom{00}109 \\ \hline \end{array}$$

4.
$$\begin{array}{r} 7,608 \\ -\phantom{0}935 \\ \hline \end{array}$$

5.
$$\begin{array}{r} \square\square\square\square \\ -2,481 \\ \hline \end{array}$$

6.
$$\begin{array}{r} \square\square\square\square \\ -\phantom{0}507 \\ \hline \end{array}$$

7.
$$\begin{array}{r} 3,685 \\ -\phantom{0}188 \\ \hline \end{array}$$

8.
$$\begin{array}{r} \square\square\square\square \\ -\phantom{000}46 \\ \hline \end{array}$$

9.
$$\begin{array}{r} \square\square\square\square \\ -\phantom{00}391 \\ \hline \end{array}$$

10.
$$\begin{array}{r} 3,060 \\ -\phantom{0}674 \\ \hline \end{array}$$

11.
$$\begin{array}{r} \square\square\square\square \\ -\phantom{0}534 \\ \hline \end{array}$$

12.
$$\begin{array}{r} \square\square\square\square \\ -\phantom{0}917 \\ \hline \end{array}$$

13.
$$\begin{array}{r} 935 \\ -256 \\ \hline \end{array}$$

14.
$$\begin{array}{r} \square\square\square \\ -384 \\ \hline \end{array}$$

15.
$$\begin{array}{r} \square\square\square \\ -218 \\ \hline \end{array}$$

Name _____

Date _____

# Making a Difference!

Goldie wants to keep the earth clean! She is spreading the word! Solve each problem on another sheet of paper. Write the answer on the line provided.

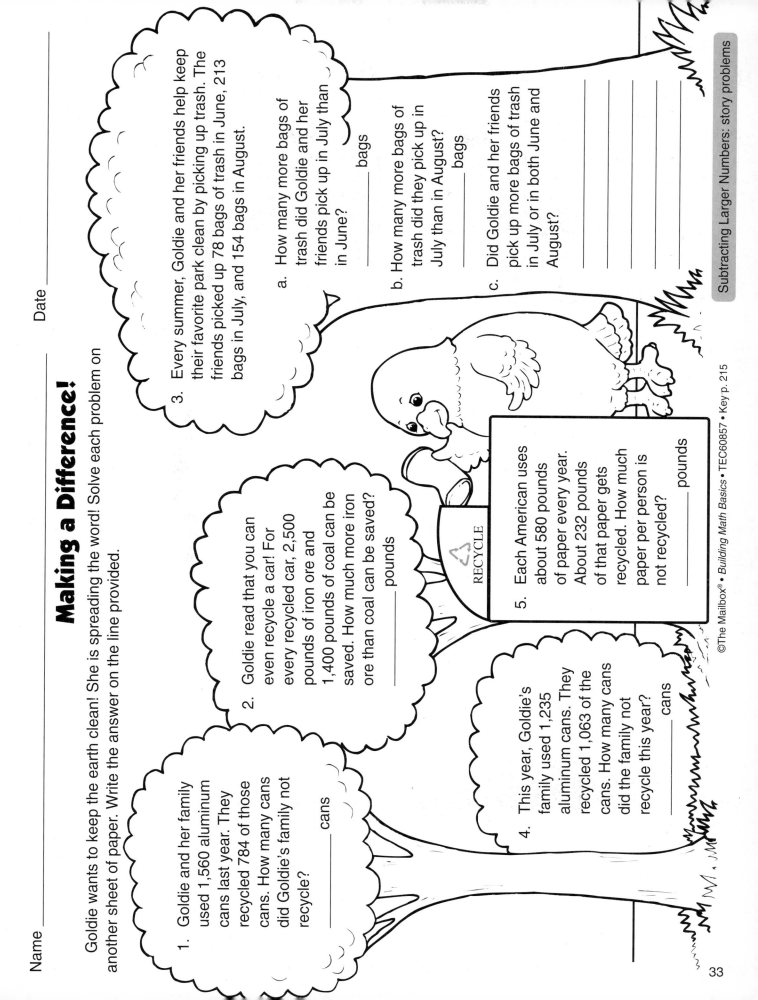

1. Goldie and her family used 1,560 aluminum cans last year. They recycled 784 of those cans. How many cans did Goldie's family not recycle?

_____ cans

2. Goldie read that you can even recycle a car! For every recycled car, 2,500 pounds of iron ore and 1,400 pounds of coal can be saved. How much more iron ore than coal can be saved?

_____ pounds

3. Every summer, Goldie and her friends help keep their favorite park clean by picking up trash. The friends picked up 78 bags of trash in June, 213 bags in July, and 154 bags in August.

a. How many more bags of trash did Goldie and her friends pick up in July than in June?

_____ bags

b. How many more bags of trash did they pick up in July than in August?

_____ bags

c. Did Goldie and her friends pick up more bags of trash in July or in both June and August?

_____

4. This year, Goldie's family used 1,235 aluminum cans. They recycled 1,063 of the cans. How many cans did the family not recycle this year?

_____ cans

RECYCLE

5. Each American uses about 580 pounds of paper every year. About 232 pounds of that paper gets recycled. How much paper per person is not recycled?

_____ pounds

©The Mailbox® • *Building Math Basics* • TEC60857 • Key p. 215

Subtracting Larger Numbers: story problems

33

# Basic Multiplication Facts

## Mend My Broken Heart

Challenge students to piece together a multiplication puzzle with this high-energy activity. Pair students and give each twosome a sheet of pink, white, or red construction paper. Have the pair draw and cut out a large heart. Next, direct the twosome to draw a zigzag line down the middle of the heart. Instruct the pair to write a multiplication fact on the left side of the line, write the fact's answer on the right side, and then cut the heart in half along the line. Collect and shuffle the hearts. Take the class to a large open area and give each child half of a heart. Allow students one minute to mend their broken hearts by finding their missing halves. After one minute, call time and have each pair with a complete heart read its fact aloud. Continue play by collecting and redistributing the hearts as many times as your heart desires!

4 x 7 = 28

12 x 12 = 144

## Rhyme Time

Have students create rhymes to help them remember challenging multiplication facts! Share with students the following example for remembering that eight times eight equals 64: Eight times eight fell on the floor; I picked it up, and it was 64. Then have each student write her own short rhyme to help her remember a fact that she frequently forgets. Finally, invite students to share their rhymes with the class.

Two times seven equals 14!

2 ♥

7 ♣

## Multiplication War

This variation of the card game War provides basic facts practice. Remove the face cards, aces, and jokers from a deck of cards and place the remaining cards in a center. To play, a pair of students deals the cards equally between themselves. Together the two players count to three and then simultaneously turn their top cards faceup. The first student to multiply the two displayed numbers and call out the answer takes both cards. Play continues in this manner until all the cards have been played. The student with more cards at the end of play is the winner.

**Find more student practice on pages 35–38.**

# Zany Zoo Facts

Multiply the problem in parentheses to complete each animal fact.

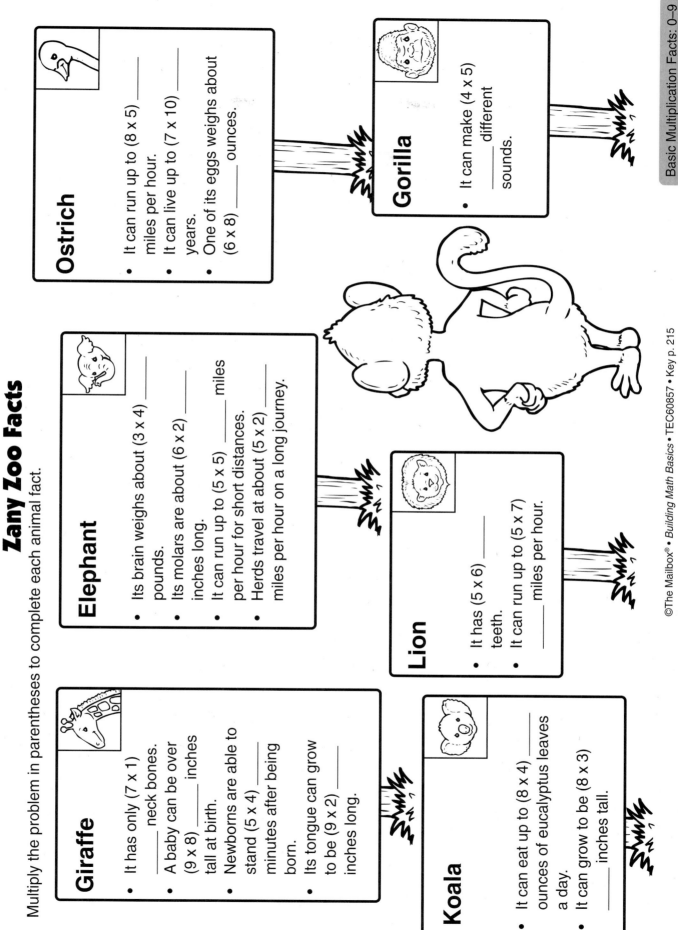

**Ostrich**

- It can run up to (8 x 5) _____ miles per hour.
- It can live up to (7 x 10) _____ years.
- One of its eggs weighs about (6 x 8) _____ ounces.

**Gorilla**

- It can make (4 x 5) _____ different sounds.

**Elephant**

- Its brain weighs about (3 x 4) _____ pounds.
- Its molars are about (6 x 2) _____ inches long.
- It can run up to (5 x 5) _____ miles per hour for short distances.
- Herds travel at about (5 x 2) _____ miles per hour on a long journey.

**Lion**

- It has (5 x 6) _____ teeth.
- It can run up to (5 x 7) _____ miles per hour.

**Giraffe**

- It has only (7 x 1) _____ neck bones.
- A baby can be over (9 x 8) _____ inches tall at birth.
- Newborns are able to stand (5 x 4) _____ minutes after being born.
- Its tongue can grow to be (9 x 2) _____ inches long.

**Koala**

- It can eat up to (8 x 4) _____ ounces of eucalyptus leaves a day.
- It can grow to be (8 x 3) _____ inches tall.

©The Mailbox® • Building Math Basics • TEC60857 • Key p. 215

Name _____    Date _____

# Stargazing

Color the star if the problem is correct. If the problem is not correct, cross out the incorrect answer and write the correct answer below it.

12 x 4 = 58

11 x 11 = 121

11 x 8 = 88

12 x 2 = 14

10 x 6 = 60

12 x 7 = 84

10 x 2 = 20

11 x 12 = 144

12 x 8 = 96

11 x 5 = 50

10 x 3 = 30

11 x 9 = 90

11 x 10 = 110

10 x 7 = 17

11 x 3 = 33

12 x 12 = 132

12 x 3 = 36

12 x 5 = 72

11 x 6 = 66

12 x 9 = 96

Name _____     Date _____

# Taking Flight

Use a ruler to draw a straight line from each problem to its answer. The first one has been done for you.

| Problem | | Answer |
|---|---|---|
| 1. 9 x 3 = | T | 66 |
| 2. 11 x 7 = | N | 80 |
| 3. 5 x 8 = | Z  X | 27 |
| 4. 6 x 11 = | D | 24 |
| 5. 3 x 4 = | U | 77 |
| 6. 8 x 3 = | | 20 |
| 7. 4 x 9 = | S | 15 |
| 8. 8 x 10 = | | 108 |
| 9. 5 x 3 = | V  Y  G | 42 |
| 10. 12 x 5 = | | 36 |
| 11. 6 x 7 = | | 40 |
| 12. 7 x 8 = | H  J  T | 54 |
| 13. 12 x 9 = | W | 60 |
| 14. 8 x 4 = | B | 0 |
| 15. 11 x 0 = | O | 45 |
| 16. 4 x 5 = | A | 56 |
| 17. 9 x 6 = | M | 28 |
| 18. 8 x 8 = | Q  T | 25 |
| 19. 4 x 11 = | | 12 |
| 20. 12 x 4 = | E  I | 64 |
| 21. 7 x 4 = | | 32 |
| 22. 5 x 5 = | G | 44 |
| 23. 10 x 7 = | F | 144 |
| 24. 9 x 5 = | I | 70 |
| 25. 12 x 12 = | | 48 |

## FLIGHT SCHOOL

### How do baby birds learn to fly?

To solve the riddle, write the circled letter that your line crossed through for each number below.

| 22 | 13 | 21 | 7 |
|---|---|---|---|

| 16 | 6 | 9 | **T** 1 |
|---|---|---|---|

| 12 | 25 | 4 | 20 | | 19 | 10 |
|---|---|---|---|---|---|---|
! 

Note to the teacher: Each student will need a ruler.

# Sunken Treasure

Multiply. Color the box if the problem is correct.
Connect the colored boxes to show a path to the
treasure.

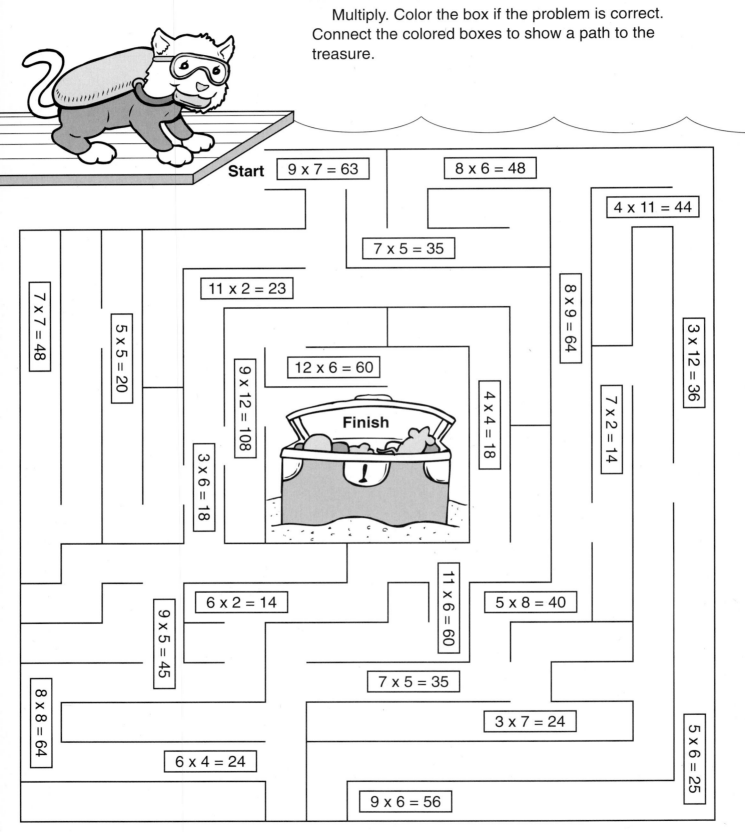

Start | 9 x 7 = 63

8 x 6 = 48

4 x 11 = 44

7 x 5 = 35

11 x 2 = 23

7 x 7 = 48

5 x 5 = 20

8 x 9 = 64

3 x 12 = 36

12 x 6 = 60

9 x 12 = 108

4 x 4 = 18

7 x 2 = 14

Finish

3 x 6 = 18

6 x 2 = 14

9 x 5 = 45

11 x 6 = 60

5 x 8 = 40

8 x 8 = 64

7 x 5 = 35

3 x 7 = 24

5 x 6 = 25

6 x 4 = 24

9 x 6 = 56

# Multiplying Larger Numbers

## Multiplication Grids

This simple tip makes multiplying large numbers a snap! In advance, make a transparency of a sheet of centimeter grid paper. Then give each child a sheet of the same grid paper and several colored pencils. Display a sample problem on the transparency, placing one digit in each box as shown. Have the student use his colored pencils to copy the problem on his paper. Next, model how to multiply, using a matching colored pencil for each place value in the bottom factor and writing only one digit in each box. Then provide additional problems for students to solve independently. Students are sure to line up numbers correctly, and they will easily see the multiplication process at work!

## Box It Up!

Add a little punch to multiplication practice with a class game of Box It Up! First, prepare two sets of ten index cards by numbering the cards in each set 0–9. Then divide students into two teams and draw on the chalkboard a 2 x 2 or 3 x 3 grid for each team. Explain that the goal is to create a multiplication problem that when solved will result in the larger product. Have the first student from each team draw a card from her team's deck, write the number anywhere on her team's grid, and then place the card in a discard pile. Repeat the process with a different student from each team until the grids are full. Then direct a student from each team to solve her team's problem. The team with the larger product earns a point. Combine and reshuffle each team's card deck and continue play in this manner until one team reaches a predetermined number of points. Follow up this activity with even more multiplication practice using the student reproducibles on pages 42–45.

# Multiplication Made Personal

This partner activity makes solving multiplication problems a bit more fun! Gather a supply of measuring tapes, rulers, and yardsticks. Begin the activity by giving each child an index card and telling her that she will have ten minutes to write three multiplication problems on the card. Explain that she can use any of the ideas below or her own ideas to personalize the problems. Have the child write her name on the back of the card and then exchange cards with a partner. Direct the student to answer her classmate's problems on scrap paper. When both students have found the solutions, have them return the cards and check one another's answers. Collect the cards and place them in a center to help keep students' multiplication skills sharp all year!

- any of the digits in her phone number
- height in inches
- house number
- birth month and date
- length of an arm or a leg
- shoe size

1. What is the product of 456 (the first three digits of my phone number) x 8 (my shoe size)?

2. What is 49 (my height in inches) x 272 (the first three digits of my zip code)?

3. Multiply 345 (my house number) x 13 (the date of my birthday).

## Hoop Properties

Hoop it up with this creative way to reinforce the properties of multiplication! Prior to the lesson, cut a large plastic hoop into fourths. Then write each digit 0–9 and the symbols "x" and "+" on separate sheets of 8½" x 11" white paper (one number or symbol per page) so that you have three of each. Begin by reviewing with the class the associative and distributive properties. Next, invite pairs of students to use the programmed papers and hoop pieces to model for the class the associative property. Explain that the hoop pieces represent the parentheses in the problem. Have classmates check the accuracy of each model. Then allow additional student pairs to try their hand at the distributive property.

$$2 \times (9 + 3)$$

**Find more student practice on pages 41 and 46.**

Name_____  Date _____

# Turn Up the Heat!

Multiply.

**Spice-o-Meter**

This is ten times hotter than last time!

| | | | |
|---|---|---|---|
| 1.   32<br>    x 5 | 2.   57<br>    x 8 | 3.   96<br>    x 2 | 4.   74<br>    x 6 |
| 5.   23<br>    x 3 | 6.   85<br>    x 9 | 7.   46<br>    x 4 | 8.   86<br>    x 5 |
| 9.   281<br>    x 4 | 10.   932<br>    x 9 | 11.   450<br>    x 6 | 12.   549<br>    x 7 |
| 13.   848<br>    x 7 | 14.   327<br>    x 2 | 15.   650<br>    x 3 | 16.   399<br>    x 8 |
| 17.   501<br>    x 5 | 18.   285<br>    x 6 | 19.   737<br>    x 4 | 20.   982<br>    x 8 |

# Zany Zebra

Give Zack a new look. Solve each problem. Then color the stripe with the matching answer. Two stripes will not be colored.

| | | | | |
|---|---|---|---|---|
| 1.   61<br>x 49 | 2.   71<br>x 65 | 3.   99<br>x 64 | 4.   52<br>x 73 | 5.   85<br>x 76 |
| 6.   48<br>x 21 | 7.   91<br>x 36 | 8.   42<br>x 83 | 9.   59<br>x 61 | 10.  66<br>x 35 |
| 11.  63<br>x 21 | 12.  72<br>x 50 | | | 13.  47<br>x 71 |
| 14.  78<br>x 16 | 15.  80<br>x 39 | | | |

Stripes: 1,006  3,486  3,276  3,796  4,615  3,599  3,120  6,336  2,989  6,460  3,600  1,248  1,008  2,310  3,337  1,323  2,640

Name_____    Date _____

# Showing Off!

Sammy Seal loves to show off his skills. Now it's your turn! Complete the puzzle below to show off your multiplication skills. Show your work on another sheet of paper.

**Across**
1. 52 x 31 =
3. 74 x 56 =
5. 61 x 37 =
7. 55 x 15 =
9. 99 x 83 =
10. 90 x 69 =
12. 33 x 16 =
14. 57 x 15 =
16. 19 x 18 =
17. 31 x 28 =
18. 65 x 64 =
19. 43 x 39 =

**Down**
1. 48 x 41 =
2. 91 x 15 =
3. 66 x 63 =
4. 83 x 59 =
5. 88 x 27 =
6. 93 x 57 =
8. 75 x 33 =
11. 50 x 51 =
13. 98 x 89 =
14. 91 x 88 =
15. 28 x 28 =
16. 21 x 17 =

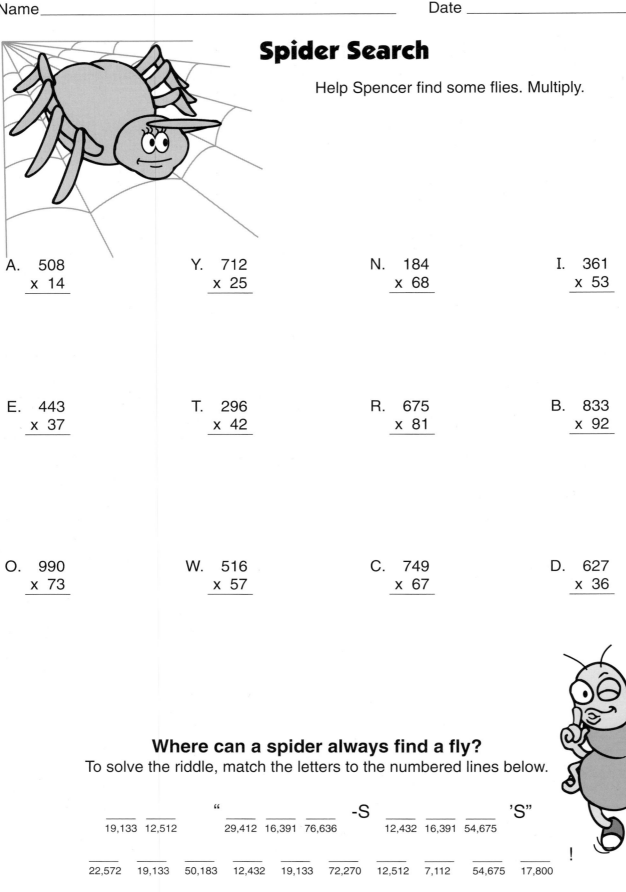

# Spider Search

### Help Spencer find some flies. Multiply.

A.  508
  x 14

Y.  712
  x 25

N.  184
  x 68

I.  361
  x 53

E.  443
  x 37

T.  296
  x 42

R.  675
  x 81

B.  833
  x 92

O.  990
  x 73

W.  516
  x 57

C.  749
  x 67

D.  627
  x 36

## Where can a spider always find a fly?
To solve the riddle, match the letters to the numbered lines below.

____  ____  "____  ____  ____ -S  ____  ____  ____ 'S"
19,133 12,512    29,412 16,391 76,636   12,432 16,391 54,675

____  ____  ____  ____  ____  ____  ____  ____  ____  ____  !
22,572 19,133 50,183 12,432 19,133 72,270 12,512 7,112  54,675 17,800

Name _____     Date _____

# Moose at the Movies

Multiply to find each answer. Show your work on another sheet of paper. Then color the path to reveal Molly and Marvin's favorite movie.

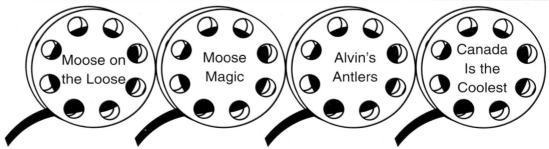

| | | | | |
|---|---|---|---|---|
| 1. 208 x 153 = | 31,804 | 31,814 | 32,124 | 31,824 |
| 2. 481 x 117 = | 56,286 | 54,286 | 56,277 | 55,197 |
| 3. 336 x 132 = | 45,258 | 41,358 | 44,352 | 42,352 |
| 4. 292 x 264 = | 77,808 | 77,088 | 76,186 | 77,188 |
| 5. 623 x 417 = | 259,791 | 259,790 | 259,781 | 258,790 |
| 6. 742 x 536 = | 397,621 | 397,712 | 395,712 | 396,718 |
| 7. 280 x 199 = | 55,710 | 55,719 | 55,720 | 56,717 |
| 8. 195 x 431 = | 84,086 | 83,080 | 85,085 | 84,045 |
| 9. 357 x 285 = | 101,752 | 100,765 | 101,745 | 103,752 |
| 10. 401 x 378 = | 153,778 | 151,578 | 152,046 | 151,529 |
| 11. 559 x 604 = | 337,636 | 337,366 | 337,663 | 337,633 |
| 12. 834 x 723 = | 601,982 | 602,982 | 602,988 | 602,987 |

Moose on the Loose     Moose Magic     Alvin's Antlers     Canada Is the Coolest

©The Mailbox® • Building Math Basics • TEC60857 • Key p. 216

Multiplying Larger Numbers: three digits by three digits  45

# Leopardville Library

Larry runs the Leopardville Library. Help him keep the library running smoothly by solving the problems below. Show your work on another sheet of paper.

1. The library has 32 tables. Each table has 12 chairs. How many people can sit in all the chairs?

   _____ people

2. The library just bought new encyclopedias. The set has 26 volumes, and each volume has 388 pages. How many pages are in the set?

   _____ pages

3. Each library shelf can hold 240 books. There are 315 shelves in the library. How many total books can the shelves hold?

   _____ books

4. A new shipment of books arrived today. There are 7 boxes, and each box contains 48 books. How many new books did the library receive?

   _____ books

5. Larry is the main librarian. He works 42 hours each week and 50 weeks each year. How many hours does he work in one year?

   _____ hours

6. There are 458 books that need new labels. Each book needs 2 labels. How many labels are needed for these books?

   _____ labels

7. The library gets 34 different magazines each month. How many magazines will the library receive in 12 months?

   _____ magazines

8. The library has a small section of audio books. Each month for the next 6 months, 115 titles will be added. How many audio books will be added?

   _____ audio books

# Basic Division Facts

## Higher or Lower?

This whole-class activity reviews basic division facts and sharpens students' mental math skills. To prepare, give each student a large index card. Have her draw an arrow on the card similar to the one shown. Then ask students a division fact question, such as "Is 16 divided by four higher or lower than 30 divided by six?" Each student holds up her card with the arrow pointing up if the answer is higher or with the arrow pointing down if the answer is lower. Call on a student to explain her answer. Then continue the activity by asking additional questions in the same manner. With a visual scan of the displayed cards, you can easily see which students are mastering their division facts!

## Math Fact Relay

Keep division facts in line with this fast-paced team game. Divide your students into two equal teams. Have each team form a straight line with one student lining up behind another. Start the game by calling out a division fact for Team 1. The first student in Team 1's line has five seconds to give the answer. If correct, he rushes to the back of the line. If incorrect, or if time runs out before he answers, he is out of the game and sits down. Next, call out another division fact, this time for the first student in Team 2's line. Continue play in this manner until only one student is left standing or as time allows. Declare the team with a student or with more students standing at the end of play the winner.

**Find more student practice on pages 48–51.**

Name _____    Date _____

# Boogie Down

Divide.

| E | O | I |
|---|---|---|
| 8 ÷ 2 = _____ | 48 ÷ 6 = _____ | 81 ÷ 9 = _____ |

| Y | T | Y | D | Y |
|---|---|---|---|---|
| 56 ÷ 8 = _____ | 18 ÷ 3 = _____ | 49 ÷ 7 = _____ | 40 ÷ 8 = _____ | 63 ÷ 9 = _____ |

| R | T | O | T | R |
|---|---|---|---|---|
| 27 ÷ 9 = _____ | 12 ÷ 2 = _____ | 64 ÷ 8 = _____ | 42 ÷ 7 = _____ | 21 ÷ 7 = _____ |

| N | D | H | I | W |
|---|---|---|---|---|
| 18 ÷ 9 = _____ | 25 ÷ 5 = _____ | 0 ÷ 9 = _____ | 36 ÷ 4 = _____ | 9 ÷ 9 = _____ |

## What dance are Pat and Peg Pretzel practicing?
To solve the riddle, match the letters to the numbered lines below.

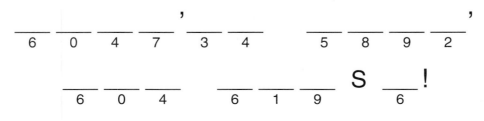

Name _____  Date _____

# Get the Picture?

Divide. Then color by the code to reveal the picture.

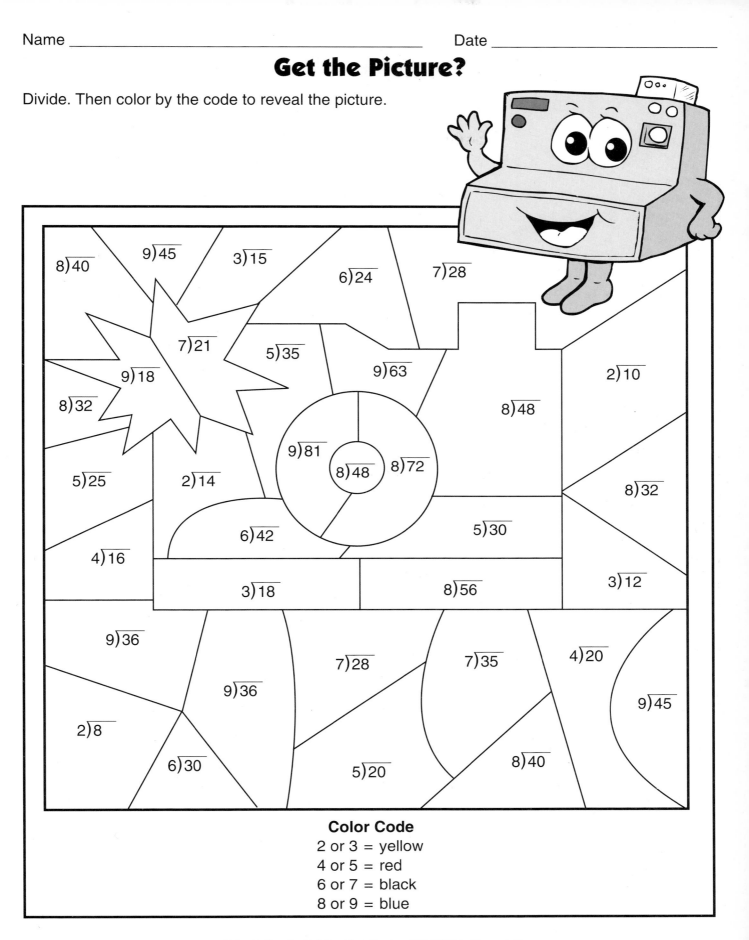

$8\overline{)40}$  $9\overline{)45}$  $3\overline{)15}$  $6\overline{)24}$  $7\overline{)28}$

$7\overline{)21}$  $5\overline{)35}$  $9\overline{)63}$  $2\overline{)10}$

$9\overline{)18}$  $8\overline{)48}$

$8\overline{)32}$  $9\overline{)81}$  $8\overline{)72}$

$5\overline{)25}$  $2\overline{)14}$  $8\overline{)48}$  $8\overline{)32}$

$6\overline{)42}$  $5\overline{)30}$

$4\overline{)16}$  $3\overline{)12}$

$3\overline{)18}$  $8\overline{)56}$

$9\overline{)36}$

$7\overline{)28}$  $7\overline{)35}$  $4\overline{)20}$

$9\overline{)36}$  $9\overline{)45}$

$2\overline{)8}$

$6\overline{)30}$  $5\overline{)20}$  $8\overline{)40}$

**Color Code**
2 or 3 = yellow
4 or 5 = red
6 or 7 = black
8 or 9 = blue

Name _____   Date _____

# Tee Time

**Divide.**

(H) 10)‾10‾   (S) 12)‾144‾   (L) 11)‾66‾   (B) 12)‾108‾

(E) 11)‾22‾   (O) 12)‾60‾   (C) 10)‾100‾   (I) 11)‾77‾   (N) 10)‾80‾

(U) 11)‾121‾   (D) 10)‾40‾   (A) 12)‾36‾   (S) 11)‾132‾   (N) 11)‾88‾

(I) 10)‾70‾   (E) 12)‾24‾   (E) 10)‾20‾   (L) 12)‾72‾   (H) 11)‾11‾

(O) 11)‾55‾   (B) 10)‾90‾   (I) 12)‾84‾   (C) 11)‾110‾   (A) 10)‾30‾

**Why did the golfer wear two pairs of pants?**
To solve the riddle, match the letters to the numbered
lines below.

__ __ __ __ __ __ __   __ __
9  2  10  3  11  12  2   1  2

__ __ __  __  __ __ __ __
1  3  4   3   1  5  6  2

__ __  __ __ __!
7  8   5  8  2

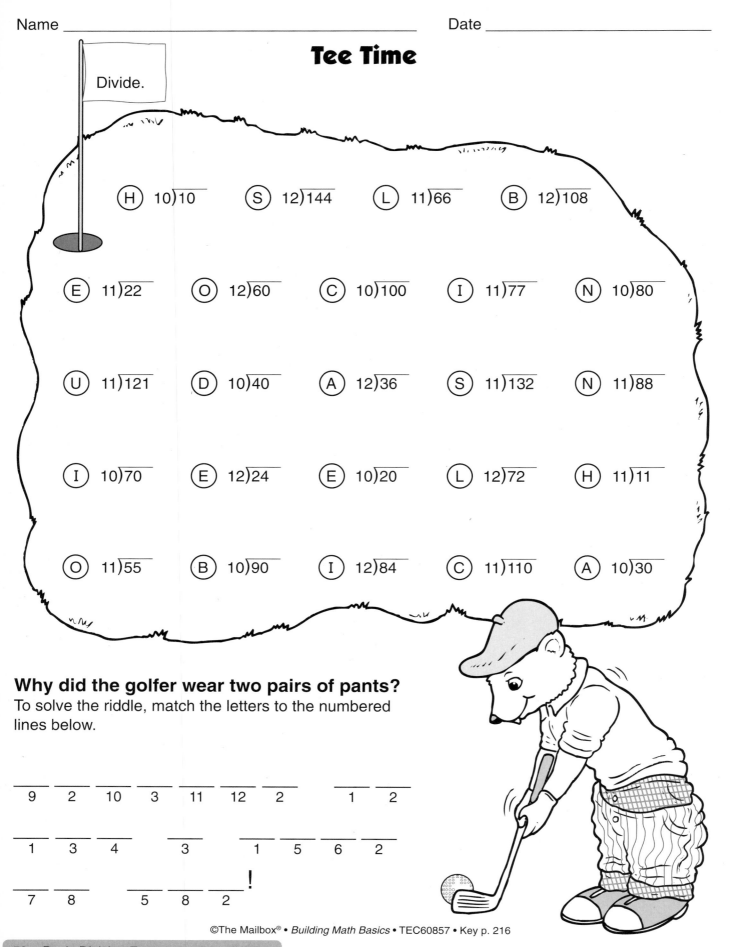

# Green Cheese

Which chunks of Moe's cheese have molded? Divide. If correct, color the cheese chunk yellow. If incorrect, color the cheese chunk green.

1. $10\overline{)10}$ = 0

2. $10\overline{)10}$ = 1

3. $12\overline{)96}$ = 3

4. $10\overline{)40}$ = 4

5. $11\overline{)0}$ = 1

6. $11\overline{)0}$ = 0

7. $10\overline{)70}$ = 6

8. $11\overline{)99}$ = 9

9. $12\overline{)48}$ = 4

10. $10\overline{)100}$ = 10

11. $12\overline{)108}$ = 8

12. $12\overline{)36}$ = 3

13. $11\overline{)121}$ = 12

14. $11\overline{)88}$ = 8

15. $12\overline{)24}$ = 2

16. $11\overline{)44}$ = 2

17. $10\overline{)90}$ = 9

18. $12\overline{)72}$ = 8

19. $11\overline{)22}$ = 11

20. $12\overline{)60}$ = 6

21. $10\overline{)20}$ = 2

22. $12\overline{)132}$ = 11

23. $11\overline{)121}$ = 11

24. $10\overline{)40}$ = 2

25. $10\overline{)70}$ = 7

Yuck!

# Dividing Larger Numbers

## Just Right for Any Season

Why not use the excitement of the season to draw students in to division practice? First, cut out a supply of seasonal shapes. Number each shape and program it with a division problem. Then post the shapes in accessible spots around your classroom. Also place a container of small treats and a numbered answer key in a designated location. As students have free time, guide them to rotate around the room, copying and solving each problem. Have students check their work against the answer key and reward themselves with a treat!

1. $2\overline{)437}$

2. $3\overline{)164}$

4. $4\overline{)484}$

1. $3\overline{)189}$

3. $5\overline{)255}$

6. $6\overline{)636}$

# Remainder Theater

Introduce dividing with remainders by having students act out division problems! Using the number of students in your class as the dividend, write on the board a division problem that will result in a remainder. For example, write "23 ÷ 5" and begin dividing students into groups of five, having each group stand together. When you can no longer form a complete group of five, point out that 23 divided by five is equal to four groups of five with a remainder of three. Finally, model how to work through the written problem on the board. Then write a new problem on the board and repeat. For even more practice, follow up this activity with the reproducible on page 58.

# Cafeteria Challenge

Reinforce division skills and interpreting remainders with this real-world challenge. Pair students and have them imagine that they are in charge of ordering tables for a new school cafeteria. Explain that they will need to have enough seating for 112 students (or any desired number of students). Have each group figure out how many tables would be needed if they purchased tables that seat four students. Then have them repeat the process with tables that seat five, six, eight, ten, and 12 students. Finally, have each pair recommend the table size it thinks is best and draw a diagram showing how to arrange the tables in the cafeteria. Be sure to set aside time for each pair to share its plan.

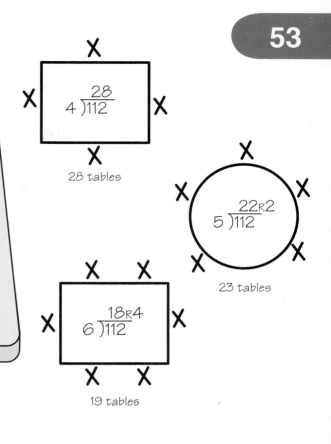

$$4\overline{)112} = 28$$
28 tables

$$5\overline{)112} = 22\text{R}2$$
23 tables

$$6\overline{)112} = 18\text{R}4$$
19 tables

## Build a Problem

Watch division skills take shape as students build their own division problems. Divide students into small groups, giving each group a sheet of light-colored construction paper. Have each group divide its paper into sections as shown. Then explain to students that each group should write ten division problems and record them on its paper. What's the catch? The first problem must have a remainder of ten, the second a remainder of nine, the third a remainder of eight, and so on until they write a tenth problem with a remainder of one. Encourage groups to first work on scrap paper and then record their final problems (without the solutions) on the construction paper. Afterward, have groups switch papers and solve each other's problems. Or, if desired, laminate the papers and place them at your math center along with dry-erase markers for an instant center activity.

| | | | | |
|---|---|---|---|---|
| $20\overline{)710}$ 35R10 $-60$ $110$ $100$ $10$ | $11\overline{)273}$ 24R9 $-22$ $53$ $44$ $9$ | $9\overline{)62}$ | $12\overline{)139}$ | $7\overline{)55}$ |
| $15\overline{)200}$ | $24\overline{)28}$ | $6\overline{)87}$ | $34\overline{)104}$ | $5\overline{)56}$ |

# Division Steps Reminder

Do your students need help remembering the steps to solve a division problem? Try using the mnemonic device **Does Mrs. Starr's Cat Bite Dogs?** to remind students to divide, multiply, subtract, check, and bring down. Even better, after sharing this example, have students make up their own reminder sentences.

**Find more student practice on pages 54–59.**

Name _____

Date _____

# A Spider With Skills

Sandy is spinning a giant web. Draw a line from each problem to the matching rounded problem. Then draw a line to the correct estimate. The first one has been done for you.

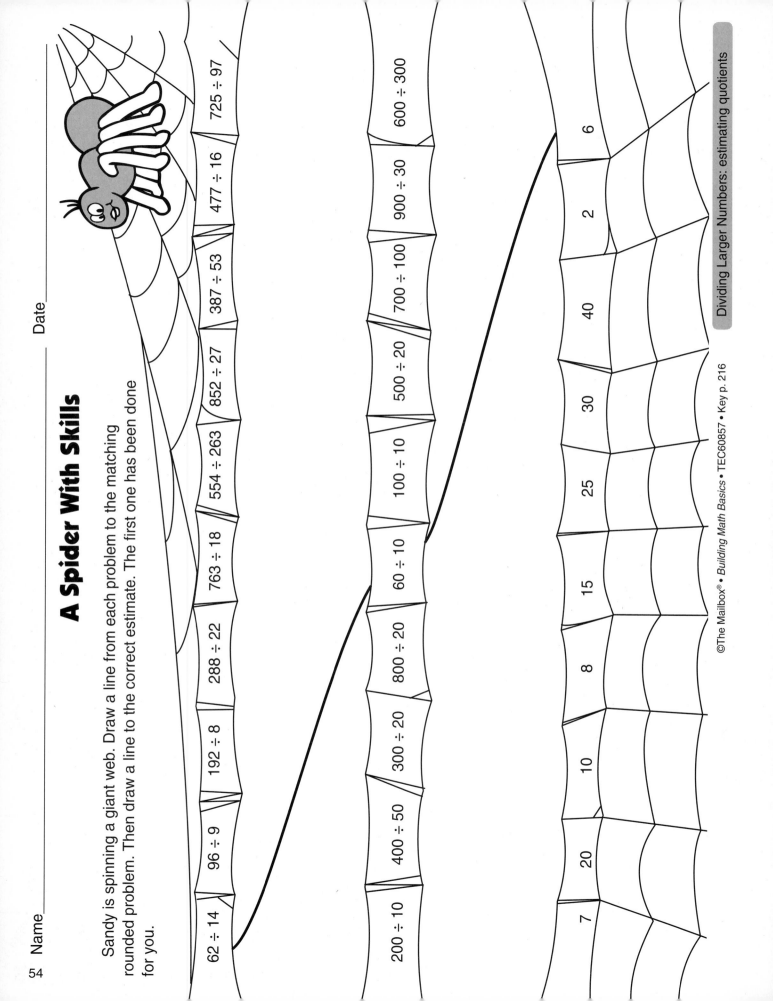

| 62 ÷ 14 | 96 ÷ 9 | 192 ÷ 8 | 288 ÷ 22 | 763 ÷ 18 | 554 ÷ 263 | 852 ÷ 27 | 387 ÷ 53 | 477 ÷ 16 | 725 ÷ 97 |

| 200 ÷ 10 | 400 ÷ 50 | 300 ÷ 20 | 800 ÷ 20 | 60 ÷ 10 | 100 ÷ 10 | 500 ÷ 20 | 700 ÷ 100 | 900 ÷ 30 | 600 ÷ 300 |

| 7 | 20 | 10 | 8 | 15 | 25 | 30 | 40 | 2 | 6 |

54

Dividing Larger Numbers: estimating quotients

©The Mailbox® • *Building Math Basics* • TEC60857 • Key p. 216

Name_____ Date _____

# Snowy Days?

Help Pete figure out when it will snow in the next ten days. Solve each problem on another sheet of paper. If the answer is 32 or below, color the box under "Snow." If the answer is above 32, color the box under "No Snow."

| Snow Forecast | | | |
|:---:|:---:|:---:|:---:|
| **Day** | **Temperature** | **Snow** | **No Snow** |
| 1 | $301 \div 7 =$ | R | D |
| 2 | $192 \div 6 =$ | F | P |
| 3 | $360 \div 12 =$ | S | L |
| 4 | $333 \div 9 =$ | E | A |
| 5 | $588 \div 21 =$ | N | M |
| 6 | $525 \div 15 =$ | K | I |
| 7 | $116 \div 4 =$ | Y | O |
| 8 | $414 \div 23 =$ | B | C |
| 9 | $527 \div 17 =$ | S | T |
| 10 | $850 \div 25 =$ | U | X |

To find how many days it will snow, match the colored letters to the numbered lines below.

___ ___ ___          ___ ___ ___ ___
31   35   34          43   37   29   30

When is it going to snow?

Name_____ Date _____

# Mad for Mud Pies!

The mud pie–making contest just ended! Each pig made mud pies for as long as he or she wanted. The pig that made the most pies per minute is the winner. Write and solve a division problem for each pig below. The first one has been done for you.

1. Bertie made 98 pies in 7 minutes.

$$\begin{array}{r} 14 \\ 7\overline{)98} \\ -7\phantom{8} \\ \hline 28 \\ -28 \\ \hline 0 \end{array}$$

2. Velma made 798 pies in 19 minutes.

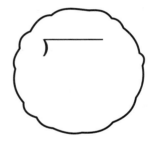

3. Muddy made 198 pies in 9 minutes.

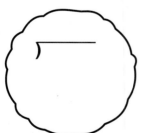

4. Snouty made 560 pies in 16 minutes.

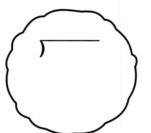

5. Curly made 188 pies in 4 minutes.

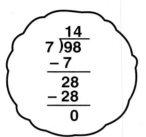

6. Pokey made 693 pies in 21 minutes.

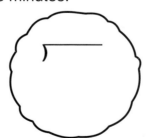

7. Pinky made 184 pies in 8 minutes.

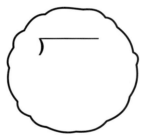

8. Floyd made 800 pies in 20 minutes.

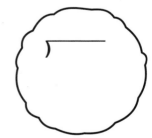

9. Hamilton made 138 pies in 3 minutes.

10. Buster made 312 pies in 12 minutes.

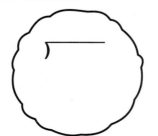

**Which pig came in first place?**

_____
name

Name _____

Date _____

# Crunchy Quotients

Solve each problem below. Color by the code.

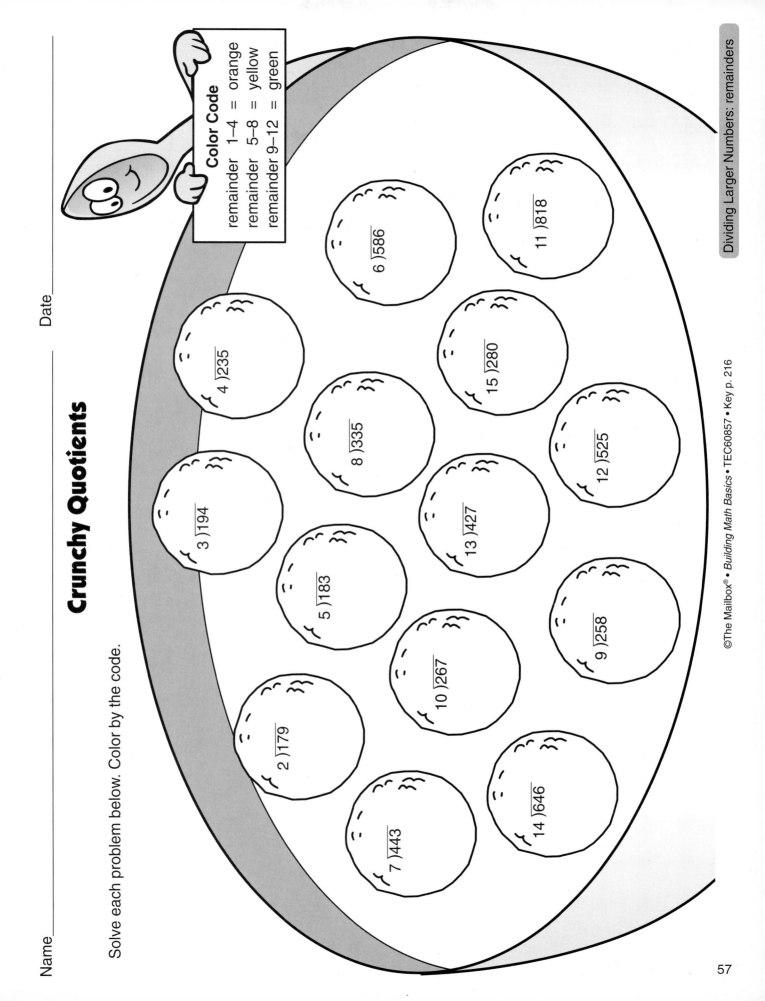

**Color Code**
remainder 1–4 = orange
remainder 5–8 = yellow
remainder 9–12 = green

$4\overline{)235}$

$6\overline{)586}$

$11\overline{)818}$

$3\overline{)194}$

$8\overline{)335}$

$15\overline{)280}$

$5\overline{)183}$

$13\overline{)427}$

$12\overline{)525}$

$2\overline{)179}$

$10\overline{)267}$

$9\overline{)258}$

$7\overline{)443}$

$14\overline{)646}$

Dividing Larger Numbers: remainders

# Shopping Spree

The Acorn Trading Store opens today! Scott and his friends have been saving acorns for weeks. Solve each problem on another sheet of paper.

1.  Scott has 83 acorns to buy Squirrel Scout cards. Each set of cards costs 6 acorns. How many card sets can Scott buy? _____ How many acorns will he have left? _____

2.  Sandy has 64 acorns to buy fancy tail combs. Each comb costs 5 acorns. How many combs can Sandy buy? _____ How many acorns will she have left? _____

3.  Sid has 120 acorns to buy Squirrel Scout comic books. Each comic book costs 7 acorns. How many comic books can Sid buy? _____ How many acorns will he have left? _____

4.  Sasha has 263 acorns to buy Squirrel Scout video games. Each game costs 23 acorns. How many games can Sasha buy? _____ How many acorns will she have left? _____

5.  Sophie has 219 acorns to buy Save the Woods T-shirts. Each T-shirt costs 12 acorns. How many T-shirts can Sophie buy? _____ How many acorns will she have left? _____

6.  Simon has 396 acorns to buy Stick-to-It gloves. Each pair of gloves costs 14 acorns. How many pairs can Simon buy? _____ How many acorns will he have left? _____

7.  Staci has 482 acorns to buy Superstacker squirrel snacks. Each bag of snacks costs 15 acorns. How many bags can Staci buy? _____ How many acorns will she have left? _____

8.  Sal has 415 acorns to buy Store-It-All storage crates. Each crate costs 25 acorns. How many crates can Sal buy? _____ How many acorns will he have left? _____

# Forgetful Freida

Freida is always leaving things behind. Solve each problem. Then match the letters to the numbered lines below to find out what Freida left at the picnic.

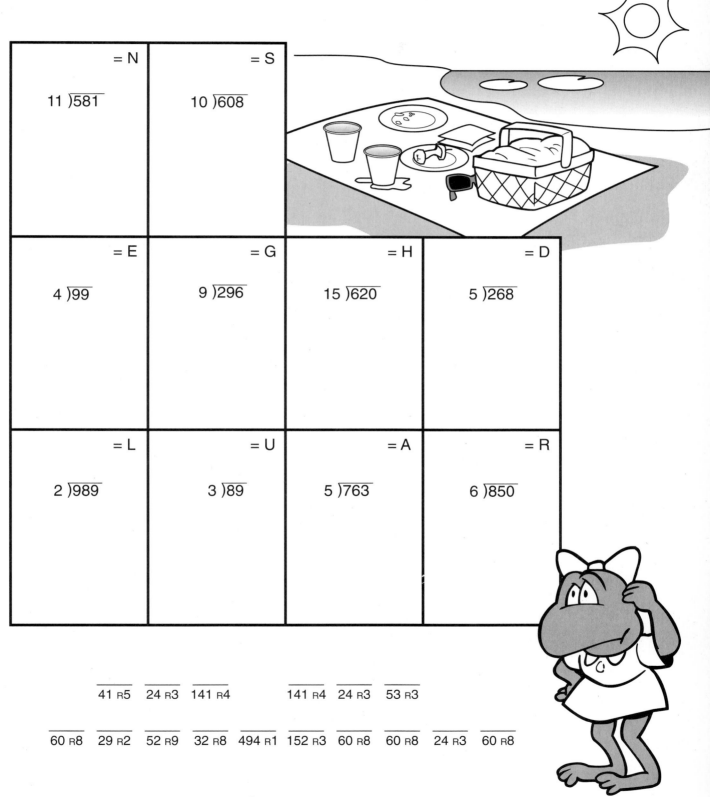

= N

11 )581

= S

10 )608

= E

4 )99

= G

9 )296

= H

15 )620

= D

5 )268

= L

2 )989

= U

3 )89

= A

5 )763

= R

6 )850

____  ____  ____    ____  ____  ____
41 R5  24 R3  141 R4    141 R4  24 R3  53 R3

____  ____  ____  ____  ____  ____  ____  ____  ____  ____
60 R8  29 R2  52 R9  32 R8  494 R1  152 R3  60 R8  60 R8  24 R3  60 R8

# Fraction Basics

## Fashionable Fractions

A fashion show runway won't be needed for this fraction identification activity! Simply choose a color and ask everyone wearing a clothing item of that color to stand. Have the class identify what fraction of the class is wearing that color; then repeat with other colors. Next, provide each student with scissors, glue, a sheet of construction paper, and access to old magazines. Direct him to cut out pictures of different colors of clothing that would make a unique outfit and glue them to a stick figure he draws on his paper. Finally, have him list somewhere on the paper the outfit's total number of pieces and what fraction of them is represented by each color. For additional practice with identifying with fractions, see the reproducible on page 64.

12 pieces of clothing

$\frac{3}{12}$ = red

$\frac{1}{12}$ = green

$\frac{1}{12}$ = blue

$\frac{2}{12}$ = white

$\frac{3}{12}$ = black

$\frac{1}{12}$ = purple

$\frac{2}{12}$ = yellow

amphibian

$\frac{4}{9}$ = vowels

$\frac{5}{9}$ = consonants

## Fraction Spelling

Make your next lesson on fractional parts of whole numbers a "spell-eriffic" one! Write one of the class's spelling words on the board. Instruct students to write a fraction that tells what part of the word is spelled with vowels and another that tells the part that is spelled with consonants. Then have the class repeat the process with the rest of the spelling list.

## Edible Fractions

Finding fractional parts of whole numbers is more fun when the manipulatives are munchable! Give each child a bag filled with 25 pieces of Fruit Loops cereal or a similar cereal. Instruct the student to take 12 pieces from her bag. Guide her to find two-thirds of 12 by having her notice the fraction's denominator (3). Instruct the student to divide her 12 cereal pieces into three groups of four pieces each. Next, point out the numerator (2). After directing her to combine two groups of four into one group of eight, help her conclude that two-thirds of 12 is eight. Have her use her cereal pieces to solve additional problems. Then share the shortcut method (divide the whole number by the denominator and multiply the quotient by the numerator). After the class solves more problems using the shortcut, allow students to eat their manipulatives!

## Equivalent Fractions Aid

What can help students understand equivalent fractions better? A ready reference they make and keep at their desks! Give each child a ruler and four pieces of construction paper, each a different color and size: 7" x 8", 8" x 9", 8" x 11", and 8" x 18". (The 8" x 18" piece should have the top five inches folded down.) Direct him to staple the first three pieces of paper under the fold of the longest piece so that the 11-inch piece is at the bottom and the seven-inch piece is on top. Next, instruct him to label the folded portion "1 whole" and then divide the successive layers into halves, thirds, fourths, and eighths and label them as shown. When students need to see which fractions are equivalent or how fractions compare in size, have them whip out their handy aids!

# Factoring With Venn Diagrams

Use students' familiarity with Venn diagrams to sharpen their understanding of finding the greatest common factor (GCF) and the least common multiple (LCM). The next time the class has to simplify a fraction (or add or subtract two unlike fractions), draw a Venn diagram on the board. Using a factor tree, guide students to list in the diagram's sections the prime factors of both the numerator and denominator if simplifying a fraction (or if adding or subtracting unlike fractions, only the denominators' prime factors). To find the GCF, direct each child to multiply the prime factors in the middle section. To find the LCM, instruct her to multiply the factors in all three sections. Have students color-code the sections if you wish!

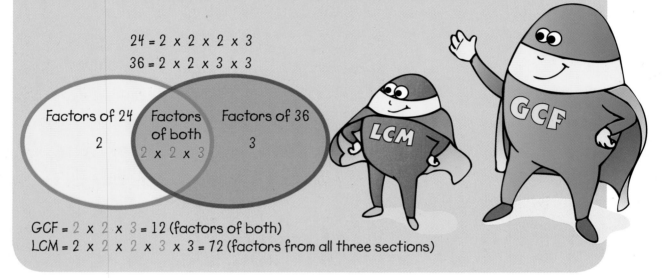

$$24 = 2 \times 2 \times 2 \times 3$$
$$36 = 2 \times 2 \times 3 \times 3$$

Factors of 24
2

Factors of both
$2 \times 2 \times 3$

Factors of 36
3

GCF = $2 \times 2 \times 3$ = 12 (factors of both)
LCM = $2 \times 2 \times 2 \times 3 \times 3$ = 72 (factors from all three sections)

# Bottoms Up!

To compare unlike fractions quickly, teach students the phrase "Bottoms Up!" Write two unlike fractions on the board. Demonstrate how to multiply the first fraction's denominator (the bottom number) by the second fraction's numerator (the number up at the top); then record the product as shown. Repeat to multiply the second fraction's denominator by the first fraction's numerator. Finally, compare the two products and write the correct symbol between the fractions. This method works every time! Students can practice this new method by completing the reproducible on page 65.

$$9 \quad \frac{3}{4} \bowtie \frac{2}{3} \quad 8$$

$$\frac{3}{4} > \frac{2}{3}$$

# Domino Fractions

Dust off the dominoes for great practice with comparing, ordering, and sorting fractions!

- **To compare fractions:** Have each pair of students place 20 dominoes facedown. Direct each partner to turn one domino faceup vertically. Explain that the top half of the domino represents the numerator and the bottom half represents the denominator. The player whose domino represents the greater fraction wins both dominoes. If the dominoes represent equal fractions, have the players keep turning two dominos faceup until one is greater. The player with the greater fraction gets all of the faceup dominoes. After ten rounds, declare the partner with more dominoes the winner.
- **To order fractions:** Have each child draw three dominoes from a set and list the fractions they represent in order from least to greatest.
- **To sort fractions:** Have each child sort ten dominoes into three groups according to the value they represent: zero (a blank domino), the whole number one, or an improper fraction.

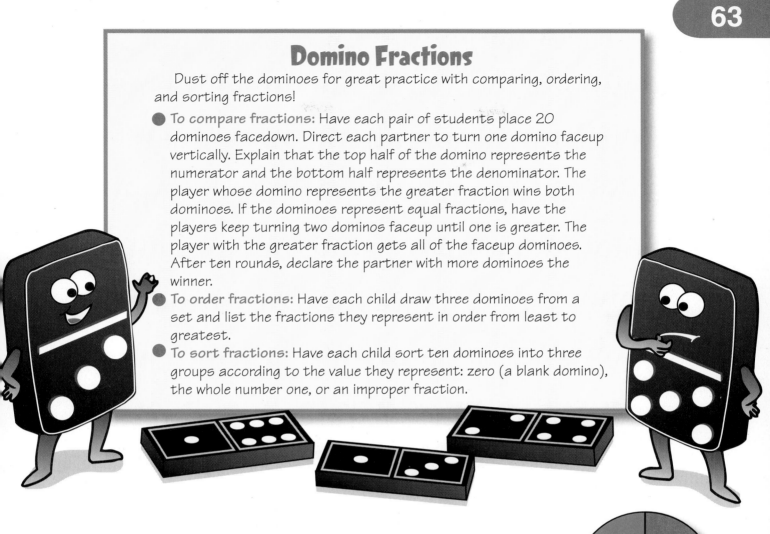

## The Renaming Game

Take students for a spin that has them review not only how to rename fractions but to compare, order, and simplify them as well! Give each student group a stack of construction paper cards programmed with numbers as follows: red with a mixed number, blue with an improper fraction, yellow with two fractions with unlike denominators, green with three fractions with unlike denominators, white with a fraction not in simplest form. Also give each group a matching five-color spinner.

To play, one child spins the spinner and draws a card of the color that the spinner lands on. Then each group member copies on paper the card's fraction(s) and renames it (them) accordingly: red—change the mixed number to an improper fraction, blue—changes the improper fraction to a mixed number, yellow—finds equivalent fractions and compares, green—finds equivalent fractions and orders, white—simplifies. Then the groupmates compare answers. If they agree, each person earns 100 points. If not, they must work together to find the mistake(s) before getting the points. Everyone wins! To continue, have group members take turns spinning and drawing cards.

**Find more student practice on pages 66–67.**

Name _____  Date _____

# Picture-Perfect Canvasses

Zeb loves painting! Write a fraction at the top of each canvas to tell what part of the picture is shaded.

**What is black and white and red all over?**
To solve the riddle, match each letter to the lines below.

$\dfrac{1}{2}$  $\dfrac{7}{10}$  $\dfrac{4}{9}$   $\dfrac{3}{8}$  $\dfrac{4}{9}$  $\dfrac{2}{3}$  $\dfrac{3}{4}$  $\dfrac{3}{4}$  $\dfrac{5}{12}$

$\dfrac{4}{9}$  $\dfrac{1}{4}$  $\dfrac{5}{6}$  $\dfrac{2}{3}$  $\dfrac{3}{8}$  $\dfrac{3}{8}$  $\dfrac{2}{3}$  $\dfrac{2}{5}$  $\dfrac{2}{5}$  $\dfrac{4}{9}$  $\dfrac{5}{8}$   $\dfrac{4}{5}$  $\dfrac{4}{9}$  $\dfrac{5}{6}$  $\dfrac{3}{8}$  $\dfrac{2}{3}$

Name _____

Date _____

# Dino's Debut

If the fractions are compared correctly, color the pencil.
If the fractions are not compared correctly, write the correct symbol in the eraser.
The first one has been done for you.

B. $\frac{3}{5} < \frac{1}{3}$  [ > ]

A. $\frac{3}{5} > \frac{3}{10}$

E. $\frac{3}{16} = \frac{1}{8}$

N. $\frac{2}{3} < \frac{3}{4}$

E. $\frac{7}{20} < \frac{9}{10}$

S. $\frac{2}{3} > \frac{4}{6}$

R. $\frac{2}{4} = \frac{1}{2}$

P. $\frac{6}{7} > \frac{9}{10}$

V. $\frac{4}{5} = \frac{20}{25}$

A. $\frac{5}{6} = \frac{10}{18}$

O. $\frac{3}{8} < \frac{7}{10}$

U. $\frac{3}{4} > \frac{3}{5}$

S. $\frac{1}{5} < \frac{4}{10}$

T. $\frac{2}{3} > \frac{4}{5}$

R. $\frac{7}{9} > \frac{2}{5}$

K. $\frac{3}{4} < \frac{2}{5}$

E. $\frac{2}{5} = \frac{8}{20}$

X. $\frac{2}{9} < \frac{4}{5}$

## What was Dino on his first day of school?

To solve the riddle, write the letters of the colored pencils in order on the lines below.

"___ ___ ___ ___ ___"

65

# Big Bowls, Little Bowls

Help Duke and Little Evie sort their bones. Simplify the fraction on each bone. Write the bone's letter in the blank on the correct bowl.

J. $\frac{21}{28}$

T. $\frac{6}{18}$

L. $\frac{3}{27}$

E. $\frac{4}{16}$

I. $\frac{2}{6}$

S. $\frac{3}{24}$

D. $\frac{15}{20}$

H. $\frac{8}{10}$

R. $\frac{2}{10}$

C. $\frac{3}{6}$

G. $\frac{16}{20}$

Q. $\frac{5}{20}$

B. $\frac{14}{21}$

K. $\frac{10}{16}$

A. $\frac{2}{18}$

F. $\frac{3}{15}$

P. $\frac{5}{10}$

O. $\frac{2}{16}$

N. $\frac{15}{24}$

M. $\frac{8}{12}$

$\frac{1}{5}$

$\frac{1}{8}$

$\frac{1}{4}$

$\frac{1}{3}$

**Duke's Bowls**

$\frac{2}{3}$

**Evie's Bowls**

$\frac{4}{5}$

$\frac{3}{4}$

$\frac{5}{8}$

$\frac{1}{2}$

$\frac{1}{9}$

Name _____     Date _____

# (Almost) Magical Changes

Rename each improper fraction to a mixed number and each mixed number to an improper fraction. Show your work on another sheet of paper. Cross off each answer on the scarf at the bottom of the page. Some answers will not be crossed off. Problems 1 and 9 have been done for you.

| Improper Fraction | Mixed Number | Mixed Number | Improper Fraction |
|---|---|---|---|
| 1. $\frac{11}{4}$ | $= 2\frac{3}{4}$ | 9. $4\frac{2}{3}$ | $= \frac{14}{3}$ |
| 2. $\frac{23}{7}$ | $=$ | 10. $6\frac{1}{2}$ | $=$ |
| 3. $\frac{25}{6}$ | $=$ | 11. $2\frac{3}{10}$ | $=$ |
| 4. $\frac{10}{3}$ | $=$ | 12. $3\frac{3}{8}$ | $=$ |
| 5. $\frac{38}{7}$ | $=$ | 13. $1\frac{4}{9}$ | $=$ |
| 6. $\frac{15}{8}$ | $=$ | 14. $5\frac{2}{5}$ | $=$ |
| 7. $\frac{34}{5}$ | $=$ | 15. $1\frac{5}{8}$ | $=$ |
| 8. $\frac{29}{6}$ | $=$ | 16. $6\frac{3}{8}$ | $=$ |

$2\frac{3}{4}$   $\frac{15}{8}$   $\frac{27}{5}$   $\frac{13}{8}$   $\frac{27}{8}$   $4\frac{1}{6}$   $6\frac{4}{5}$   $5\frac{1}{7}$

$4\frac{5}{6}$   $\frac{33}{8}$   $\frac{23}{10}$   $3\frac{1}{3}$   $\frac{13}{9}$   $3\frac{2}{7}$   $\frac{51}{8}$   $\frac{13}{2}$   $5\frac{3}{7}$   $1\frac{7}{8}$   $\frac{14}{3}$

# Adding Fractions

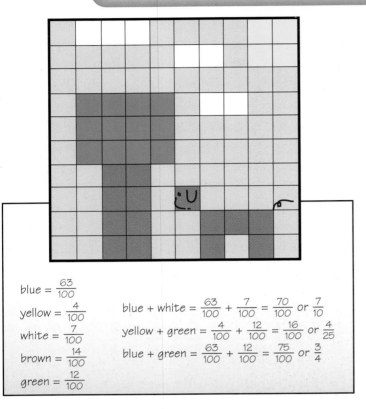

blue = $\frac{63}{100}$

yellow = $\frac{4}{100}$

white = $\frac{7}{100}$

brown = $\frac{14}{100}$

green = $\frac{12}{100}$

blue + white = $\frac{63}{100} + \frac{7}{100} = \frac{70}{100}$ or $\frac{7}{10}$

yellow + green = $\frac{4}{100} + \frac{12}{100} = \frac{16}{100}$ or $\frac{4}{25}$

blue + green = $\frac{63}{100} + \frac{12}{100} = \frac{75}{100}$ or $\frac{3}{4}$

## That's "Sum" Picture!

Here's a picture-perfect way to practice adding fractions with like denominators. Give each student a 10 x 10 grid, a large index card, and crayons or colored pencils. Instruct each student to color a simple picture or design that covers his entire grid (see the example). Next, have him write on the index card each color's total number of squares as a fractional part of the entire grid. Then guide students to create equations by adding different colors' fractions as shown. If desired, challenge students to write each fraction in its simplest form. Post the pictures and cards on a bulletin board titled "That's 'Sum' Picture!" Follow up with the reproducible on page 70 for even more practice with adding with like denominators.

Ready...rotate!

## Assembly Line Addition

Use a fun assembly line to help students practice adding fractions with unlike denominators. Divide students into groups of four and have group members sit side by side in a row. Write a fraction addition problem with unlike denominators on the board. Direct the first person in each row to copy the problem on paper and pass the paper to the person on his right. Have that child find the least common denominator and the third person make fractions with like denominators. Instruct the fourth person to add the fractions. (If students are familiar with simplifying answers, have the fourth group member pass the paper back to the first member to complete this step.) Have the groups solve a total of eight problems, directing students to rotate positions after every two problems so that each child practices every step. For additional practice with adding fractions with unlike denominators, see page 72.

# Domino Draw

This fractions center game for two is a cinch to prepare. Gather a set of dominoes and remove any pieces with blank halves. Place the set at a center along with paper, pencils, and the following directions.

## Playing the game:

1. Players place all dominoes facedown on the playing surface.
2. Player 1 draws two dominoes and writes the fractions that are created when the dominoes are in the vertical position.
3. Player 1 adds the fractions and places the dominoes in the discard pile.
4. Player 2 checks Player 1's calculation and then takes a turn in the same manner.
5. Player 1 takes another turn, this time drawing only one domino. He adds this fraction to the sum from Round 1.
6. Players continue to take turns, drawing only one domino and adding it to their sums.
7. The student with the higher sum after five rounds of play wins the game.

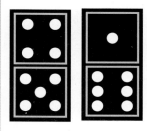

**Round 1**
$\frac{4}{5} + \frac{1}{6} = \frac{29}{30}$

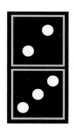

**Round 2**
$\frac{29}{30} + \frac{2}{3} = 1\frac{19}{30}$

# Three in a Row

Turn this variation of bingo into a frolicking session of adding fractions! Direct each student to draw a 3 x 3 grid on a sheet of notebook paper and program each section with one of the fractions below. Next, write on the board one randomly selected equation from the box at the left. Instruct each player to add the fractions on scrap paper, writing the answer in simplest form. If the student has the answer on his grid, he covers that square with a game marker. Continue with additional equations from the list until a student announces that he has covered three squares in a row. When this happens, verify that his answers are correct, declare the student that round's winner, and then have students clear their grids to play another round. If desired, have students add whole numbers to their fraction sheets, and call out equations that add up to mixed numbers.

| Fraction | Equations |
|---|---|
| $\frac{1}{8}$ | $\frac{1}{16} + \frac{1}{16}, \frac{1}{12} + \frac{1}{24}, \frac{1}{32} + \frac{3}{32}$ |
| $\frac{1}{6}$ | $\frac{1}{12} + \frac{1}{12}, \frac{1}{24} + \frac{1}{8}, \frac{1}{18} + \frac{1}{9}$ |
| $\frac{1}{4}$ | $\frac{1}{8} + \frac{1}{8}, \frac{3}{16} + \frac{1}{16}, \frac{1}{12} + \frac{1}{6}$ |
| $\frac{1}{3}$ | $\frac{1}{6} + \frac{1}{6}, \frac{1}{15} + \frac{4}{15}, \frac{1}{8} + \frac{5}{24}$ |
| $\frac{1}{2}$ | $\frac{1}{4} + \frac{1}{4}, \frac{2}{7} + \frac{3}{14}, \frac{1}{3} + \frac{1}{6}$ |
| $\frac{2}{3}$ | $\frac{1}{3} + \frac{1}{3}, \frac{1}{6} + \frac{1}{2}, \frac{1}{9} + \frac{5}{9}$ |
| $\frac{3}{4}$ | $\frac{1}{4} + \frac{1}{2}, \frac{1}{3} + \frac{5}{12}, \frac{3}{8} + \frac{3}{8}$ |
| $\frac{4}{5}$ | $\frac{2}{5} + \frac{2}{5}, \frac{1}{2} + \frac{3}{10}, \frac{1}{3} + \frac{7}{15}$ |
| $\frac{5}{6}$ | $\frac{2}{3} + \frac{1}{6}, \frac{1}{2} + \frac{1}{3}, \frac{3}{4} + \frac{1}{12}$ |

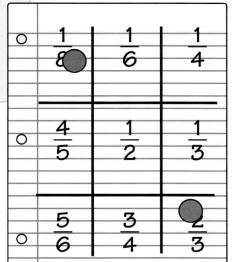

**Find more student practice on pages 71, 73–75.**

Name _____    Date _____

# Tennis, Anyone?

Add the fractions. Write the answer in simplest form. Draw a straight line from your answer to the matching paddle. The first one has been done for you.

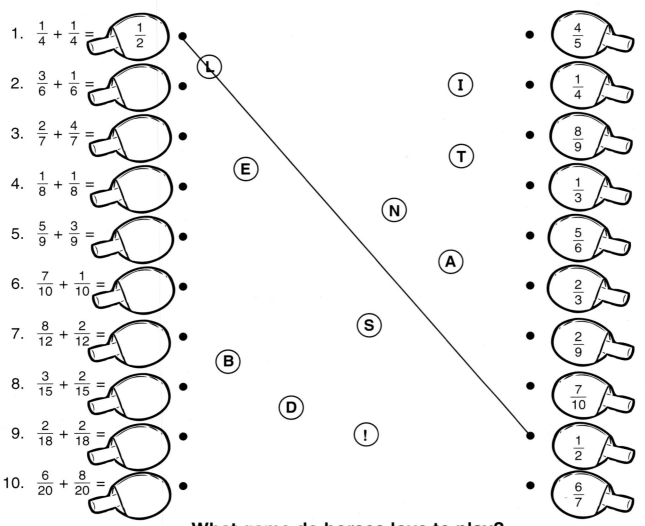

1.  $\frac{1}{4} + \frac{1}{4} = \frac{1}{2}$

2.  $\frac{3}{6} + \frac{1}{6} =$

3.  $\frac{2}{7} + \frac{4}{7} =$

4.  $\frac{1}{8} + \frac{1}{8} =$

5.  $\frac{5}{9} + \frac{3}{9} =$

6.  $\frac{7}{10} + \frac{1}{10} =$

7.  $\frac{8}{12} + \frac{2}{12} =$

8.  $\frac{3}{15} + \frac{2}{15} =$

9.  $\frac{2}{18} + \frac{2}{18} =$

10. $\frac{6}{20} + \frac{8}{20} =$

$\frac{4}{5}$  $\frac{1}{4}$  $\frac{8}{9}$  $\frac{1}{3}$  $\frac{5}{6}$  $\frac{2}{3}$  $\frac{2}{9}$  $\frac{7}{10}$  $\frac{1}{2}$  $\frac{6}{7}$

L  E  N  A  S  B  D  !  I  T

## What game do horses love to play?

To answer the riddle, match the letter or punctuation mark that each line crossed through to a numbered line below.

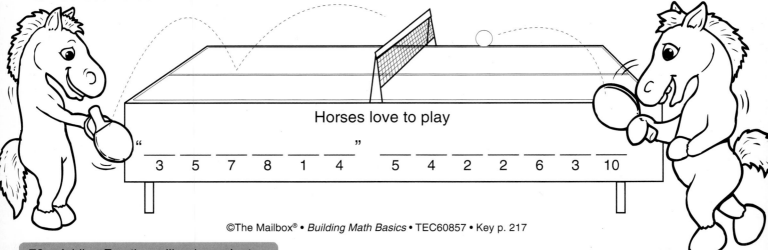

Horses love to play

"____  ____  ____  ____  ____  ____    ____  ____  ____  ____  ____  ____  ____"
 3    5    7    8    1    4      5    4    2    2    6    3    10

Name _____ Date _____

# Get the Scoop!

Estimate each sum. Then color the scoop that best matches the estimate on the cone.

1. $\frac{7}{10} + \frac{1}{10}$ / $\frac{1}{10} + \frac{3}{10}$ — $\frac{1}{2}$

2. $\frac{4}{5} + \frac{1}{5}$ / $\frac{3}{8} + \frac{1}{5}$ — $1$

3. $\frac{7}{8} + \frac{2}{5}$ / $\frac{3}{11} + \frac{6}{11}$ — $1\frac{1}{2}$

4. $\frac{6}{11} + \frac{7}{12}$ / $\frac{1}{3} + \frac{1}{4}$ — $\frac{1}{2}$

5. $\frac{7}{8} + \frac{2}{3}$ / $\frac{1}{5} + \frac{7}{8}$ — $1$

6. $\frac{1}{9} + \frac{4}{9}$ / $\frac{8}{15} + \frac{8}{9}$ — $1\frac{1}{2}$

7. $\frac{1}{11} + \frac{5}{11}$ / $\frac{3}{5} + \frac{8}{9}$ — $\frac{1}{2}$

8. $\frac{4}{9} + \frac{1}{4}$ / $\frac{6}{7} + \frac{1}{4}$ — $1$

9. $\frac{3}{4} + \frac{1}{5}$ / $\frac{2}{3} + \frac{6}{7}$ — $1$

10. $\frac{5}{12} + \frac{1}{7}$ / $\frac{3}{7} + \frac{4}{7}$ — $\frac{1}{2}$

11. $\frac{1}{3} + \frac{1}{3}$ / $\frac{5}{12} + \frac{7}{8}$ — $1\frac{1}{2}$

12. $\frac{13}{15} + \frac{5}{8}$ / $\frac{7}{15} + \frac{3}{8}$ — $1\frac{1}{2}$

Name _____          Date _____

# Royal Workout

Solve each problem below. Write each answer in simplest form.

**I**    $\frac{1}{2} + \frac{3}{4} =$ _____

**C**    $\frac{2}{3} + \frac{5}{6} =$ _____

**H**    $\frac{3}{4} + \frac{5}{8} =$ _____

**E**    $\frac{1}{3} + \frac{1}{4} =$ _____

**B**    $\frac{3}{5} + \frac{7}{20} =$ _____

**S**    $\frac{5}{18} + \frac{5}{6} =$ _____

**L**    $\frac{3}{7} + \frac{3}{14} =$ _____

**A**    $\frac{5}{8} + \frac{1}{16} =$ _____

**D**    $\frac{1}{8} + \frac{5}{24} =$ _____

**R**    $\frac{4}{9} + \frac{5}{18} =$ _____

**N**    $\frac{7}{12} + \frac{1}{6} =$ _____

**T**    $\frac{2}{5} + \frac{7}{15} =$ _____

## What did King Freddie lose while working out at the gym?

To solve the riddle, match the letters to the numbered lines below. Some letters will not be used.

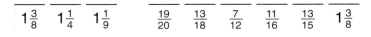

$1\frac{3}{8}$   $1\frac{1}{4}$   $1\frac{1}{9}$     $\frac{19}{20}$   $\frac{13}{18}$   $\frac{7}{12}$   $\frac{11}{16}$   $\frac{13}{15}$   $1\frac{3}{8}$

Name _____

Date _____

## Crack the Case

Help solve the mystery of the missing fractions. Solve each problem.
Write the number of the problem in the matching briefcase.

$4\frac{1}{2}$ _____

$6\frac{2}{3}$ _____

$8$ _____

$2\frac{3}{4}$ _____

1. $1\frac{1}{4} + 3\frac{1}{4} =$ _____

2. $5\frac{2}{3} + 1 =$ _____

3. $4\frac{1}{5} + 3\frac{4}{5} =$ _____

4. $3\frac{1}{9} + 3\frac{5}{9} =$ _____

5. $1\frac{5}{8} + 1\frac{1}{8} =$ _____

6. $1\frac{3}{10} + 6\frac{7}{10} =$ _____

7. $2\frac{1}{8} + 2\frac{3}{8} =$ _____

8. $2\frac{9}{16} + \frac{3}{16} =$ _____

9. $4\frac{1}{3} + 2\frac{1}{3} =$ _____

10. $1\frac{11}{24} + 1\frac{7}{24} =$ _____

11. $3\frac{1}{2} + 1 =$ _____

12. $5\frac{5}{7} + 2\frac{2}{7} =$ _____

13. $3\frac{1}{3} + 3\frac{1}{3} =$ _____

14. $1 + 1\frac{3}{4} =$ _____

15. $2\frac{1}{4} + 2\frac{1}{4} =$ _____

16. $4\frac{2}{3} + 3\frac{1}{3} =$ _____

17. $5\frac{5}{6} + 2\frac{1}{6} =$ _____

18. $4\frac{1}{3} + 2\frac{1}{3} =$ _____

19. $1\frac{1}{4} + 1\frac{2}{4} =$ _____

20. $1\frac{1}{2} + 3 =$ _____

73

# On a Roll!

Add the mixed number on each egg to the mixed number on the egg before it. Show your work on another sheet of paper. The first one has been done for you.

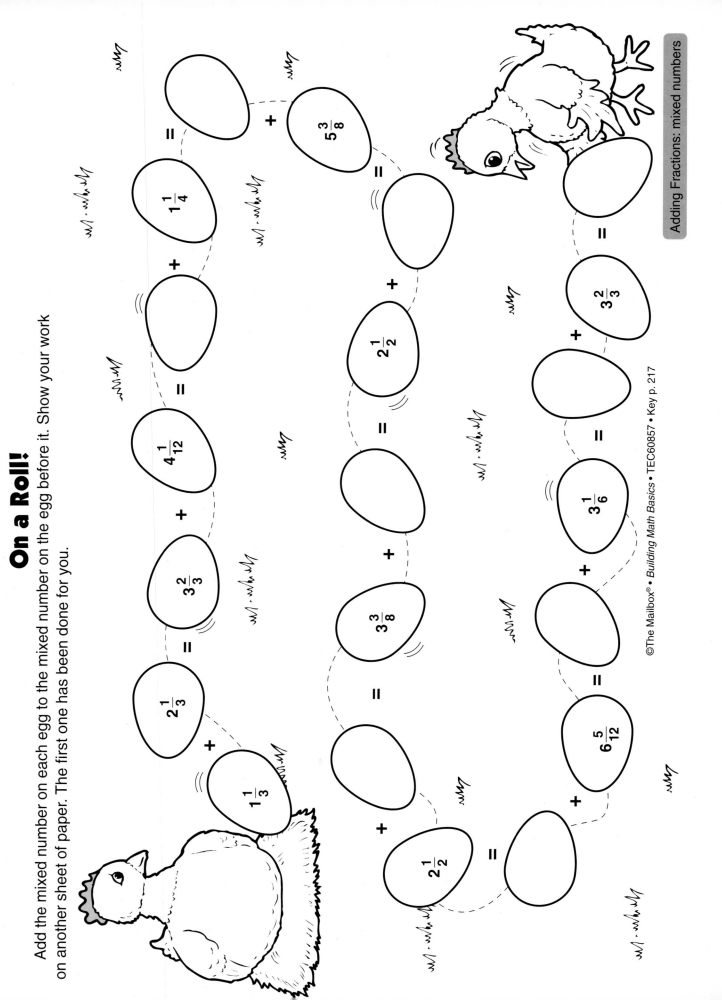

Name _____     Date _____

# Froggy Fractions

Solve each problem. Write your answer on the line.

1. Fiona and Fay feasted on flapjacks before school. Fiona ate $2\frac{1}{3}$ flapjacks. Fay ate $3\frac{1}{6}$ flapjacks. How many flapjacks did Fiona and Fay eat in all?

_____ flapjacks

2. Franco and Fran found time to read their favorite books. Franco read $18\frac{1}{2}$ pages. Fran read $27\frac{3}{4}$ pages. How many pages did they read in all?

_____ pages

3. Felix and Fay made fancy fudge for their class. The students ate $2\frac{1}{8}$ pans of fudge before lunch. They ate $3\frac{1}{4}$ pans after lunch. How many pans of fudge did the students eat in all?

_____ pans of fudge

4. Fanny plays the French horn in the band. She practiced for $1\frac{7}{8}$ hours Monday. She practiced for $1\frac{1}{4}$ hours Tuesday and $1\frac{3}{4}$ hours Thursday. How many hours did Fanny practice in all?

_____ hours

5. Fran collected $4\frac{3}{4}$ bags of canned food for Freemont School's food drive. Felix brought in $2\frac{1}{2}$ bags. How many bags of food did Fran and Felix collect?

_____ bags of food

6. Fanny's morning bus ride took $\frac{1}{2}$ of an hour. The bus broke down on the way home, making that ride take $1\frac{5}{6}$ hours. How many hours did Fanny spend on the bus in all?

_____ hours

$\frac{3}{17}$  $\frac{5}{21}$  $\frac{1}{5}$  $\frac{6}{11}$  $\frac{1}{10}$

# Subtracting Fractions

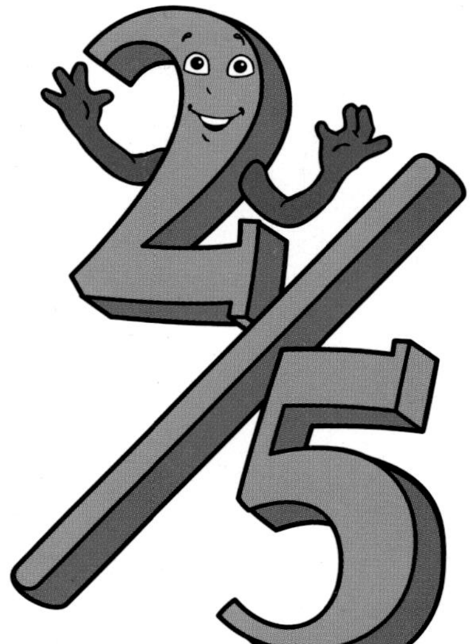

$\frac{3}{16}$

$\frac{2}{3}$  $\frac{1}{3}$  $\frac{9}{14}$  $\frac{5}{27}$

$\frac{5}{8}$

## Subtraction Stories

Reinforce fraction subtraction with student-created story problems. Give each child a sheet of paper. Direct him to fold it into thirds and then write his name on the back. Write on the board the six section topics shown below. Instruct students to write a different subtraction story problem related to one of the six topics in each section of his paper. Collect the papers and redistribute them, making sure no student receives his own paper. Challenge each student to solve the three problems and show his work on the paper. When he is finished, have him return the paper to its original owner to have the owner check the solutions.

**Section Topics:**
food
school supplies
entertainment
afterschool activity
family event
animals

Five-sixths of my cookies were chocolate. I ate ½ of my chocolate cookies. How many chocolate cookies are left?

$$\frac{5}{6} = \frac{5}{6}$$
$$-\frac{1}{2} = \frac{3}{6}$$
$$\frac{2}{6} = \frac{1}{3}$$

Three-fourths of the students in our class prefer using pencils and ¼ prefer using pens. How many more students prefer using pencils than pens?

One-half of the people at the movie theater went to see a comedy. One-fourth of the people went to see an action movie. How many more people saw a comedy than an action movie?

## How Low Can You Go?

Use this whole-class game to sharpen students' skills with mixed numbers! Give each student an index card and have her program it with a mixed number less than ten. Collect and shuffle the cards. Place them face-down in a stack near the board. Divide your class into two teams. Write on the board the mixed number 50½ for each team. One student from each team comes to the board and draws a card from the stack. Each student subtracts the mixed number on her card from 50½. If a student's answer is correct, her team earns a point, and play continues with a new team member's drawing a new card from the deck and subtracting the number on her card from the answer resulting from the first problem. If a student's answer is incorrect, the next team member comes to the board and attempts to solve the existing problem. Continue play in this manner. The first team to draw a card that cannot be subtracted from the previous answer is the winner.

# Yours Minus Mine

Pair students for this game, which reinforces subtracting fractions with unlike denominators. Program a copy of the spinner pattern below with fractions similar to those shown. Then give each pair a copy of the programmed spinner, a paper clip, and a pencil. To play, each partner takes a turn spinning the spinner. Then both students use the two resulting fractions to write a subtraction problem on a sheet of paper, making sure that the larger fraction is on top. Each partner works the subtraction problem independently and then compares his answer to his partner's. If both answers are correct, each partner earns a point. If not, only the player with the correct answer earns the point. Players repeat this process to continue play. The player with more points at the end of ten rounds is the winner.

To modify the game for practice with subtracting mixed numbers, simply give each pair two spinners, one programmed with whole numbers and one programmed with fractions. Students play in a similar manner, with each partner spinning both spinners to create a mixed number at the beginning of each round.

**Find more student practice on pages 78–83.**

## Spinner Pattern
Use with "Yours Minus Mine" above.

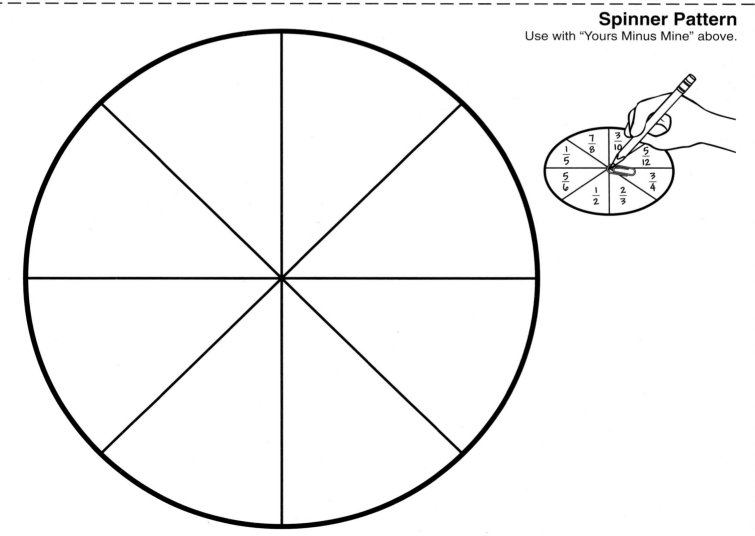

# Slam Dunk Subtraction

Help George score a slam dunk by solving each problem. Write the answer in simplest form. Color the basketball with the matching answer. Some of the balls will not be colored.

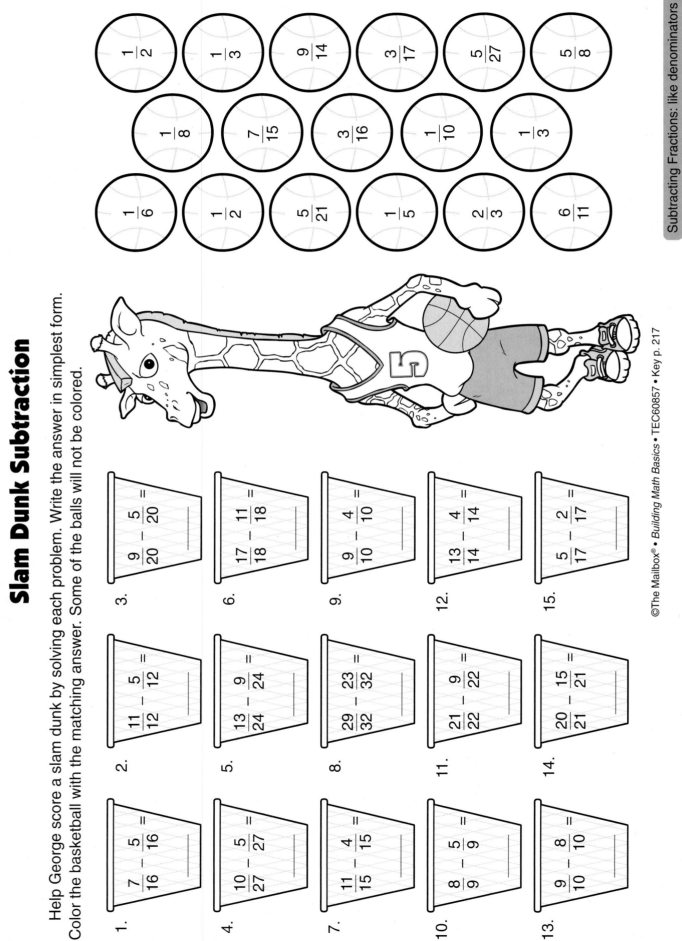

Basketballs:

$\frac{1}{6}$   $\frac{1}{8}$   $\frac{1}{2}$

$\frac{1}{2}$   $\frac{7}{15}$   $\frac{1}{3}$

$\frac{5}{21}$   $\frac{3}{16}$   $\frac{9}{14}$

$\frac{1}{5}$   $\frac{1}{10}$   $\frac{3}{17}$

$\frac{2}{3}$   $\frac{1}{3}$   $\frac{5}{27}$

$\frac{6}{11}$        $\frac{5}{8}$

Problems:

1. $\dfrac{7}{16} - \dfrac{5}{16} =$ _____

2. $\dfrac{11}{12} - \dfrac{5}{12} =$ _____

3. $\dfrac{9}{20} - \dfrac{5}{20} =$ _____

4. $\dfrac{10}{27} - \dfrac{5}{27} =$ _____

5. $\dfrac{13}{24} - \dfrac{9}{24} =$ _____

6. $\dfrac{17}{18} - \dfrac{11}{18} =$ _____

7. $\dfrac{11}{15} - \dfrac{4}{15} =$ _____

8. $\dfrac{29}{32} - \dfrac{23}{32} =$ _____

9. $\dfrac{9}{10} - \dfrac{4}{10} =$ _____

10. $\dfrac{8}{9} - \dfrac{5}{9} =$ _____

11. $\dfrac{21}{22} - \dfrac{9}{22} =$ _____

12. $\dfrac{13}{14} - \dfrac{4}{14} =$ _____

13. $\dfrac{9}{10} - \dfrac{8}{10} =$ _____

14. $\dfrac{20}{21} - \dfrac{15}{21} =$ _____

15. $\dfrac{5}{17} - \dfrac{2}{17} =$ _____

Subtracting Fractions: like denominators

# The Right Combination

Subtract. Write each answer in simplest form. Write the number
of the problem on the matching padlock.

1. $\frac{5}{12} - \frac{1}{6}$

2. $\frac{9}{10} - \frac{2}{5}$

3. $\frac{7}{10} - \frac{1}{2}$

4. $\frac{14}{15} - \frac{3}{5}$

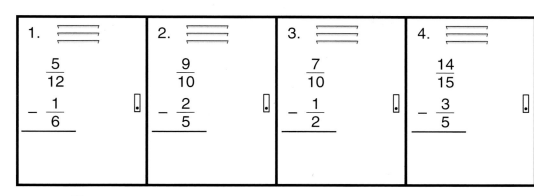

5. $\frac{1}{2} - \frac{1}{4}$

6. $\frac{16}{21} - \frac{3}{7}$

7. $\frac{32}{35} - \frac{5}{7}$

8. $\frac{4}{5} - \frac{11}{20}$

9. $\frac{5}{6} - \frac{1}{3}$

10. $\frac{11}{14} - \frac{2}{7}$

11. $\frac{1}{2} - \frac{3}{10}$

12. $\frac{5}{6} - \frac{1}{2}$

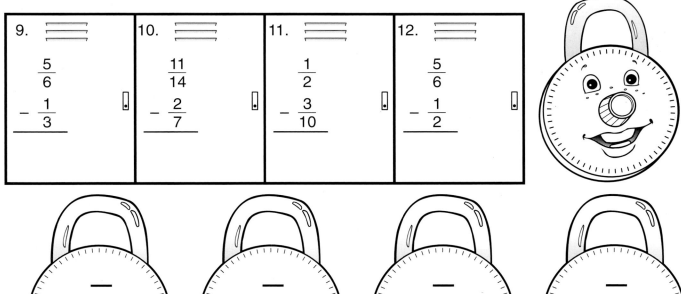

$\frac{1}{2}$   $\frac{1}{3}$   $\frac{1}{4}$   $\frac{1}{5}$

Subtracting Fractions: unlike denominators  79

Name _____

Date _____

# Ready, Set, Subtract!

Estimate each difference. Color the flag to show whether the answer is closer to $\frac{1}{2}$ or 0.

1. $\frac{5}{8} - \frac{1}{4} =$    $\frac{1}{2}$   0

2. $\frac{1}{2} - \frac{1}{3} =$    $\frac{1}{2}$   0

3. $1 - \frac{4}{5} =$    $\frac{1}{2}$   0

4. $\frac{6}{8} - \frac{1}{4} =$    $\frac{1}{2}$   0

5. $\frac{7}{10} - \frac{1}{2} =$    $\frac{1}{2}$   0

6. $\frac{4}{5} - \frac{2}{3} =$    $\frac{1}{2}$   0

7. $\frac{6}{7} - \frac{3}{7} =$    $\frac{1}{2}$   0

8. $\frac{7}{8} - \frac{3}{4} =$    $\frac{1}{2}$   0

9. $\frac{5}{8} - \frac{1}{12} =$    $\frac{1}{2}$   0

10. $\frac{3}{4} - \frac{1}{4} =$    $\frac{1}{2}$   0

11. $\frac{17}{18} - \frac{1}{15} =$    $\frac{1}{2}$   0

12. $\frac{3}{4} - \frac{3}{12} =$    $\frac{1}{2}$   0

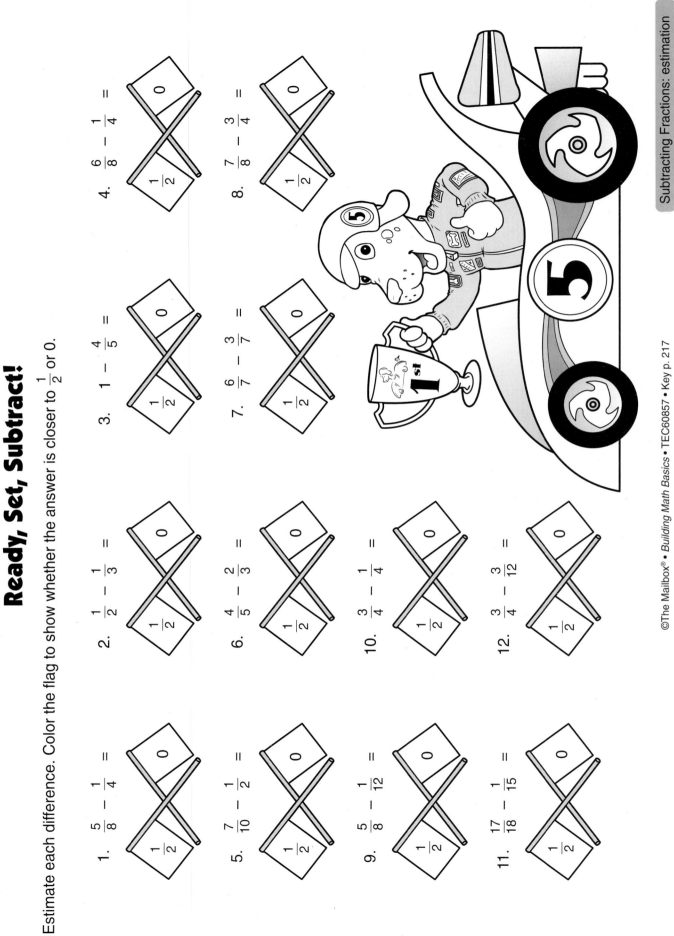

80

# Teamwork

Subtract. Color the gumball if the answer is correct. Cross out each incorrect answer and write the right answer next to it.

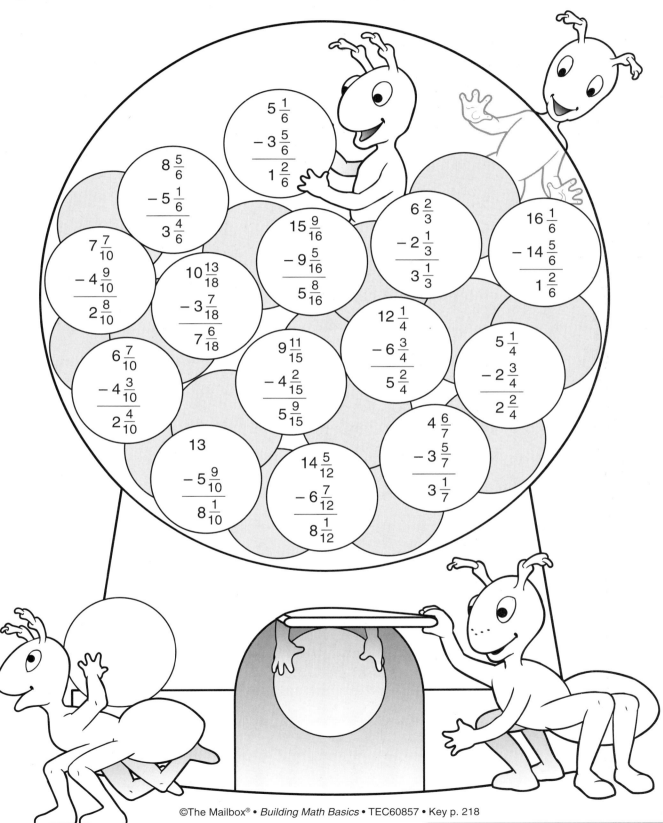

$$8\frac{5}{6} - 5\frac{1}{6} = 3\frac{4}{6}$$

$$5\frac{1}{6} - 3\frac{5}{6} = 1\frac{2}{6}$$

$$6\frac{2}{3} - 2\frac{1}{3} = 3\frac{1}{3}$$

$$16\frac{1}{6} - 14\frac{5}{6} = 1\frac{2}{6}$$

$$7\frac{7}{10} - 4\frac{9}{10} = 2\frac{8}{10}$$

$$10\frac{13}{18} - 3\frac{7}{18} = 7\frac{6}{18}$$

$$15\frac{9}{16} - 9\frac{5}{16} = 5\frac{8}{16}$$

$$12\frac{1}{4} - 6\frac{3}{4} = 5\frac{2}{4}$$

$$5\frac{1}{4} - 2\frac{3}{4} = 2\frac{2}{4}$$

$$6\frac{7}{10} - 4\frac{3}{10} = 2\frac{4}{10}$$

$$9\frac{11}{15} - 4\frac{2}{15} = 5\frac{9}{15}$$

$$4\frac{6}{7} - 3\frac{5}{7} = 3\frac{1}{7}$$

$$13 - 5\frac{9}{10} = 8\frac{1}{10}$$

$$14\frac{5}{12} - 6\frac{7}{12} = 8\frac{1}{12}$$

©The Mailbox® • *Building Math Basics* • TEC60857 • Key p. 218

# Penguin in Paradise

Subtract. Show your work on another sheet of
paper. Write each answer in simplest form. Then color
the answer to reveal the path to Penny Penguin's
favorite vacation spot.

1. $7\frac{1}{5} - 2\frac{3}{10} =$

2. $8\frac{2}{3} - 6\frac{1}{9} =$

3. $3\frac{3}{10} - \frac{1}{2} =$

4. $10\frac{1}{6} - 1\frac{3}{4} =$

5. $9\frac{2}{3} - 6\frac{3}{4} =$

6. $13\frac{3}{16} - 5\frac{3}{8} =$

7. $9\frac{2}{15} - 4\frac{4}{5} =$

8. $16\frac{5}{18} - 7\frac{4}{9} =$

9. $22 - 1\frac{7}{24} =$

10. $13\frac{5}{12} - 6\frac{1}{2} =$

11. $6\frac{1}{10} - 3\frac{2}{3} =$

12. $18\frac{3}{14} - 11\frac{5}{7} =$

| | | | |
|---|---|---|---|
| $5\frac{2}{5}$ | $4\frac{9}{10}$ | $4\frac{1}{10}$ | $5\frac{1}{10}$ |
| $1\frac{2}{9}$ | $2\frac{5}{9}$ | $2\frac{2}{9}$ | $2\frac{3}{9}$ |
| $2\frac{4}{5}$ | $3\frac{5}{10}$ | $3\frac{1}{2}$ | $2\frac{8}{10}$ |
| $9\frac{6}{12}$ | $8\frac{5}{12}$ | $8\frac{1}{2}$ | $9\frac{5}{12}$ |
| $3\frac{3}{12}$ | $2\frac{1}{2}$ | $2\frac{11}{12}$ | $3\frac{11}{12}$ |
| $8\frac{2}{16}$ | $8\frac{13}{16}$ | $7\frac{3}{16}$ | $7\frac{13}{16}$ |
| $5\frac{1}{3}$ | $4\frac{4}{15}$ | $4\frac{1}{3}$ | $5\frac{1}{5}$ |
| $9\frac{2}{18}$ | $8\frac{5}{6}$ | $9\frac{1}{3}$ | $8\frac{2}{3}$ |
| $21\frac{14}{24}$ | $20\frac{7}{12}$ | $20\frac{17}{24}$ | $21\frac{7}{12}$ |
| $7\frac{4}{12}$ | $6\frac{11}{12}$ | $7\frac{1}{3}$ | $6\frac{3}{4}$ |
| $2\frac{1}{2}$ | $2\frac{13}{30}$ | $3\frac{1}{3}$ | $3\frac{17}{30}$ |
| $6\frac{1}{2}$ | $7\frac{5}{7}$ | $6\frac{3}{7}$ | $7\frac{1}{2}$ |

**Seashell Beach**  **Painted Desert**  **Serenity Springs**  **Soothe-Your-Spirit Spa**

Name_____     Date _____

# Meow Meow Diner

Carrie and Candy work at the Meow Meow Diner. Solve each problem on another sheet of paper. Write your answer in simplest form on the blank provided.

1. The diner is $\frac{2}{3}$ of a mile from Carrie's house and $\frac{1}{7}$ of a mile from Candy's house. How much farther is the diner from Carrie's house than from Candy's?

   _____ of a mile

2. Candy scrambled $\frac{11}{12}$ of a carton of eggs for breakfast. Two customers ate a total of $\frac{5}{6}$ of the eggs. What portion of the scrambled eggs were not eaten?

   _____ of the eggs

3. It took Carrie $\frac{3}{4}$ of an hour to make biscuits. Candy needed $\frac{2}{5}$ of an hour to make gravy. How much longer did Carrie spend making biscuits than Candy spent making gravy?

   _____ of an hour

4. Carrie used $9\frac{3}{8}$ ounces of a 16-ounce bottle of juice. How much juice was left in the bottle?

   _____ ounces

5. Candy made 5 gallons of spaghetti sauce. One and two-fifths gallons of it spilled on the floor. How much sauce did not spill on the floor?

   _____ gallons

6. Two-thirds of the diner's customers ordered ravioli for dinner. One-fourth of the customers ordered spaghetti. How many more customers ordered ravioli than spaghetti?

   _____ of the customers

7. Carrie and Candy both love kibble cake. Carrie ate $2\frac{4}{5}$ slices and Candy ate $2\frac{1}{10}$ slices. How much more cake did Carrie eat?

   _____ more cake

8. Carrie is famous for her dessert pizza. She cooked an apple pizza and cut it into 15 slices. Two customers ate a total of $7\frac{3}{5}$ of the slices. How many slices were left?

   _____ slices

# Multiplying Fractions

## Modeling Multiplication

Help students fold and color their way to a better understanding of multiplying fractions! Give each child a sheet of paper and a crayon. Also write "$\frac{2}{3} \times \frac{1}{2}$" on the board. Explain that this is the same as finding $\frac{2}{3}$ of $\frac{1}{2}$. Direct each student to fold his paper in half lengthwise. Then have him unfold it and lightly color one of the two equal sections. Next, instruct him to fold the paper in thirds. After he unfolds it, have him count the paper's total number of parts (6) and then its colored parts (3). Have the student color two of the three colored sections more heavily. Guide the class to identify the product ($\frac{2}{6}$ or $\frac{1}{3}$) and to understand that the two darker parts represent the numerator and the six total parts represent the denominator. To model another problem, have students use another sheet of paper to show the product of $\frac{3}{4} \times \frac{1}{2}$ ($\frac{3}{8}$). To provide more practice, have each child complete a copy of page 86 as directed.

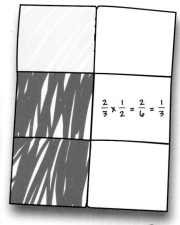

$$\frac{2}{3} \times \frac{1}{2} = \frac{2}{6} = \frac{1}{3}$$

## What's Speedier?

Which method is faster when finding the product of two fractions: repeated addition or multiplying? Challenge students to find out! Label several pairs of sentence strips with related addition and multiplication problems such as the ones shown. Tape one pair of strips to the chalkboard facedown in columns; then invite two students to come to the board to solve the problems. At your signal, have each child flip her strip over, retape it to the board, and race to solve the problem. When the students are finished, have the class check their work and note which student finished first. Continue the challenge, using a new set of problems and a different pair of volunteers until all the problems have been solved. It won't take long for students to decide that multiplication is faster!

$$\frac{1}{3} + \frac{1}{3} + \frac{1}{3} + \frac{1}{3} + \frac{1}{3} + \frac{1}{3} + \frac{1}{3} = ?$$

$$\frac{1}{3} \times 7 = ?$$

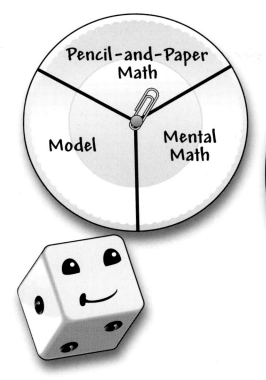

# Three-Method Spin

Make multiplying fractions "spinner-ific" with this multi method practice! Create a paper plate spinner and label it as shown. Then obtain a die and stack a deck of cards (with face cards removed) facedown. Next, choose three students. Have the first student roll the die twice and use the numbers rolled (in any order) to write on the board a fraction followed by a multiplication symbol. Have the second student draw two cards and use their values in a similar way to write a second fraction followed by an equal sign. Instruct the third student to spin the spinner to determine the problem-solving method for the class to use to find the product. When everyone has solved the problem, choose a volunteer to share her answer and how she got it (or explain the math process she used). If correct, allow her to choose two other students to help her roll, write, and spin for the next round!

# Bargain Shopping

Need an activity that can help students appreciate the usefulness of multiplying fractions? Try using sales ads! Ask students to bring in various ads that offer a fraction off the original price or advertise products with fewer carbs or calories, and place them in a container. (If some ads offer a percentage off instead of a fraction, create a set of index cards labeled with common fractions that students can substitute.) Next, use an ad to model how to estimate and find the actual amounts saved and spent. Copy the example on chart paper and display it near the container. Select a different ad each day for the class to use as a review problem and a different child to explain its solution when checking. Follow up by having each student complete page 91 as directed.

**Find more student practice on pages 87–89 and 92.**

Name _____     Date _____

# Keeping Hilda Happy

Hilda loves s'mores! And the bigger the piece, the better!
Write the fraction for each cracker in the box.
Compare the two fractions.
Write the letter of the larger cracker in the blank.
Use the example for help.

Example: Which piece is bigger: $\frac{1}{3}$ of $\frac{1}{2}$ OR $\frac{1}{3}$ of $\frac{1}{4}$?

I.     J.

OR

$\frac{1}{3}$ of $\frac{1}{2} = \boxed{\frac{1}{6}}$     $\frac{1}{3}$ of $\frac{1}{4} = \boxed{\frac{1}{12}}$

Cracker ____I____ is bigger.

I'll take $\frac{1}{3}$ of $\frac{1}{2}$!

1.
A.     B.
OR
$\frac{2}{3}$ of $\frac{1}{4} = \boxed{\phantom{x}}$     $\frac{2}{3}$ of $\frac{1}{2} = \boxed{\phantom{x}}$

Cracker _____ is bigger.

2.
C.     D.
OR
$\frac{2}{3}$ of $\frac{1}{2} = \boxed{\phantom{x}}$     $\frac{1}{2}$ of $\frac{1}{3} = \boxed{\phantom{x}}$

Cracker _____ is bigger.

3.
E.     F.
OR
$\frac{1}{3}$ of $\frac{1}{4} = \boxed{\phantom{x}}$     $\frac{1}{2}$ of $\frac{1}{5} = \boxed{\phantom{x}}$

Cracker _____ is bigger.

4.
G.     H.
OR
$\frac{2}{5}$ of $\frac{1}{2} = \boxed{\phantom{x}}$     $\frac{1}{4}$ of $\frac{1}{4} = \boxed{\phantom{x}}$

Cracker _____ is bigger.

Name _____    Date _____

# Clyde's Ride

Clyde is biking to a friend's house. Find out which friend!
Solve each problem and write its answer in simplest form.
Then find the gate with that answer. Draw a line connecting
each correct answer to see the path he will take!

1. $\frac{1}{2} \times \frac{3}{4} =$ _____

2. $\frac{2}{6} \times \frac{4}{6} =$ _____

3. $\frac{5}{6} \times \frac{1}{4} =$ _____

4. $\frac{5}{7} \times \frac{2}{3} =$ _____

5. $\frac{1}{2} \times \frac{2}{5} =$ _____

6. $\frac{5}{6} \times \frac{1}{5} =$ _____

7. $\frac{2}{5} \times \frac{2}{3} =$ _____

8. $\frac{5}{6} \times \frac{2}{3} =$ _____

9. $\frac{1}{3} \times \frac{5}{8} =$ _____

10. $\frac{7}{8} \times \frac{6}{7} =$ _____

Clyde is visiting _____.

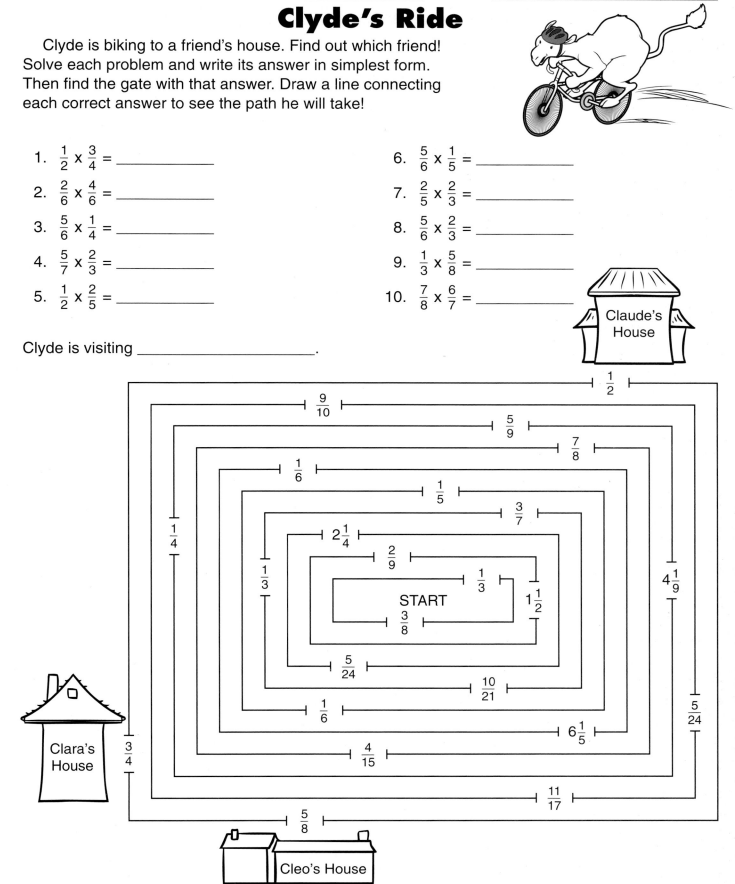

Name _____ Date _____

# Awesome Apples

Multiply.
Write each answer in simplest form.
Color by the code.

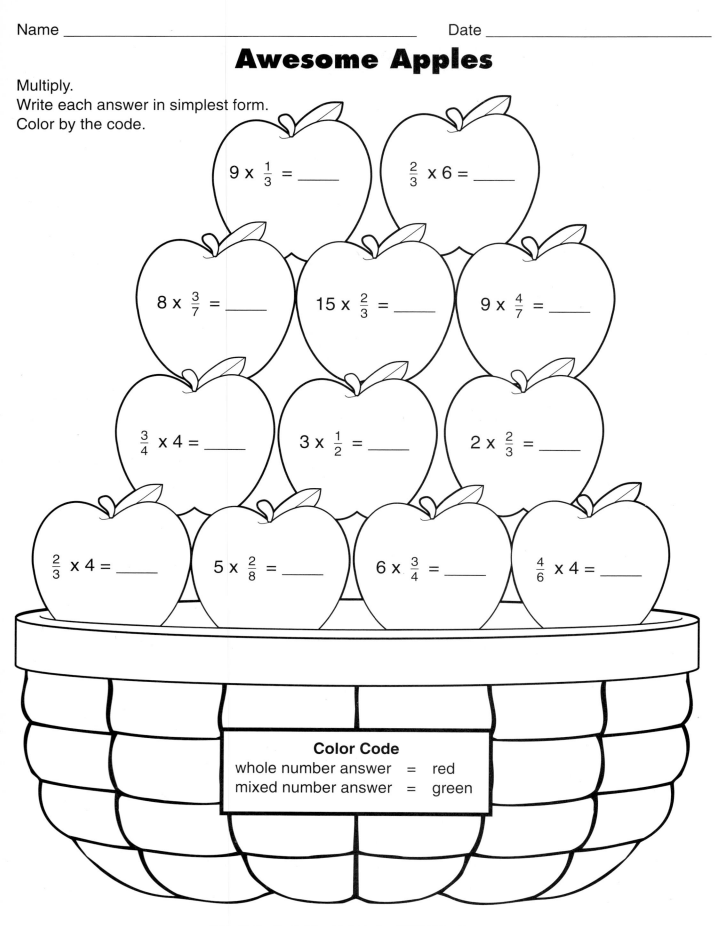

$9 \times \frac{1}{3} =$ _____

$\frac{2}{3} \times 6 =$ _____

$8 \times \frac{3}{7} =$ _____

$15 \times \frac{2}{3} =$ _____

$9 \times \frac{4}{7} =$ _____

$\frac{3}{4} \times 4 =$ _____

$3 \times \frac{1}{2} =$ _____

$2 \times \frac{2}{3} =$ _____

$\frac{2}{3} \times 4 =$ _____

$5 \times \frac{2}{8} =$ _____

$6 \times \frac{3}{4} =$ _____

$\frac{4}{6} \times 4 =$ _____

**Color Code**
whole number answer = red
mixed number answer = green

Name _____    Date _____

# Rico's Reality Check

Rico thinks he will never need to know how to multiply fractions. To convince him that he does, his friends are sharing examples. Solve each friend's example.

1. Zora Zebra wanted lemonade. Her recipe made three servings and called for 27 lemons. Since she wanted only two servings, she had to find $\frac{2}{3}$ of 27 lemons.
   _____ lemons

2. Jill Giraffe and her two sisters had a camera that took 24 photos. Since they each wanted to take the same number of pictures, they had to find $\frac{1}{3}$ of 24 pictures.
   _____ pictures

3. Freddy Frog bought 120 butterfly eggs. He was told that about $\frac{1}{10}$ of them would not hatch. To figure out how many that was, he had to find $\frac{1}{10}$ of 120 butterfly eggs.
   _____ butterfly eggs

4. Artie Ant's family had a 10-slice pizza. His little brother ate 1 slice and said he was full. Artie wanted to share the rest of the pizza equally with his mom and dad, so he had to find $\frac{1}{3}$ of 9 pieces.
   _____ pieces of pizza

5. Greta Grasshopper and her parents wanted to invite 75 people to her grandmother's 75th birthday party. So that they would each address the same number of envelopes, she had to find $\frac{1}{3}$ of 75 envelopes.
   _____ envelopes

Gunter Grasshopper

6. Lulu Ladybug wanted to create a design for her art class that had equal parts of blue, green, red, and yellow. The design she made had 56 parts. So she had to find $\frac{1}{4}$ of 56 parts.
   _____ parts

Colored Chalk

7. Nicky Gnat wanted to draw 3 scenes on the sidewalk. His cousin wanted to draw 1 scene. The sidewalk was 40 inches long, so he had to find $\frac{3}{4}$ of 40 inches.
   _____ inches

Raffle Ticket

8. Hilda Hippo sold 20 raffle tickets to 5 friends. One friend bought 4 times as many tickets as the rest. So Hilda had to give him $\frac{4}{5}$ of the 20 tickets.
   _____ tickets

# Marvin's Mistake

Marvin just canceled his last show. To find out why, solve the problem and write the answer in simplest form. Then write the letter for each answer in the matching blanks below.

**NO SHOW TONIGHT**

1. $\frac{4}{5} \times \frac{1}{6} =$ _____ (H)

2. $1\frac{2}{3} \times \frac{2}{3} =$ _____ (G)

3. $12 \times \frac{2}{3} =$ _____ (A)

4. $\frac{7}{8} \times 1\frac{1}{8} =$ _____ (W)

5. $\frac{3}{4} \times \frac{2}{3} =$ _____ (I)

6. $\frac{1}{6} \times \frac{1}{4} =$ _____ (T)

7. $\frac{3}{4} \times \frac{3}{7} =$ _____ (U)

8. $\frac{1}{6} \times \frac{1}{3} =$ _____ (O)

9. $\frac{3}{5} \times \frac{1}{2} =$ _____ (E)

10. $\frac{2}{3} \times 1\frac{4}{9} =$ _____ (N)

11. $1\frac{5}{8} \times \frac{4}{5} =$ _____ (C)

12. $\frac{2}{3} \times \frac{1}{3} =$ _____ (S)

13. $\frac{1}{2} \times 2\frac{1}{4} =$ _____ (D)

14. $2\frac{1}{6} \times 1\frac{1}{2} =$ _____ (J)

15. $\frac{2}{3} \times \frac{1}{4} =$ _____ (R)

16. $\frac{7}{8} \times 1\frac{1}{5} =$ _____ (L)

**Why did Marvin cancel the magic show?**

$\overline{\frac{2}{15}}$ $\overline{\frac{3}{10}}$  $\overline{\frac{2}{15}}$ $\overline{8}$ $\overline{1\frac{1}{8}}$  $\overline{3\frac{1}{4}}$ $\overline{\frac{9}{28}}$ $\overline{\frac{2}{9}}$ $\overline{\frac{1}{24}}$  $\overline{\frac{63}{64}}$ $\overline{8}$ $\overline{\frac{2}{9}}$ $\overline{\frac{2}{15}}$ $\overline{\frac{3}{10}}$ $\overline{1\frac{1}{8}}$   **,**

$\overline{\frac{2}{15}}$ $\overline{\frac{1}{2}}$ $\overline{\frac{2}{9}}$  $\overline{\frac{2}{15}}$ $\overline{8}$ $\overline{\frac{1}{6}}$ $\overline{\frac{3}{10}}$  $\overline{8}$ $\overline{\frac{26}{27}}$ $\overline{1\frac{1}{8}}$  $\overline{1\frac{3}{10}}$ $\overline{\frac{1}{18}}$ $\overline{\frac{9}{28}}$ $\overline{1\frac{1}{20}}$ $\overline{1\frac{1}{8}}$ $\overline{\frac{26}{27}}$ $\overline{\frac{1}{24}}$

$\overline{1\frac{1}{8}}$ $\overline{\frac{1}{18}}$  $\overline{8}$  $\overline{\frac{1}{24}}$ $\overline{\frac{2}{15}}$ $\overline{\frac{1}{2}}$ $\overline{\frac{26}{27}}$ $\overline{1\frac{1}{9}}$  $\overline{\frac{63}{64}}$ $\overline{\frac{1}{2}}$ $\overline{\frac{1}{24}}$ $\overline{\frac{2}{15}}$  $\overline{\frac{1}{2}}$ $\overline{\frac{1}{24}}$ **!**

Name _____  Date _____

# "Bee-utiful" Hive

Multiply.
Write your answer in simplest form.

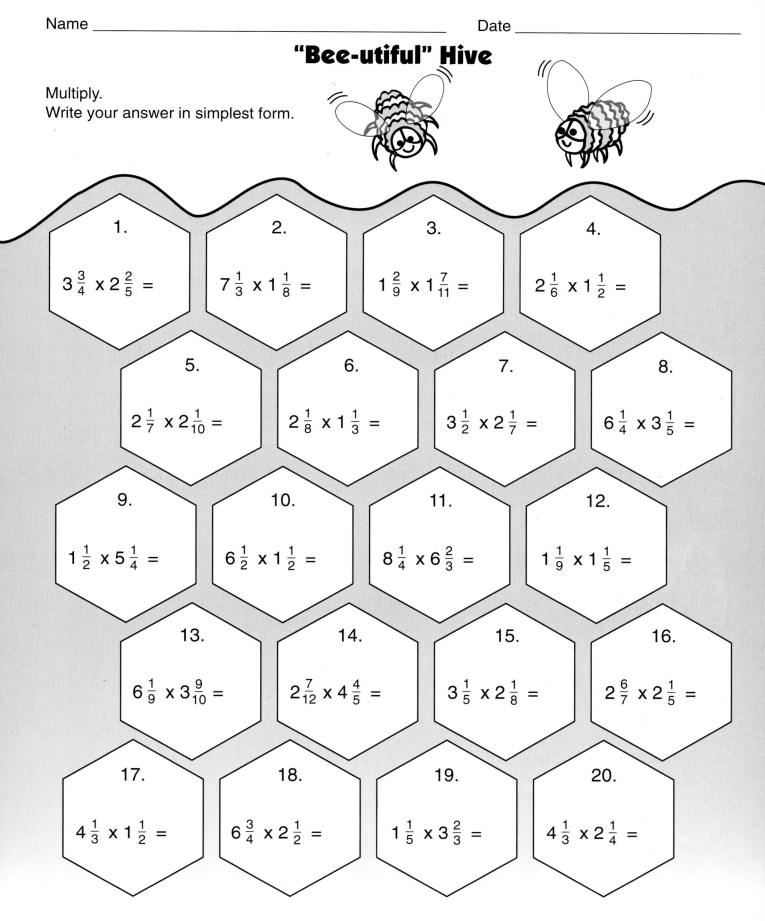

1. $3\frac{3}{4} \times 2\frac{2}{5} =$

2. $7\frac{1}{3} \times 1\frac{1}{8} =$

3. $1\frac{2}{9} \times 1\frac{7}{11} =$

4. $2\frac{1}{6} \times 1\frac{1}{2} =$

5. $2\frac{1}{7} \times 2\frac{1}{10} =$

6. $2\frac{1}{8} \times 1\frac{1}{3} =$

7. $3\frac{1}{2} \times 2\frac{1}{7} =$

8. $6\frac{1}{4} \times 3\frac{1}{5} =$

9. $1\frac{1}{2} \times 5\frac{1}{4} =$

10. $6\frac{1}{2} \times 1\frac{1}{2} =$

11. $8\frac{1}{4} \times 6\frac{2}{3} =$

12. $1\frac{1}{9} \times 1\frac{1}{5} =$

13. $6\frac{1}{9} \times 3\frac{9}{10} =$

14. $2\frac{7}{12} \times 4\frac{4}{5} =$

15. $3\frac{1}{5} \times 2\frac{1}{8} =$

16. $2\frac{6}{7} \times 2\frac{1}{5} =$

17. $4\frac{1}{3} \times 1\frac{1}{2} =$

18. $6\frac{3}{4} \times 2\frac{1}{2} =$

19. $1\frac{1}{5} \times 3\frac{2}{3} =$

20. $4\frac{1}{3} \times 2\frac{1}{4} =$

# Dividing Fractions

## Roll 'em!

Roll out this fun center activity to give students quick practice with dividing fractions! Place paper, two pencils, and a die at a center. Invite student pairs visiting the center to take turns rolling the die twice. The first child uses his rolls to create a dividend. The other child uses hers to create a divisor. Have each student solve the resulting problem and check each other's work. Then direct each player with a correct answer to roll the die and use the number rolled as his score. After students play as many rounds as time allows, declare the player with the higher score the winner. As a variation, have students roll the die three times each to divide a mixed number by a mixed number! Follow up this activity with the reproducible on page 93 for additional practice.

| Player 1 | Score |
|---|---|
| 1. $\frac{2}{3} \div \frac{5}{6} = \frac{2}{3} \times \frac{6}{5} = \frac{12}{15} = \frac{4}{5}$ | 2 |
| 2. $\frac{6}{4} \div \frac{1}{2} = \frac{6}{4} \times \frac{2}{1} = \frac{12}{4} = 3$ | 5 |
| 3. | |

## Scavenging for Quotients

Challenge students to practice dividing fractions using real-life objects! On each of ten to 20 index cards, write a different sentence about fractions that represents a classroom object. (See the examples.) Include several cards with incorrect answers. Place the cards at a free-time center along with paper, pencils, and a bag labeled "Scavenger Hunt." When a student finishes her work, invite her to choose a card and try to identify on a sheet of paper the object it describes. Then have her write and solve the corresponding math problem to determine whether the sentence is correct. Next, have her write her name on the paper, fold it with the card inside, and place it in the bag. At the end of the day (or week), check the bag's contents and award a small treat to each student whose paper has a correct answer!

**Example Sentences**
1. Twelve half-inch-wide books could fit on this six-foot-long shelf.

2. If this five-inch-long candy bar were divided into half-inch-long pieces, there would be enough for ten people to have an equal share.

3. If this $8\frac{1}{2}$-inch-wide paper were divided into $3\frac{1}{4}$-inch-wide sections, there would be $10\frac{3}{4}$ sections in all.

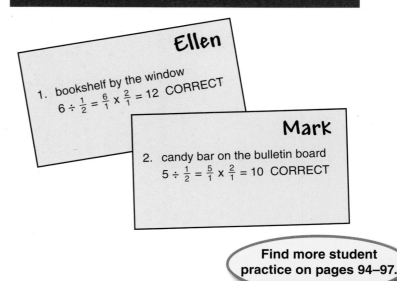

**Ellen**
1. bookshelf by the window
$6 \div \frac{1}{2} = \frac{6}{1} \times \frac{2}{1} = 12$ CORRECT

**Mark**
2. candy bar on the bulletin board
$5 \div \frac{1}{2} = \frac{5}{1} \times \frac{2}{1} = 10$ CORRECT

**Find more student practice on pages 94–97.**

Name _____

Date _____

# Rent a Wreck!

Which cars have not been rented? Divide. Write each quotient in simplest terms. Show your work on another sheet of paper. Then color each car whose quotient is on an exhaust cloud. The cars that are left have not been rented!

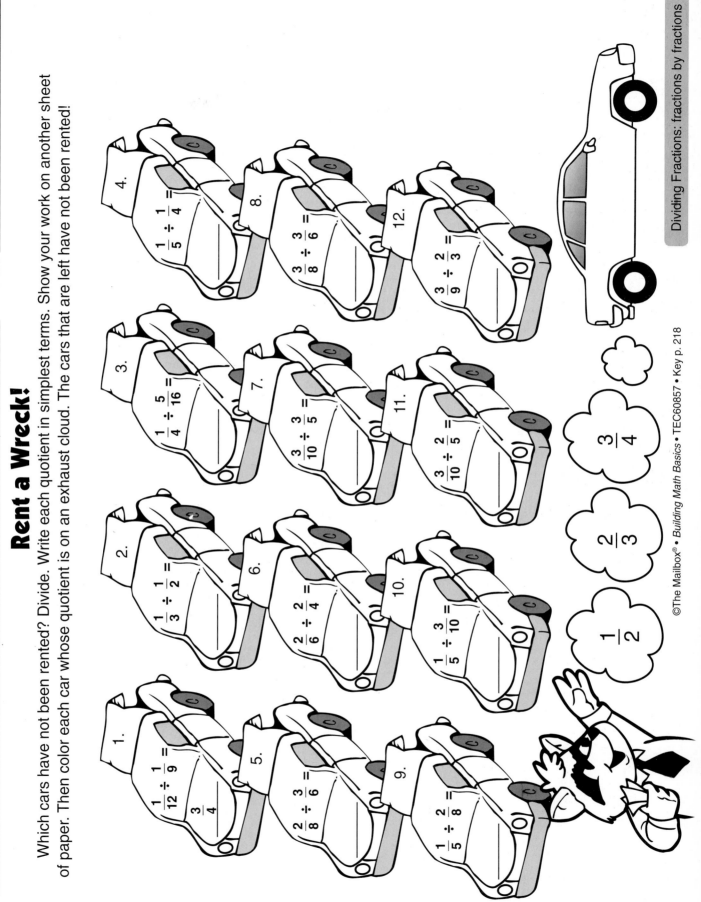

1. $\dfrac{1}{12} \div \dfrac{1}{9} = \dfrac{3}{4}$

2. $\dfrac{1}{3} \div \dfrac{1}{2} =$

3. $\dfrac{1}{4} \div \dfrac{5}{16} =$

4. $\dfrac{1}{5} \div \dfrac{1}{4} =$

5. $\dfrac{2}{8} \div \dfrac{3}{6} =$

6. $\dfrac{2}{6} \div \dfrac{2}{4} =$

7. $\dfrac{3}{10} \div \dfrac{3}{5} =$

8. $\dfrac{3}{8} \div \dfrac{3}{6} =$

9. $\dfrac{1}{5} \div \dfrac{2}{8} =$

10. $\dfrac{1}{5} \div \dfrac{3}{10} =$

11. $\dfrac{3}{10} \div \dfrac{2}{5} =$

12. $\dfrac{3}{9} \div \dfrac{2}{3} =$

$\dfrac{1}{2}$     $\dfrac{2}{3}$     $\dfrac{3}{4}$

Dividing Fractions: fractions by fractions

# Sweet Dreams

Mavis is dreaming of ice cream. Divide. Write each quotient in simplest terms. Color the matching answer. The number of colored cones is how many she could eat!

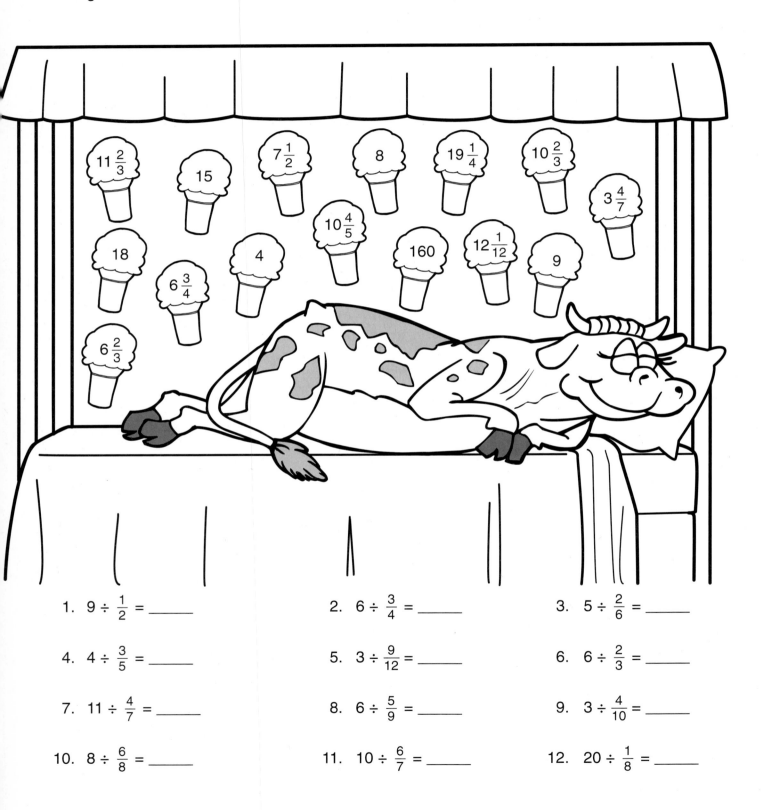

1. $9 \div \frac{1}{2} =$ _____

2. $6 \div \frac{3}{4} =$ _____

3. $5 \div \frac{2}{6} =$ _____

4. $4 \div \frac{3}{5} =$ _____

5. $3 \div \frac{9}{12} =$ _____

6. $6 \div \frac{2}{3} =$ _____

7. $11 \div \frac{4}{7} =$ _____

8. $6 \div \frac{5}{9} =$ _____

9. $3 \div \frac{4}{10} =$ _____

10. $8 \div \frac{6}{8} =$ _____

11. $10 \div \frac{6}{7} =$ _____

12. $20 \div \frac{1}{8} =$ _____

Name _____     Date _____

# Pen Pals

Which pens have red ink? Which have blue? To find out, divide! Show your work on another sheet of paper. If the quotient is a whole number, color the pen blue. If the quotient is a mixed number, color it red.

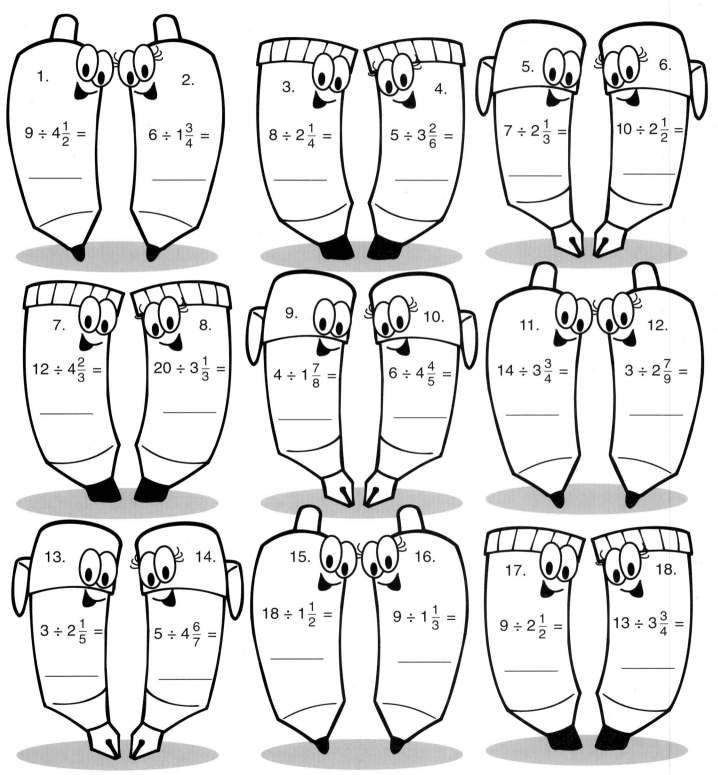

1. $9 \div 4\frac{1}{2} =$ _____

2. $6 \div 1\frac{3}{4} =$ _____

3. $8 \div 2\frac{1}{4} =$ _____

4. $5 \div 3\frac{2}{6} =$ _____

5. $7 \div 2\frac{1}{3} =$ _____

6. $10 \div 2\frac{1}{2} =$ _____

7. $12 \div 4\frac{2}{3} =$ _____

8. $20 \div 3\frac{1}{3} =$ _____

9. $4 \div 1\frac{7}{8} =$ _____

10. $6 \div 4\frac{4}{5} =$ _____

11. $14 \div 3\frac{3}{4} =$ _____

12. $3 \div 2\frac{7}{9} =$ _____

13. $3 \div 2\frac{1}{5} =$ _____

14. $5 \div 4\frac{6}{7} =$ _____

15. $18 \div 1\frac{1}{2} =$ _____

16. $9 \div 1\frac{1}{3} =$ _____

17. $9 \div 2\frac{1}{2} =$ _____

18. $13 \div 3\frac{3}{4} =$ _____

# Shaggy Chic!

Why does Charlotte have so many fancy clothes? To find out, divide to solve the problems, and write the quotients in simplest terms. Show your work on another sheet of paper. Then use the code to write the letter for each problem's quotient in its matching blank below.

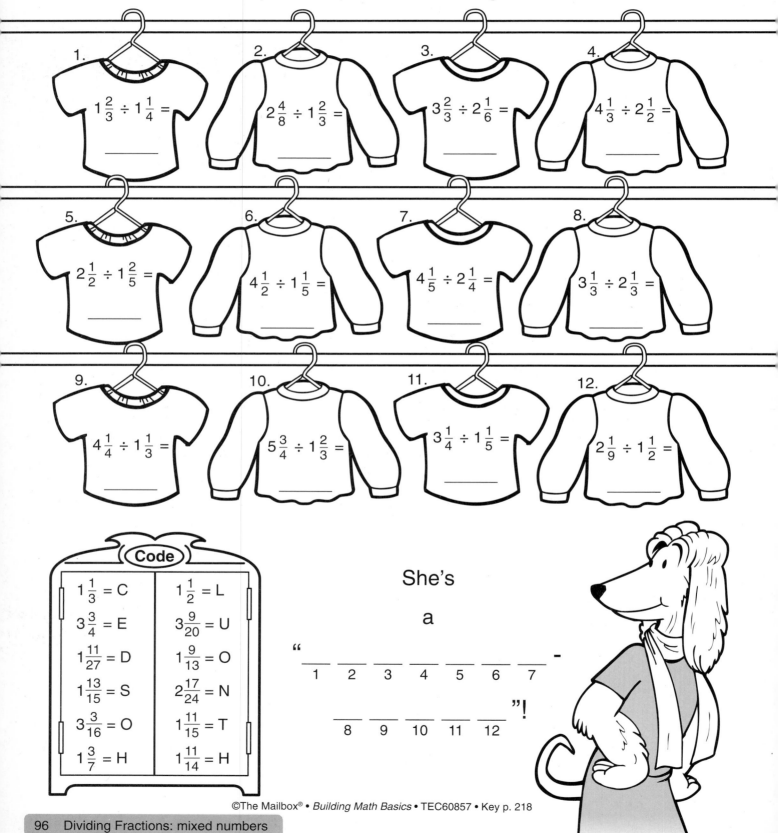

1. $1\frac{2}{3} \div 1\frac{1}{4} =$ ____

2. $2\frac{4}{8} \div 1\frac{2}{3} =$ ____

3. $3\frac{2}{3} \div 2\frac{1}{6} =$ ____

4. $4\frac{1}{3} \div 2\frac{1}{2} =$ ____

5. $2\frac{1}{2} \div 1\frac{2}{5} =$ ____

6. $4\frac{1}{2} \div 1\frac{1}{5} =$ ____

7. $4\frac{1}{5} \div 2\frac{1}{4} =$ ____

8. $3\frac{1}{3} \div 2\frac{1}{3} =$ ____

9. $4\frac{1}{4} \div 1\frac{1}{3} =$ ____

10. $5\frac{3}{4} \div 1\frac{2}{3} =$ ____

11. $3\frac{1}{4} \div 1\frac{1}{5} =$ ____

12. $2\frac{1}{9} \div 1\frac{1}{2} =$ ____

**Code**

| | |
|---|---|
| $1\frac{1}{3}$ = C | $1\frac{1}{2}$ = L |
| $3\frac{3}{4}$ = E | $3\frac{9}{20}$ = U |
| $1\frac{11}{27}$ = D | $1\frac{9}{13}$ = O |
| $1\frac{13}{15}$ = S | $2\frac{17}{24}$ = N |
| $3\frac{3}{16}$ = O | $1\frac{11}{15}$ = T |
| $1\frac{3}{7}$ = H | $1\frac{11}{14}$ = H |

She's

a

" __ __ __ __ __ __ __ -
   1   2   3   4   5   6   7

__ __ __ __ __ "!
 8  9  10  11  12

Name _____    Date _____

# Good Eggs

Which eggs will pass inspection? To find out, estimate the quotient of each problem. Divide on another sheet of paper to check your answer. Then color the egg in each basket whose number is closer to that problem's actual quotient. Good luck!

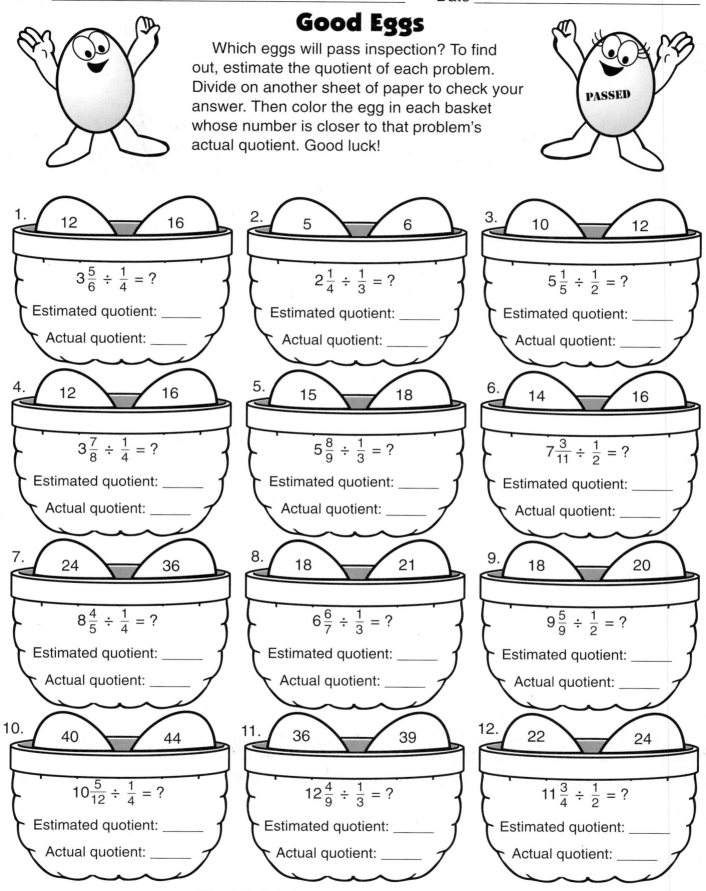

1.  12    16

$3\frac{5}{6} \div \frac{1}{4} = ?$

Estimated quotient: _____

Actual quotient: _____

2.  5    6

$2\frac{1}{4} \div \frac{1}{3} = ?$

Estimated quotient: _____

Actual quotient: _____

3.  10    12

$5\frac{1}{5} \div \frac{1}{2} = ?$

Estimated quotient: _____

Actual quotient: _____

4.  12    16

$3\frac{7}{8} \div \frac{1}{4} = ?$

Estimated quotient: _____

Actual quotient: _____

5.  15    18

$5\frac{8}{9} \div \frac{1}{3} = ?$

Estimated quotient: _____

Actual quotient: _____

6.  14    16

$7\frac{3}{11} \div \frac{1}{2} = ?$

Estimated quotient: _____

Actual quotient: _____

7.  24    36

$8\frac{4}{5} \div \frac{1}{4} = ?$

Estimated quotient: _____

Actual quotient: _____

8.  18    21

$6\frac{6}{7} \div \frac{1}{3} = ?$

Estimated quotient: _____

Actual quotient: _____

9.  18    20

$9\frac{5}{9} \div \frac{1}{2} = ?$

Estimated quotient: _____

Actual quotient: _____

10.  40    44

$10\frac{5}{12} \div \frac{1}{4} = ?$

Estimated quotient: _____

Actual quotient: _____

11.  36    39

$12\frac{4}{9} \div \frac{1}{3} = ?$

Estimated quotient: _____

Actual quotient: _____

12.  22    24

$11\frac{3}{4} \div \frac{1}{2} = ?$

Estimated quotient: _____

Actual quotient: _____

# Decimal Basics

### Reading and Writing Relay

Reading and writing decimals can be "relay" fun with this class game! Have each child label an index card with the number and word form of a decimal to the hundredths place. Check the cards, asking students to correct any mistakes. Then shuffle the cards and stack them facedown in a pile. After dividing the class into two teams, have Player 1 on Team A draw a card and read its word form aloud. Ask Player 1 on Team B to come to the board and write that decimal in number form. Have Player 2 on Team B check the number and advise his teammate of any needed corrections. Then ask the reader to announce whether the recorded number is correct. If so, award Team B a point. If not, have Player 3 on Team B draw a card and read its word form aloud for Team A's Player 2 to write on the board and Team A's Player 3 to check. Continue in this manner until one team earns 15 points. For a partner game on reading and writing decimals, see page 101.

304.52

three hundred four and
fifty-two hundredths

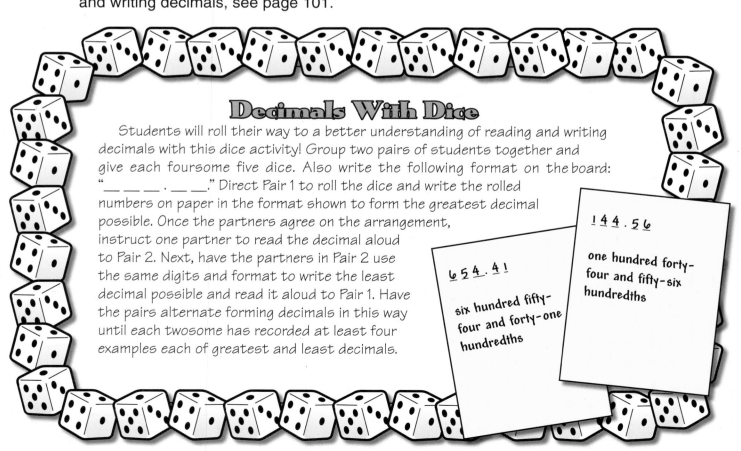

### Decimals With Dice

Students will roll their way to a better understanding of reading and writing decimals with this dice activity! Group two pairs of students together and give each foursome five dice. Also write the following format on the board: "__ __ __ . __ __." Direct Pair 1 to roll the dice and write the rolled numbers on paper in the format shown to form the greatest decimal possible. Once the partners agree on the arrangement, instruct one partner to read the decimal aloud to Pair 2. Next, have the partners in Pair 2 use the same digits and format to write the least decimal possible and read it aloud to Pair 1. Have the pairs alternate forming decimals in this way until each twosome has recorded at least four examples each of greatest and least decimals.

144.56

one hundred forty-four and fifty-six hundredths

654.41

six hundred fifty-four and forty-one hundredths

## Bargain Bingo

Turn practice with rounding hundredths to the nearest tenth into a favorite free-time activity! Place old catalogs, store advertisements and flyers, scissors, and glue in a convenient location in the classroom. Give each child a 5 x 6 grid in which you have written a different amount in dollars and dimes at the top of each column. Challenge each student to search the catalogs, advertisements, and flyers for prices that can be rounded to each amount. When she finds an example, have her cut out the price and glue it to her card in the appropriate column. Give a small treat to each child who fills her entire card! For additional practice rounding decimals, see the reproducible on page 103.

| $1.20 | $4.30 | $6.90 | $9.50 | $10.80 |
|-------|-------|-------|-------|--------|
| $1.19 | $4.28 | $6.89 |       | $10.78 |
|       |       | $6.93 |       | $10.83 |
|       |       |       |       | $10.79 |
|       |       |       |       |        |
|       |       |       |       |        |
|       |       |       |       |        |

## Four in a Row

Make rounding decimals a much-requested activity with this team game! Draw a 4 x 4 grid on a transparency with a permanent marker. Use a wipe-off marker to fill each box with a decimal that can be rounded to the nearest tenth or hundredth. Next, divide the class into two teams: the Xs and the Os. Have Player 1 on Team X select any decimal in the grid. Direct her to round that decimal to the nearest tenth or hundredth. If she is correct, make a large X in that box. If she is incorrect, make no mark at all. Then have Player 1 on Team O select any decimal and round it to the place you announce. Continue play in this manner until one team gets four marks in a row vertically, horizontally, or diagonally. To play another round, just wipe the grid clean and fill its boxes with different decimals!

| 6.09 | 3.15 | 25.856 | 1.067 |
|------|------|--------|-------|
| 4.86 | 3.247 | 8.482 | 9.663 |
| 14.56 | 45.369 | 63.914 | 0.114 |
| 72.39 | 58.153 | 2.555 | 1.840 |

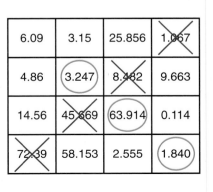

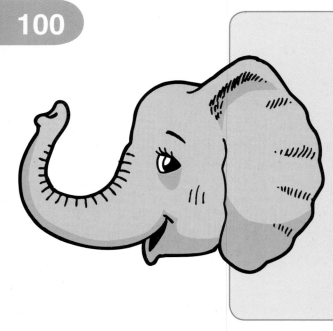

## Bigger or Smaller

Boost students' skills with ordering decimals using this quick mental-math workout! Write three different decimals on the board, such as "5.33," "5.61," and "5.04." Next, make a statement that includes a similar decimal, such as "Ellie the elephant weighs five and four tenths tons." Then ask students which decimal choices on the board are bigger (or smaller) than the decimal used in the statement (5.61 is bigger; 5.33 and 5.04 are smaller). To vary the exercise, provide only one correct answer, two correct answers, all correct answers, or even no correct answers. Once students get the idea down pat, let them take turns writing the decimals and providing the statements!

## Odd One Out

How sharp is your class when it comes to writing decimal equivalents? Find out! Assign each student a different decimal, such as 0.8. Direct him to use equivalent decimals or fractions to express the assigned decimal in three other ways, such as 0.80, ⁸/₁₀, and ⁴/₅. In addition, instruct him to add to the list a decimal or fraction that is *not* equivalent, such as 0.08 or ⁶/₈. Then call on a student to write his five numbers on the board in random order. Invite his classmates to raise their hands when they can identify the number that does not belong in the list. Allow the first child to find the error to be the next person to write her five numbers on the board. Continue in this manner as time permits. Was anyone able to stump the class?

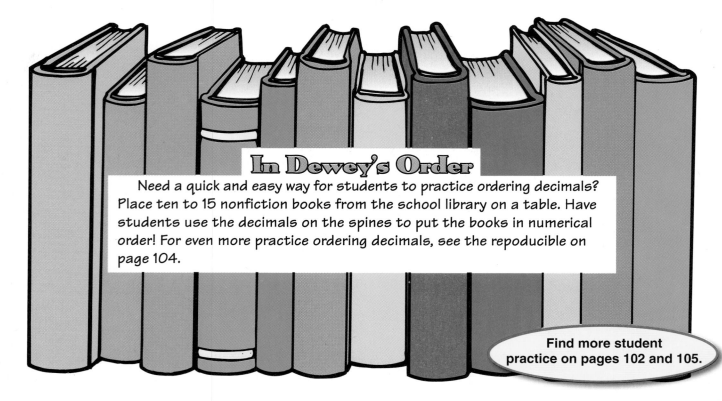

## In Dewey's Order

Need a quick and easy way for students to practice ordering decimals? Place ten to 15 nonfiction books from the school library on a table. Have students use the decimals on the spines to put the books in numerical order! For even more practice ordering decimals, see the repoducible on page 104.

**Find more student practice on pages 102 and 105.**

Name _____  Date _____

# Decimal Dash

**Playing the game:**

1. Player 1 rolls the die and moves his game piece that number of spaces. If the number on that space is in word form, Player 1 writes the number in standard form on another sheet of paper. If the number on the space is in standard form, he writes that number in word form.
2. Player 2 checks Player 1's answer. If correct, Player 1 initials that space.
3. Player 2 takes a turn. If she lands on an initialed space, she moves her game piece to the next open space.
4. The first player to initial ten squares is the winner.

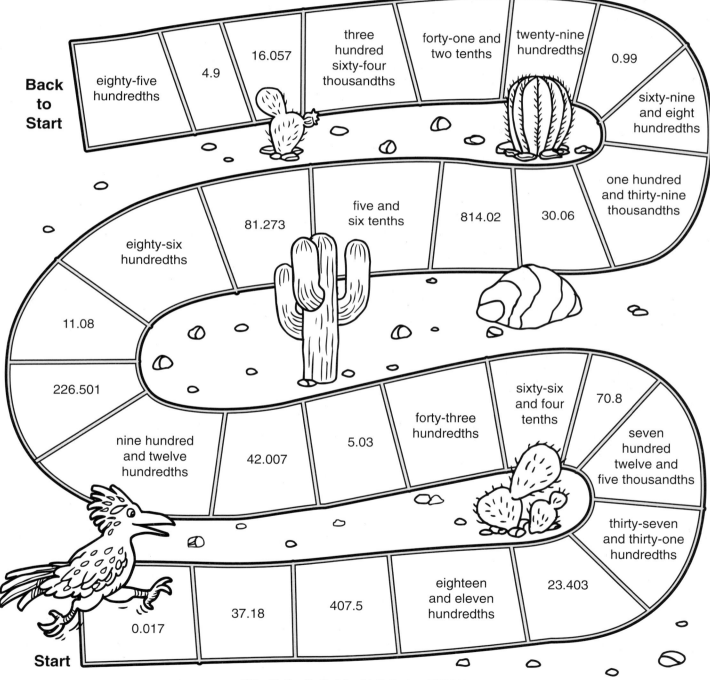

Back to Start

eighty-five hundredths | 4.9 | 16.057 | three hundred sixty-four thousandths | forty-one and two tenths | twenty-nine hundredths | 0.99 | sixty-nine and eight hundredths

one hundred and thirty-nine thousandths

eighty-six hundredths | 81.273 | five and six tenths | 814.02 | 30.06

11.08

226.501

nine hundred and twelve hundredths | 42.007 | 5.03 | forty-three hundredths | sixty-six and four tenths | 70.8

seven hundred twelve and five thousandths

thirty-seven and thirty-one hundredths

23.403

eighteen and eleven hundredths

37.18 | 407.5

0.017

Start

©The Mailbox® • *Building Math Basics* • TEC60857

**Note to the teacher:** Each student pair will need a copy of this page, a die, and game markers to play this game.

# Robo-Rob's Job

Help Robo-Rob file decimals. In the blank on each drawer, write the letter(s) of the numbers on Rob's list that match each description. If no number matches a description, write "none." (Hint: Some numbers can be placed in more than one drawer.) The first one has been done for you.

**Numbers to File**

A.  345.967

B.  9,084.61

C.  27.346

D.  472.68

E.  113.445

F.  2,056.056

G.  9.038

H.  7,946.195

I.  678.901

J.  0.430

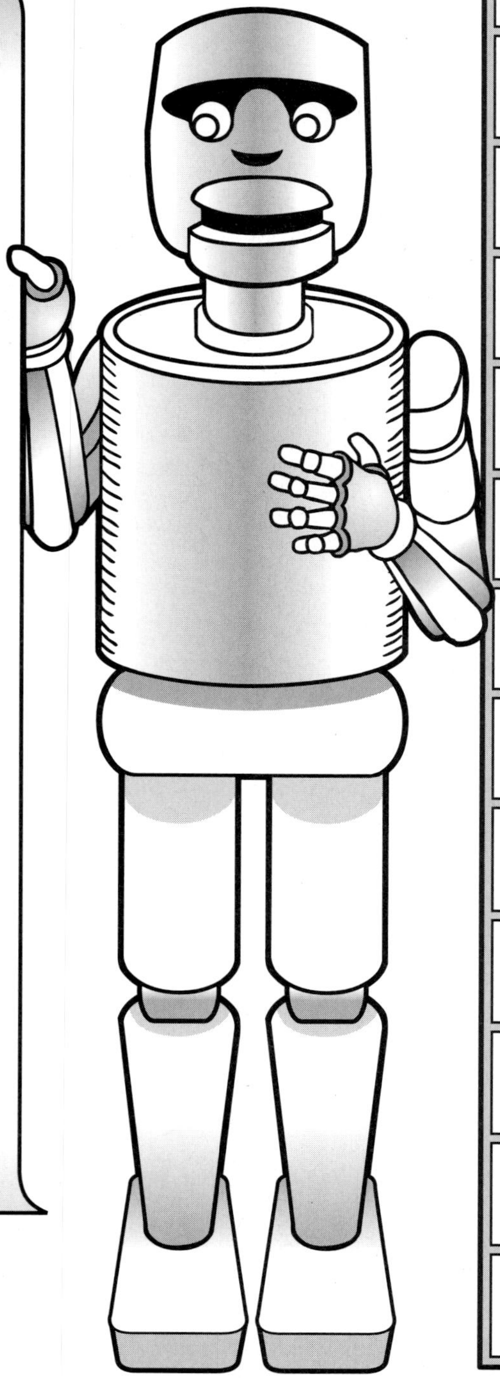

|  | |  |  |
|---|---|---|---|
| Drawer 1 | | 4 tenths | E, J |
| Drawer 2 | | 7 thousandths | |
| Drawer 3 | | 6 hundredths | |
| Drawer 4 | | 5 thousandths | |
| Drawer 5 | | 0 hundredths | |
| Drawer 6 | | 4 hundredths | |
| Drawer 7 | | 1 tenth | |
| Drawer 8 | | 9 tenths | |
| Drawer 9 | | 3 hundredths | |
| Drawer 10 | | 3 thousandths | |
| Drawer 11 | | 0 thousandths | |
| Drawer 12 | | 8 hundredths | |
| Drawer 13 | | 6 thousandths | |
| Drawer 14 | | 2 thousandths | |
| Drawer 15 | | 6 tenths | |

Name _____  Date _____

# Dollar Day at the Flea Market

Freddy loves coming to the flea market on dollar day. Round each
price tag to the nearest dollar. Color each rounded tag by the code.

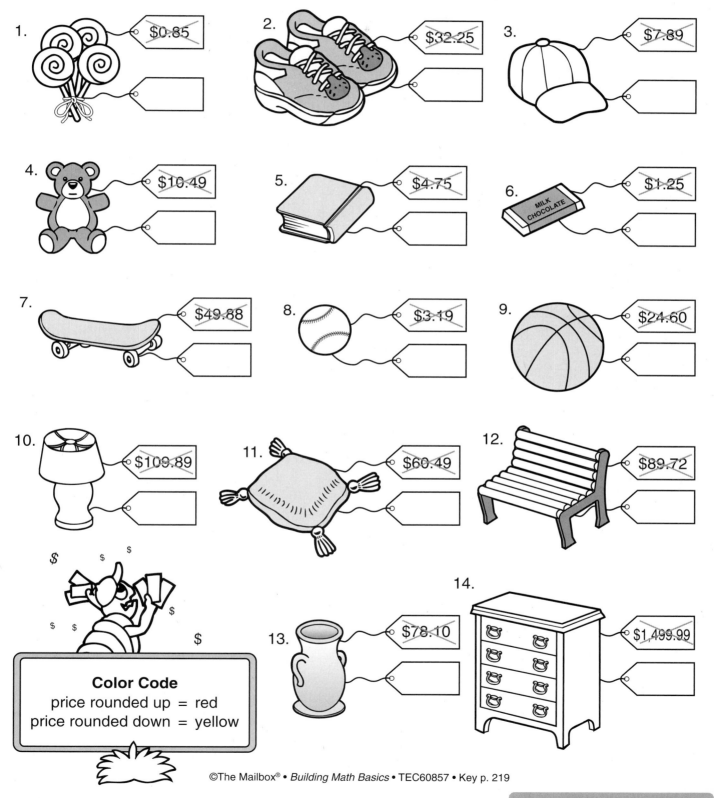

1. $0.85

2. $32.25

3. $7.89

4. $10.49

5. $4.75

6. MILK CHOCOLATE  $1.25

7. $49.88

8. $3.19

9. $24.60

10. $109.89

11. $60.49

12. $89.72

13. $78.10

14. $1,499.99

**Color Code**
price rounded up = red
price rounded down = yellow

# Speeding Through Sherwood

Who's the new member of the Sherwood Racing Club? To find out, use the chart to decide whether each statement below is true or false. Shade a box to show your answer. Then write the letters of the unshaded boxes in order in the blanks. If your answers are correct, you'll know the animal's name!

| Club Member | Speed |
|---|---|
| Bugsy Bee | 6.684 mph |
| Benjy Butterfly | 6.689 mph |
| Charlie Crow | 25.910 mph |
| Daisy Deer | 33.678 mph |
| Freddy Fox | 42.811 mph |
| Harry Horse | 47.801 mph |
| Henry Hawk | 110.154 mph |
| Oscar Owl | 18.941 mph |
| Rhonda Rabbit | 35.278 mph |
| Sammy Skunk | 6.278 mph |

|  | True | False |
|---|---|---|
| 1. The fastest animal shown on the chart is Henry Hawk. | E | B |
| 2. The slowest animal shown is Benjy Butterfly. | E | D |
| 3. The second fastest animal shown is Harry Horse. | S | N |
| 4. Oscar Owl is about three times slower than Sammy Skunk. | E | Q |
| 5. Daisy Deer is slower than Rhonda Rabbit. | U | B |
| 6. Freddy Fox is about five mph faster than Harry Horse. | E | I |
| 7. Benjy Butterfly is slightly faster than Bugsy Bee. | R | A |
| 8. Rhonda Rabbit is about six times faster than Sammy Skunk. | R | V |
| 9. Only three animals shown travel more slowly than Charlie Crow. | E | E |
| 10. No two animals on the chart have exactly the same speed. | L | R |

The new club member is ___ ___ ___  ___.  ___ ___ ___ ___ ___ ___.

©The Mailbox® • *Building Math Basics* • TEC60857 • Key p. 219

104  Decimal Basics: comparing and ordering

Name _____  Date _____

# Porkey's Dinner Palace

Porkey bought a dinner theater that seats 100 people!
Follow the directions to show how well it is doing.

Now Showing:
Piglets in a Blanket

Shade the models to show the decimal for each fraction.

1. Tickets sold Friday night: $\frac{88}{100}$

2. Tickets sold Saturday night: $\frac{93}{100}$

3. Tickets sold Sunday night: $\frac{75}{100}$

4. Friday night no-shows: $\frac{30}{100}$

5. Saturday night no-shows: $\frac{2}{100}$

6. Sunday night no-shows: $\frac{7}{100}$

Write a fraction for each model.

7. Profit from food: _____

8. Persons buying 1–4 tickets: ____

9. Persons buying 5 or more tickets: _____

10. Average pasta dinners eaten per person: _____

11. Average vegetable platters eaten per person: _____

12. Average desserts eaten per person: _____

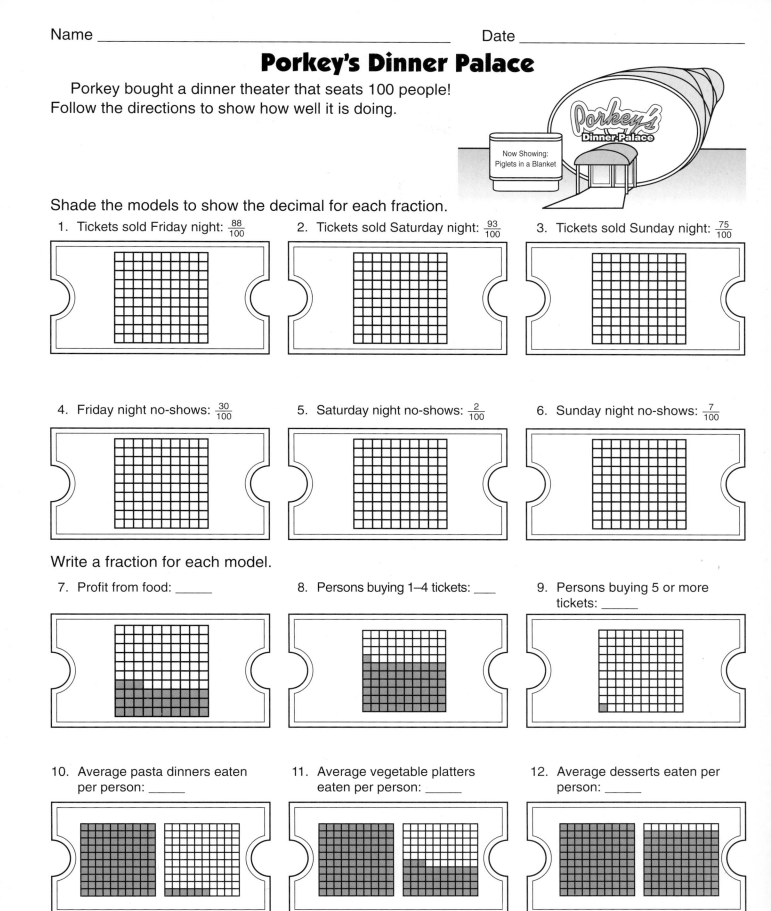

# ADDING DECIMALS

## Line 'em Up!

Keep decimal skills in line with this simple tip. When working with decimals, have each child turn a sheet of notebook paper horizontally. The student records his addition problem on the page, writing one number in each column as shown. If desired, he can even label each column with the place value. Then he solves the problem, knowing exactly where to place the sum and decimal point. This tip works great for subtraction and multiplication too!

| tens | ones | tenths | hundredths | thousandths |
|------|------|--------|------------|-------------|
| 1 | 5 . | 2 | 3 | |
| + 0 | . | 6 | 5 | 8 |
| 1 | 5 . | 8 | 8 | 8 |

## SHOPPING FRENZY!

Improve students' addition skills with this real-world math game! Collect a supply of grocery store flyers from your newspaper. Next, divide your class into groups of four or five and give each group several fliers. Explain that each group has $150.00 to spend on groceries using the prices from the fliers. Tell the group that no more than two of the same item can be purchased. Then have the group list on a sheet of paper each item it wants to purchase and the item's price. Direct the group to keep a running total of the items it purchases. The team that comes the closest to spending $150.00 without going over wins!

**Alexander's Food Stores**

**Martin's Grocery Store**

**FOOD QUEEN**

Group A

$2.89   pound of coffee
+ $0.50   candy bar
———
$3.39

+ $2.59   2 jars of
———   spaghetti sauce
$5.98

# Target 30

This partner game adds up to decimal fun! Pair students and give each twosome a pair of dice. Then guide pairs through the directions below to play Target 30.

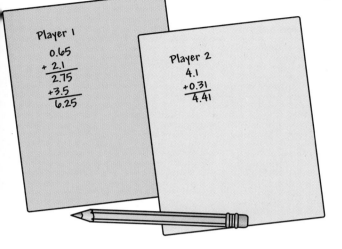

Player 1
0.65
+ 2.1
2.75
+3.5
6.25

Player 2
4.1
+0.31
4.41

**To Play:**

1. Player 1 rolls the dice and uses the resulting two numbers to write a decimal on a sheet of paper. (For example, after rolling a six and a five, she may write 5.6, 6.5, 0.56, or 0.65.)
2. Player 2 takes a turn in the same manner.
3. Player 1 takes another turn and adds the decimal from this turn to her original decimal.
4. Play continues with each player rolling the dice and adding her newly formed decimal to the previous total.
5. The winner is the player whose final total is closer to 30.0 without going over.

# MENU

## MENU CREATIONS

What's today's special? Making decimal addition fun! In advance, gather a supply of restaurant menus. Pair students and give each twosome a 12" x 18" sheet of light-colored construction paper and several menus. Have each pair create its own menu for an imaginary restaurant, including three to five menu items each for beverages, main dishes, and desserts. Explain that each menu item should include a short description and a price. Next, have the pair use the information on the menu to write five story problems with solutions that require adding decimals. Finally, have each pair switch menus and problems with another twosome and solve the problems. Afterward, place the menus and problems in a center to challenge students during free time.

Matt and Jared's Restaurant
MENU

1. One customer ordered a soft drink, a turkey sandwich, and a slice of cheesecake. How much did his meal cost?

2.

**Find more student practice on pages 108–112.**

Name _____    Date _____

# A Day at the Beach

Add.
Color by the code.

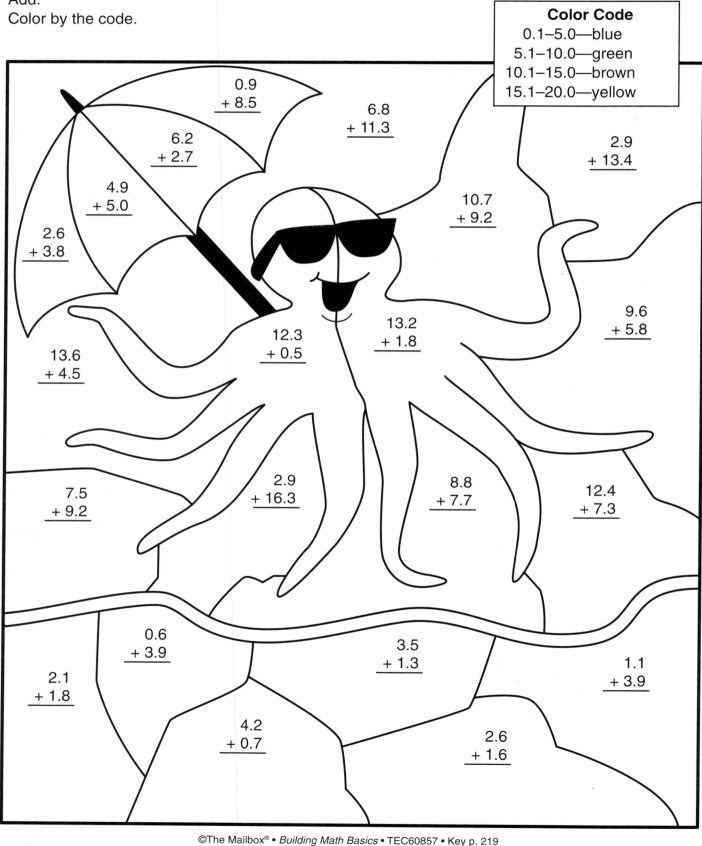

Name_____ Date _____

# Veggie Magic

Add. Write the answers in the magic square.
The sum of each row and column should equal 100.

1. 13.8 + 10.8 =     2. 19.3 + 16.4 =     3. 9.5 + 3.8 =     4. 19.5 + 6.9 =

5. 15.2 + 13.2 =     6. 15.2 + 17.6 =     7. 6.8 + 2.9 =     8. 14.6 + 14.5 =

9. 16.7 + 10.9 =     10. 9.1 + 5.2 =     11. 16.8 + 15.4 =     12. 19.3 + 6.6 =

13. 10.9 + 8.5 =     14. 11.8 + 5.4 =     15. 31.5 + 13.3 =     16. 12.7 + 5.9 =

Name_____  Date _____

# Patsy's Pet Store

Patsy's Pet Store is featuring the following coupons. Use the pet store coupons to answer each question. Write your answer on the line. Then color the M if you used mental math to solve the problem. Color the P if you used paper and pencil.

_____ 1. How much will you save on dog food if coupon C is tripled?   | M | P |

_____ 2. What are the savings if coupons A and E are used?   | M | P |

_____ 3. Will you save more using coupons B and C or D and G?   | M | P |

_____ 4. Will you save more or less than $1.00 using coupons C, E, and G?   | M | P |

_____ 5. Exactly how much can you save by using coupons B and F?   | M | P |

_____ 6. If you have four E coupons, how much will you save in all?   | M | P |

_____ 7. Patsy will double coupon D's value. About how much will you save?   | M | P |

_____ 8. What are the savings if coupons D, F, and G are used?   | M | P |

_____ 9. What three coupons can you use to save about $2.00?   | M | P |

_____ 10. What is the exact value of all the coupons added together?   | M | P |

Name_____  Date _____

# Inch by Inch

Help Seth make his way through the Snailtown mini maze. Add each problem on another sheet of paper. If the problem is correct, circle it. Connect the circled problems to show the path to the finish.

$6.37 + 10.5 = 16.87$

$26.9 + 13.51 = 40.41$

$16.71 + 3.7 = 17.08$

$36.15 + 5.28 = 41.43$

$2.14 + 93.23 = 95.37$

**Start**

$6.99 + 2.6 = 7.25$

$1.95 + 6.54 = 8.49$

$9.98 + 18.2 = 28.18$

$17.3 + 65.41 = 82.71$

$19.12 + 36.92 = 55.04$

$12.74 + 37.8 = 16.52$

**FINISH**

$19.7 + 8.42 = 28.12$

$41.23 + 7.97 = 49.2$

$17.45 + 19.26 = 36.71$

$24.32 + 19.8 = 44.18$

$63.2 + 14.78 = 77.98$

$9.17 + 8.8 = 17.97$

$71.6 + 18.96 = 26.12$

$16.33 + 81.05 = 97.48$

$23.56 + 31.48 = 55.04$

# Sweet Treat

Add.

(A)  16.25
    + 8.487

(C)  11.019
    + 4.279

(D)  17.839
    + 8.166

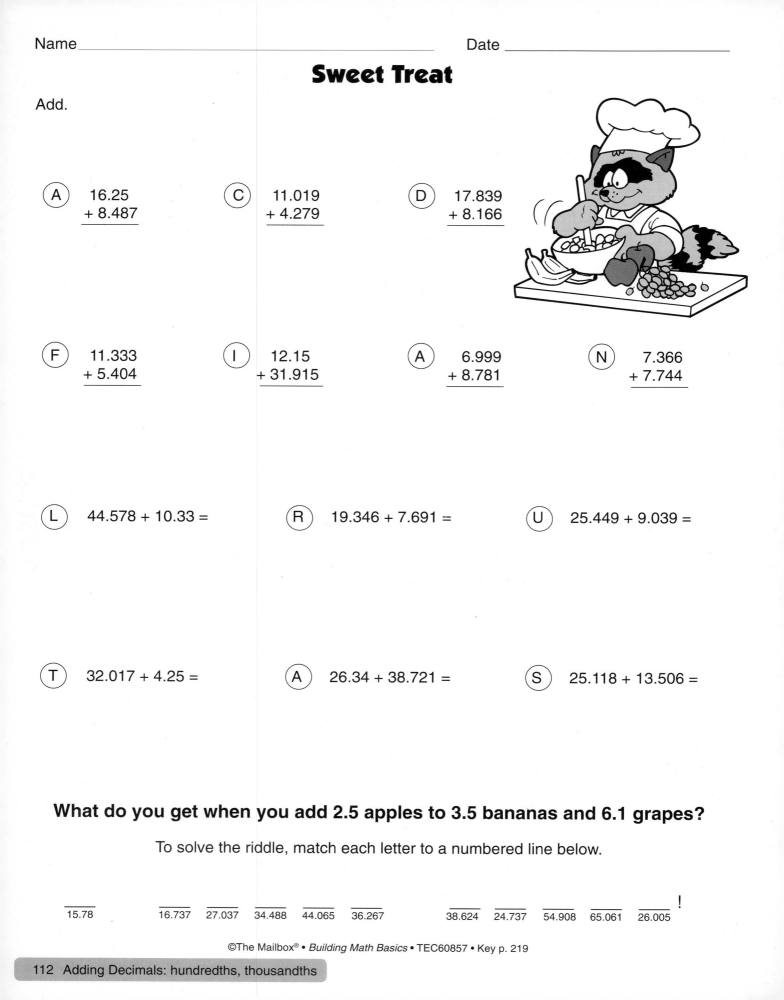

(F)  11.333
    + 5.404

(I)  12.15
    + 31.915

(A)  6.999
    + 8.781

(N)  7.366
    + 7.744

(L)  44.578 + 10.33 =

(R)  19.346 + 7.691 =

(U)  25.449 + 9.039 =

(T)  32.017 + 4.25 =

(A)  26.34 + 38.721 =

(S)  25.118 + 13.506 =

## What do you get when you add 2.5 apples to 3.5 bananas and 6.1 grapes?

To solve the riddle, match each letter to a numbered line below.

___     ___ ___ ___ ___ ___    ___ ___ ___ ___ ___ !
15.78    16.737  27.037  34.488  44.065  36.267    38.624  24.737  54.908  65.061  26.005

# Subtracting Decimals

## Spin to Win!

This fun partner game reinforces subtracting decimals. Pair students, giving each student one copy of page 115, a paper clip, a pencil, and a calculator. Refer students to the diagram on page 115 that shows how to use the spinner. Then guide students through the steps below to play the game.

### To Play:
1. Player 1 spins his spinner and writes the number in a box for Round 1. He continues spinning until all the boxes have been filled, creating a subtraction problem. (Remind students to make the top number in the problem larger than the bottom number.)
2. Player 2 takes a turn in the same manner.
3. Players 1 and 2 both solve their subtraction problems independently and then use their calculators to check each other's answer.
4. If a player's answer is correct, he earns one point and records it in the chart. If incorrect, he reworks the problem to earn one-half of a point.
5. Repeat Steps 1–4 to complete nine rounds. The player with more points at the end is the winner.

## Spicy Subtraction

Raid your kitchen cabinets to spice up subtracting decimals from whole numbers. For every two students, collect one spice container whose content's weight is a decimal number less than five ounces. To begin, give each pair a spice container to share and guide the pair in locating the spice's weight. Allow each student a few minutes to write the name of the spice on a sheet of paper, subtract the spice's weight from five, and then compare his answer to his partner's. Then, on your signal, have each pair exchange spice containers with another pair and repeat the process. Continue until each pair has solved a subtraction problem for each spice container.

Bay Leaves

$$\begin{array}{r} 5.00 \\ -\ 1.4 \\ \hline 3.60 \end{array}$$

Mustard Seed

$$\begin{array}{r} 5.00 \\ -\ 1.58 \\ \hline 3.42 \end{array}$$

BAY LEAVES

NET WT 1.4 OZ

# Dwindling Balances!

This center gives students real-world practice with subtracting decimals. In advance, collect a variety of cash register receipts, each with a total less than $50.00. Circle each total and place the receipts in a lunch-size paper bag at a center along with lined paper, pencils, and a calculator. To use the center, a student writes "$500.00" at the top of her paper. This is the amount of money she has for an imaginary shopping spree. Then she pulls a receipt out of the bag and subtracts the circled total from her $500.00 balance as if she purchased the items on the receipt. She lays this receipt aside and continues pulling out receipts and subtracting the totals from her most recent balance until she has collected ten receipts. Finally, she circles her ending balance and uses the calculator to check her work. If desired, invite students to write about how it felt to watch that dwindling balance! For even more practice subtracting money, see the reproducible on page 117.

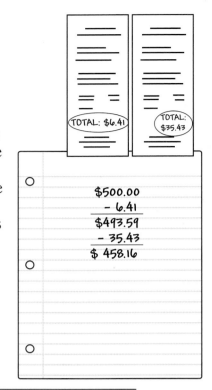

# Nibble by Nibble

This small-group game improves students' decimal skills one nibble at a time! Divide your class into groups, giving 20 small cards to each group. Instruct students to program the cards with different numbers from 0.1 to 0.499. To initiate play, direct each student to imagine that he has one pound of chocolate and have him write "1.0" on a sheet of paper. Then guide the group through the steps below.

## To Play:

1. One player shuffles all of the cards and places them facedown in a stack.
2. Each player draws a card from the pile and lays it faceup on the playing surface. Players identify the largest decimal displayed.
3. The player with the largest decimal does nothing. The remaining players subtract the decimals on their cards from 1.0. The decimal represents how much chocolate each player has eaten, and the difference is how much chocolate he now has left.
4. Each player discards his played card, draws a new card from the pile, and repeats the process, this time subtracting the decimal on the card from his remaining portion of chocolate.
5. Nibble by nibble, play continues until all the cards are played or one player's remaining portion of chocolate falls below zero. The player with the smallest number at the end of the game is the winner.

# CHOCOLATE

Find more student practice on pages 116 and 118.

Name_____  Date _____

| Round 1 | Round 2 | Round 3 |
|---|---|---|
| 0.☐<br>− 0.☐ | 0.☐<br>− 0.☐ | 0.☐☐<br>− 0.☐☐ |

| Round 4 | Round 5 | Round 6 |
|---|---|---|
| 0.☐☐<br>− 0.☐☐ | 0.☐☐<br>− 0.☐☐ | ☐.☐<br>− 0.☐ |

| Round 7 | Round 8 | Round 9 |
|---|---|---|
| ☐.☐<br>− ☐.☐ | ☐.☐☐<br>− ☐.☐☐ | ☐.☐☐<br>− ☐.☐☐ |

| Round | 1 | 2 | 3 | 4 | 5 | 6 | 7 | 8 | 9 | Total |
|---|---|---|---|---|---|---|---|---|---|---|
| Points | | | | | | | | | | |

**Note to the teacher:** Use with "Spin to Win!" on page 113.

# Colorful Blooms

Subtract.
Color by the code.

1. 6.8 − 2.9

2. 1.7 − 1.5

3. 7.6 − 4.4

4. 8.6 − 7.9

5. 3.2 − 1.2

6. 8.4 − 3.5

7. 5.7 − 3.2

8. 8.1 − 6.7

9. 9.1 − 8.8

10. 10.3 − 6.2

11. 2.3 − 1.2

12. 8.1 − 4.7

**Color Code**
0.0–0.9 = red
1.0–1.9 = blue
2.0–2.9 = green
3.0–3.9 = yellow
4.0–4.9 = orange

Name_____ Date _____

# Barry's Banking

Subtract. If the answer is less than $50.00, color the box. The answer in the last colored box tells how much money Barry has in his bank account. Write this amount on his bank statement at the bottom of the page.

| | | | | |
|---|---|---|---|---|
| $719.86<br>− 311.24 | $186.43<br>− 21.56 | $157.57<br>− 28.84 | $94.00<br>− 14.03 | $125.73<br>− 76.84 |
| $636.00<br>− 87.10 | $92.93<br>− 15.27 | $426.16<br>− 318.07 | $86.71<br>− 24.69 | $219.72<br>− 171.93 |
| $844.00<br>− 703.72 | $256.18<br>− 214.92 | $222.75<br>− 214.70 | $169.49<br>− 121.56 | $179.99<br>− 56.99 |
| $419.68<br>− 407.72 | $163.26<br>− 18.69 | $509.50<br>− 79.25 | National Woodland Bank<br>Name: Barry B. Beaver<br>Address: 14 Lodge Lane | |
| $397.17<br>− 256.04 | $86.00<br>− 65.24 | $70.26<br>− 35.14 | Balance: $ _____ | |

National Woodland Bank
Name: Barry B. Beaver
Address: 14 Lodge Lane

Balance: $ _____

Where we think money grows on trees!

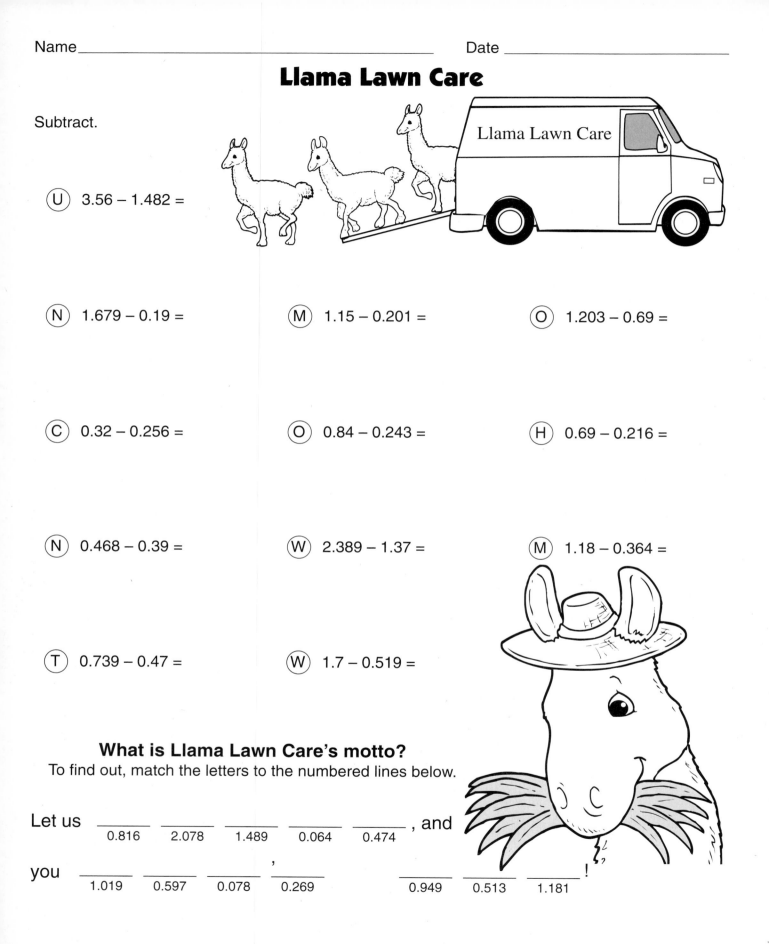

Name_____  Date _____

# Llama Lawn Care

Subtract.

(U) 3.56 – 1.482 =

(N) 1.679 – 0.19 =

(M) 1.15 – 0.201 =

(O) 1.203 – 0.69 =

(C) 0.32 – 0.256 =

(O) 0.84 – 0.243 =

(H) 0.69 – 0.216 =

(N) 0.468 – 0.39 =

(W) 2.389 – 1.37 =

(M) 1.18 – 0.364 =

(T) 0.739 – 0.47 =

(W) 1.7 – 0.519 =

## What is Llama Lawn Care's motto?
To find out, match the letters to the numbered lines below.

Let us  _____  _____  _____  _____  _____ , and
        0.816   2.078   1.489   0.064   0.474

you  _____  _____  _____  _____  ,  _____  _____  _____ !
   1.019   0.597   0.078   0.269        0.949   0.513   1.181

# Multiplying Decimals

## Square Times

Show students that there is nothing square about multiplying decimals! Direct each pair of students to draw a 7 x 7 grid, label its axes from 0 to 6, and randomly fill the grid's boxes with the digits 1–9. Next, give each duo a pair of dice and two game markers. Instruct Player 1 to roll the dice and cover the digit at the coordinate formed by the two rolled numbers. Have Player 2 cover the digit at the reversed coordinate. If a player rolls doubles, have him roll again. Then have each player multiply his covered digit by the tenths-place value of any adjacent digit (except another covered one) to form the greatest possible product. Give the player forming the greater product one point. Declare the first player to earn five points the winner. As a variation, have players multiply their covered digits by any two adjacent clockwise digits to multiply by hundredths (or by any three adjacent digits to multiply by thousandths). For a follow-up activity, see the reproducible on page 121.

### Round 1

| 6 | 4 | 7 | 9 | 8 | 2 | 9 |
|---|---|---|---|---|---|---|
| 5 | 1 | 6 | 8 | 9 | 8 | 3 |
| 4 | 5 | 6 | 5 | 5 | 6 | 7 |
| 3 | 2 | 4 | 1 | 7 | 4 | 8 |
| 2 | 6 | 3 | 5 | 2 | 3 | 3 |
| 1 | 1 | 4 | 1 | 2 | 9 | 7 |
| 0 | 1 | 2 | 3 | 4 | 5 | 6 |

(A 5 and a 4 are rolled.)
Player 1: 6 x 0.8 = 4.8

Player 2: 9 x 0.9 = 8.1 (1 point)

### Round 2

| 6 | 4 | 7 | 9 | 8 | 2 | 9 |
|---|---|---|---|---|---|---|
| 5 | 1 | 6 | 8 | 9 | 8 | 3 |
| 4 | 5 | 6 | 5 | 5 | 6 | 7 |
| 3 | 2 | 4 | 1 | 7 | 4 | 8 |
| 2 | 6 | 3 | 5 | 2 | 3 | 3 |
| 1 | 1 | 4 | 1 | 2 | 9 | 7 |
| 0 | 1 | 2 | 3 | 4 | 5 | 6 |

(A 4 and a 6 are rolled.)
Player 1: 8 x 0.9 = 7.2 (1 point)

Player 2: 7 x 0.8 = 5.6

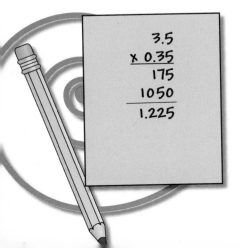

$$\begin{array}{r} 3.5 \\ \times\ 0.35 \\ \hline 175 \\ 1050 \\ \hline 1.225 \end{array}$$

## Die-to-Die Decimals

All you need for this quick multiplication-of-decimals review game is dice, paper, and pencils! Give each pair of students two dice. At your signal, direct the partners to take turns rolling the dice. Have each child record her two rolled numbers in any order to form a mixed decimal and a hundredths-place decimal; then have her find the product (see the example showing a roll of a three and a five). Next, determine the class's winner by asking a question such as the following: Who has the greatest (or least) product? The product closest to two? A product between 3.2 and 3.6? Play as long as time permits, using a different question for each round.

# The 12 Days of Multiplication

Here's a booklet-making activity that provides real-world practice with multiplying decimals no matter what the season! Gather sales flyers from various stores. Next, have each child staple 12 sheets of white paper between two colorful sheets of paper. Instruct her to decorate the cover and title it as shown. Then have her cut from a flyer an item's picture and its price and glue them to her booklet's first page. Have her also add the sentence shown, filling in the number and name of the pictured item and the name of its recipient. Finally, have the student write and solve a multiplication problem to find the cost, checking it with a calculator. Direct her to complete each successive page in a similar way, using different items and people, revising each sentence to match the day, and multiplying each item's price by two, three, and so on, until all 12 pages are done.

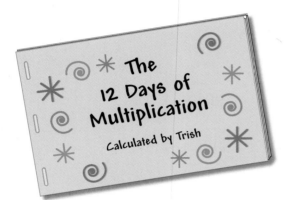

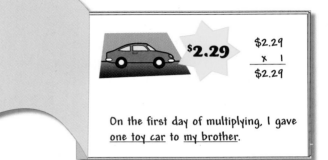

The 12 Days of Multiplication
Calculated by Trish

$2.29

$2.29
x 1
$2.29

On the first day of multiplying, I gave one toy car to my brother.

# "Dom-in-no" Products

For practice with estimating decimal products, grab sets of double-six dominoes! Draw on the board a domino, and demonstrate how to represent its pips as a mixed decimal. Next, give each pair of students a set of dominoes in a paper bag. Have each twosome divide a sheet of paper into four sections and label them as shown. (The least and greatest products using double-six dominoes are 0.01 and 43.56.) Direct each partner to draw eight dominoes from the bag and randomly place two dominoes in each section. Instruct the pair to predict whether the product of the two mixed decimals represented by each section's dominoes would fit within the labeled range. If so, have the duo write "In" on another sheet of paper and "No" if not. Then have the partners solve the problems to see whether their "dom-in-no" predictions were correct, using a calculator to check. Award the pair one point for each correct guess. To play additional rounds, have students return the dominoes to the bag, shake it, and start again!

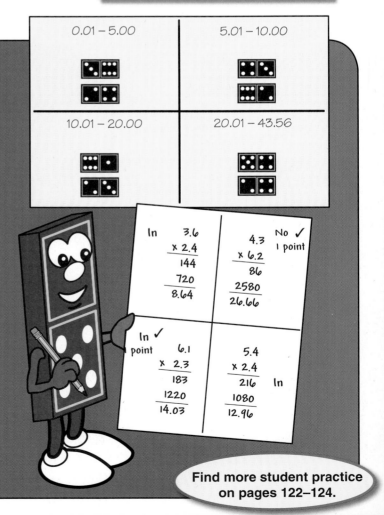

| 0.01 – 5.00 | 5.01 – 10.00 |
| --- | --- |
| 10.01 – 20.00 | 20.01 – 43.56 |

In    3.6
    x 2.4
    144
    720
    8.64

No ✓
1 point
    4.3
  x 6.2
    86
  2580
  26.66

In ✓
point    6.1
      x 2.3
      183
    1220
    14.03

    5.4
  x 2.4
    216
  1080
  12.96    In

**Find more student practice on pages 122–124.**

Name_____  Date _____

# Seaworthy Cereals

Multiply to find the total shipping weight of each type of
cereal. Show your work on each box, and write the answer in
the blank. Cross off the matching answer on the clipboard.
Some answers will not be crossed off.

**1**
12 boxes of
**Soggy Os**
0.3 oz. each

= _____ oz.

**2**
7 boxes of
**Frosted Shells**
0.8 oz. each

= _____ oz.

**3**
28 boxes of
**Coral Puffs**
0.5 oz. each

= _____ oz.

**4**
10 boxes of
**Cocoa Shells**
0.7 oz. each

= _____ oz.

**5**
33 boxes of
**Lucky Arms**
0.5 oz. each

= _____ oz.

**6**
19 boxes of
**Blowfish Puffs**
0.6 oz. each

= _____ oz.

**7**
21 boxes of
**Golden Gills**
0.3 oz. each

= _____ oz.

**8**
16 boxes of
**Raisin Sand**
0.4 oz. each

= _____ oz.

**9**
9 boxes of
**Crab Crisps**
0.3 oz. each

= _____ oz.

**10**
17 boxes of
**Sea Crunch**
0.9 oz. each

= _____ oz.

**Shipping Weights**

| | |
|---|---|
| 2.7 | 6.5 |
| 11.4 | 7 |
| 15.3 | 5.6 |
| 6.8 | 6.3 |
| 3.6 | 14 |
| 7.3 | |
| 16.5 | |
| 6.4 | |

Name _____ Date _____

# "A-peeling" Prices

Multiply to find the cost of each amount of fruit. Show your work on another sheet of paper.

Monkeys' Mart

Bananas $0.59 lb.

Limes $0.77 lb.

Lemons $0.74 lb.

Peaches $0.99 lb.

Watermelons $0.49 lb.

Pineapples $0.86 lb.

Oranges $0.53 lb.

Cherries $0.96 lb.

Grapes $0.84 lb.

1. 16 lb. of grapes = _____

2. 25 lb. of lemons = _____

3. 8 lb. of peaches = _____

4. 16 lb. of cherries = _____

5. 5 lb. of bananas = _____

6. 12 lb. of watermelons = _____

7. 10 lb. of cherries = _____

8. 15 lb. of peaches = _____

9. 30 lb. of limes = _____

10. 14 lb. of oranges = _____

11. 9 lb. of bananas = _____

12. 19 lb. of pineapples = _____

# Freda's Fabulous Fabrics

Freda loves to make colorful hand-painted fabrics!
Multiply to help her complete her newest design.
Show your work. Then color by the code.

**Color Code**

| | | |
|---|---|---|
| 0.0000 to 0.0999 | = | red |
| 0.1000 to 0.1999 | = | blue |
| 0.2000 to 0.2999 | = | purple |
| 0.3000 to 0.3999 | = | yellow |
| 0.4000 to 0.4999 | = | green |

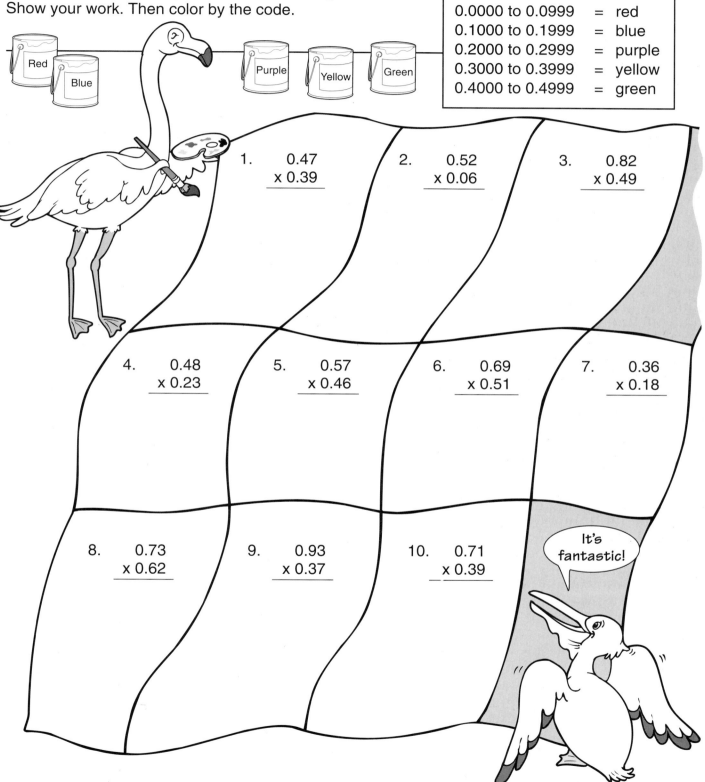

1.  0.47
    x 0.39

2.  0.52
    x 0.06

3.  0.82
    x 0.49

4.  0.48
    x 0.23

5.  0.57
    x 0.46

6.  0.69
    x 0.51

7.  0.36
    x 0.18

8.  0.73
    x 0.62

9.  0.93
    x 0.37

10.  0.71
    x 0.39

It's fantastic!

Name_____  Date _____

# Dining at Danny's Diner

What's tonight's special at the diner? To find out, multiply. Then write the letter of each matching product on the specials board.

**Welcome to DANNY'S DINER!**

(O)  3.4 x 0.3 = _____

(I)  1.7 x 12 = _____

(C)  5.4 x 1.6 = _____

(T)  4.63 x 7 = _____

(E)  9.6 x 0.26 = _____

(L)  3.11 x 0.11 = _____

(B)  2.6 x 3.2 = _____

(E)  8.5 x 0.03 = _____

(H)  2.8 x 0.05 = _____

(R)  0.8 x 2.4 = _____

**Today's Special**

| ___ | **H** | ___ | ___ | **E** | - |
|-----|-------|-----|-----|-------|---|
| 32.41 | | 1.92 | 2.496 | | |

| ___ | ___ | **N** | ___ |
|------|------|-------|------|
| 8.32 | 1.02 | | 0.255 |

| ___ | ___ | ___ | ___ | **I** |
|------|------|------|------|-------|
| 8.64 | 0.14 | 20.4 | 0.3421 | |

# Dividing Decimals

## "Stick-y" Division

Make the concept of dividing mixed decimals by whole numbers really stick! Give each group of three students 45 craft sticks, a box of toothpicks, three pens (red, blue, and black), and ten index cards labeled with the following problems: 3.4 ÷ 2, 4.8 ÷ 3, 12.5 ÷ 5, 8.1 ÷ 9, 10.2 ÷ 6, 4.4 ÷ 4, 15.4 ÷ 7, 10.8 ÷ 2, 8.4 ÷ 3, and 14.4 ÷ 8. Explain that the craft sticks represent whole numbers and the toothpicks are the numbers after the decimals. Model one problem, such as 3.4 ÷ 2. (Arrange three craft sticks and four toothpicks as shown. Next, place one craft stick and two tooth-picks in each of two groups. Trade the remaining craft stick for ten toothpicks and add five additional toothpicks to each group.) Explain that the quotient (1.7) is represented by one craft stick and seven toothpicks. Then have each group mate use a different pen to record the quotient on that card's back. Direct each child to solve the nine remaining problems in a similar way. When everyone is finished, have the members of each trio check to see whether their answers match each other. If not, have the threesome rework those problems. To provide additional practice with this skill, use the reproducible on page 127.

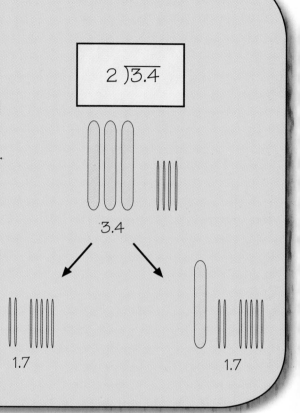

## The Great Chocolate Divide

This mouthwatering center provides plenty of practice dividing whole numbers by tenths! Program a supply of index cards with division problems similar to the one shown, writing each problem's answer on the back of its card. (Be sure that the dividend is six or less and that the divisor can be divided evenly.) Next, create six candy bars by cutting a sheet of brown construction paper into six equal strips. Then draw lines to divide each candy bar into ten equal sections as shown. Laminate the candy bars and place them in a center along with the cards, a dry-erase marker, and paper towels. To use the center, a child selects a card and uses the marker to number groupings of chocolate pieces to determine the answer to the problem. He then checks his work by turning over the index card. After wiping the candy bars clean, he repeats this process with a new card.

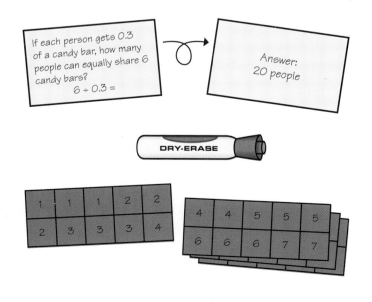

# Three in a Row

Have students play tic-tac-toe to a better understanding of dividing mixed decimals by whole numbers! List on the board the quotients from the problems shown. Then pair students and have each duo draw a tic-tac-toe grid on a sheet of paper. Also have each pair randomly write any nine of the quotients in its grid. Next, call out a problem. Direct one partner to solve the problem on another sheet of paper. If the solver finds his quotient on the grid, he makes an X on the corresponding box. If not, no mark is made. Then call out a second problem. Instruct the other partner to solve this problem. If she finds her quotient on the grid, she draws an O on the grid. The first partner to mark three Xs or Os in a row wins.

**Problems**

$5.26 \div 2 = 2.63$
$2.03 \div 7 = 0.29$
$8.88 \div 6 = 1.48$
$5.44 \div 8 = 0.68$
$9.36 \div 3 = 3.12$
$8.20 \div 5 = 1.64$
$12.44 \div 4 = 3.11$
$25.26 \div 6 = 4.21$
$21.5 \div 5 = 4.3$
$33.6 \div 7 = 4.8$
$173.6 \div 8 = 21.7$
$38.601 \div 9 = 4.289$

| 3.11 | 1.64 | 4.8 |
| --- | --- | --- |
| 0.68 | 4.21 | 21.7 |
| 4.289 | 3.12 | 2.63 |

# Prepaid Arcade

Score high points with this activity, which focuses on dividing decimals by decimals! Give each group of four students an 18" x 24" sheet of construction paper to fold into eight equal sections and label with their favorite arcade or video games. Also have the group write under each game's name any eight of the amounts and game prices listed in the chart below. Then have each group member calculate on paper how many of each game she could play at the given price using the specified amount. When group members have solved all eight problems, have them compare answers. If their answers match, have each child copy her work for two of the problems on the group's sheet. If any answers do not match, direct the students to rework those problems before adding them to the sheet and sharing their work with the class. Follow up with the reproducible on page 128 for even more practice on dividing decimals by decimals.

| Price Per Game | Amount to Spend |
| --- | --- |
| $0.15 | $4.50 |
| $0.25 | $3.75 |
| $0.80 | $3.20 |
| $0.20 | $6.00 |
| $0.85 | $7.65 |
| $1.05 | $4.20 |
| $0.80 | $4.00 |
| $0.55 | $2.75 |
| $0.95 | $3.80 |
| $0.15 | $1.35 |

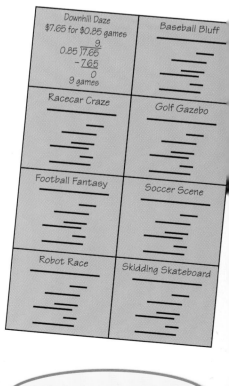

**Find more student practice on pages 129–130.**

Name_____  Date_____

# Message in a Bottle

Polly has found a bottle floating in the sea! What does it say? To find out, solve the problems. Then shade the box of each matching answer.

1.  $6\overline{)15.384}$

2.  $2\overline{)7.178}$

3.  $8\overline{)35.712}$

4.  $3\overline{)2.328}$

5.  $4\overline{)5.028}$

6.  $9\overline{)20.826}$

7.  $8\overline{)10.864}$

8.  $4\overline{)21.052}$

| 5.263 | 6.014 | 1.358 | 13.581 | 0.776 |
| 3.589 | 4.464 | 4.215 | 1.135 | 2.564 |
| 2.314 | 2.440 | 5.214 | 52.141 | 1.257 |

9.  $6\overline{)25.290}$

10.  $7\overline{)36.498}$

Name_____   Date _____

# Off on a Wild Ride

Groucho escaped from the zoo in a golf cart! Where did he go? To find out, solve the problems. Then shade the box of each matching answer to show the path to where he went.

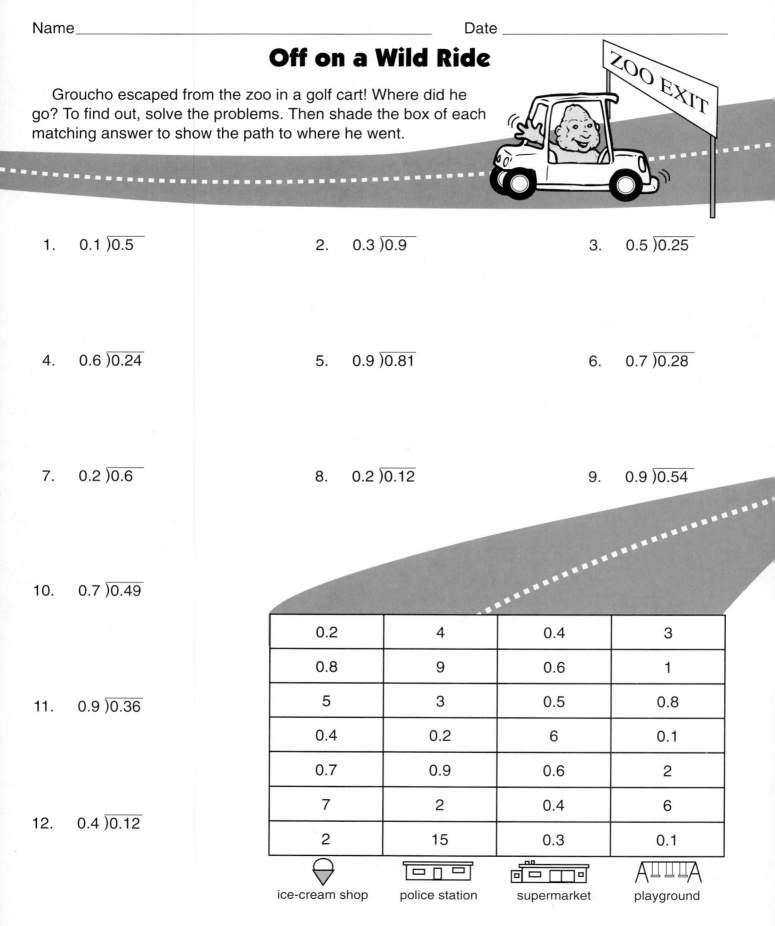

1.  $0.1\,\overline{)0.5}$

2.  $0.3\,\overline{)0.9}$

3.  $0.5\,\overline{)0.25}$

4.  $0.6\,\overline{)0.24}$

5.  $0.9\,\overline{)0.81}$

6.  $0.7\,\overline{)0.28}$

7.  $0.2\,\overline{)0.6}$

8.  $0.2\,\overline{)0.12}$

9.  $0.9\,\overline{)0.54}$

10.  $0.7\,\overline{)0.49}$

11.  $0.9\,\overline{)0.36}$

12.  $0.4\,\overline{)0.12}$

| 0.2 | 4 | 0.4 | 3 |
|---|---|---|---|
| 0.8 | 9 | 0.6 | 1 |
| 5 | 3 | 0.5 | 0.8 |
| 0.4 | 0.2 | 6 | 0.1 |
| 0.7 | 0.9 | 0.6 | 2 |
| 7 | 2 | 0.4 | 6 |
| 2 | 15 | 0.3 | 0.1 |
| ice-cream shop | police station | supermarket | playground |

Name_____    Date _____

# Divide and Hide!

Carlos the Chameleon has found a new place to hide! To find out where he is, solve the problems. Then write the letter that goes with each quotient in the matching numbered blank below.

Ⓐ  $0.25\overline{)3}$        Ⓑ  $0.24\overline{)6}$        Ⓔ  $0.15\overline{)9}$

Ⓗ  $0.08\overline{)24}$       Ⓘ  $0.09\overline{)36}$       Ⓜ  $0.03\overline{)18}$

Ⓝ  $0.27\overline{)54}$       Ⓞ  $0.13\overline{)91}$       Ⓢ  $0.05\overline{)235}$

Ⓣ  $0.17\overline{)765}$                        Ⓩ  $0.34\overline{)952}$

___ ___ ___    ___ ___ ___ ___ ___ ___    ___ ___ ___ ___ ___
4,500 300 60    12 600 12 2,800 700 200    25 12 4,700 400 200

# Drake's Dilemma

Help Drake find where he buried his bone. Follow the directions below. Color the bone containing the answer. Write the letters that are left in order to find where the bone is buried.

**Estimate each quotient.**

1. Penny Poodle spent $14.67 on 3 dog collars. About how much did each one cost? _____

2. Riley Retriever spent $8.30 on tennis balls. Each ball cost $1.05. About how many tennis balls did he buy? _____

3. Timmy Terrier ran around the park 4 times in 79.68 seconds. About how long did it take him to run around the park each time?

   _____

4. Harvey Hound howled 11 times last night for a total of 55.4 minutes. About how long did each howl last? _____

5. Gracie Greyhound ran 4.5 miles in 35 minutes. About how long did it take her to run each mile? _____

**Solve on another sheet of paper.**

6. Daisy Dalmatian spent 7.17 hours on the fire truck this week. If she spent 3 days on the truck this week, how many hours did she spend on it each day? _____

7. If Clyde Collie ate 12.25 cups of food this week, how many cups of food did he eat each day?

   _____

8. Sherman Shepherd guarded the police station for 57.75 hours this week. How many hours did he guard the station each day? _____

9. Ellie Elkhound spent $13.56 on 4 boxes of doggy biscuits. How much did each box cost?

   _____

10. Sammy Spaniel spent 5.5 days at a kennel. The total cost was $170.50. How much did it cost each day? _____

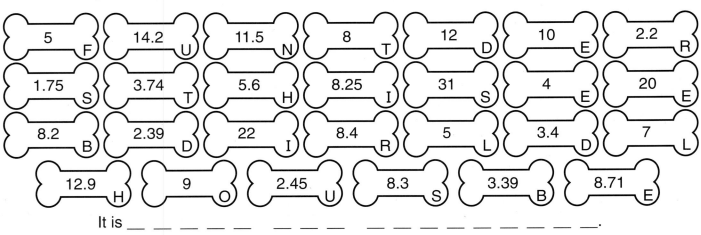

| 5 F | 14.2 U | 11.5 N | 8 T | 12 D | 10 E | 2.2 R |
| 1.75 S | 3.74 T | 5.6 H | 8.25 I | 31 S | 4 E | 20 E |
| 8.2 B | 2.39 D | 22 I | 8.4 R | 5 L | 3.4 D | 7 L |
| 12.9 H | 9 O | 2.45 U | 8.3 S | 3.39 B | 8.71 E | |

It is __ __ __ __ __ __ __ __ __ __ __ __.

# Lines, Segments, and Rays

## Show Me!

Students will be standing in line for this act-it-out activity! Just guide the class through the directions below to represent lines, segments, and rays. Then watch students' understanding of the terms soar!

- **For a line segment,** stand and make a fist with each hand. Then hold each arm out straight so that it is perpendicular to the body and parallel to the floor.

- **For a line,** use the actions for the line segment, but extend the index finger of each hand.

- **For a ray,** use the actions for the line, but hold one arm straight down along the side of the body.

- **For parallel lines,** have two students face each other and use the actions for the line.

- **For intersecting lines,** use the actions for parallel lines, but have one student twist slightly until one of his arms rests lightly on the other student's forearm or elbow.

- **For perpendicular lines,** use the actions for intersecting lines, but have one student turn 90° away from the other student.

|  | Visible | Invisible |
|---|---|---|
| Lines and line segments | • telephone lines the horizon | • underground power lines |
| Rays | • light from the sun<br>• beams of light from a lighthouse or flashlight |  |

## Searching for Samples

Send students on a scavenger hunt that has them identifying lines and rays represented in real-life objects! At the beginning of the week, ask each child to draw on a sheet of paper a chart such as the one shown. Throughout the week, have her list in her chart examples she brainstorms or personally observes that fit each description. At the end of the week, collect the papers and see who listed the most examples. Then share the most common and unique ones with the class!

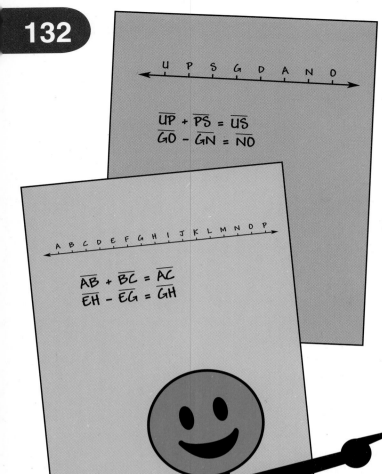

$$\overline{UP} + \overline{PS} = \overline{US}$$
$$\overline{GO} - \overline{GN} = \overline{NO}$$

$$\overline{AB} + \overline{BC} = \overline{AC}$$
$$\overline{EH} - \overline{EG} = \overline{GH}$$

# Segments Rule!

Is it possible to add and subtract with line segments? You bet! Give each student a sheet of unlined paper and a metric ruler. Direct him to draw near the top of the paper a line 15 centimeters long with points that are one centimeter apart. Have him label the points *A–P* as shown. Next, use problems such as those shown to demonstrate how to add and subtract with the segments. Afterward, instruct each child to write below his number line five problems of his own (without the answers). Then have him trade papers with a partner and solve his partner's problems. For students who need a greater challenge, have each child draw a number line labeled with different letters and create problems whose answers are two-letter words!

# Hide 'em in a Picture!

This creative review of lines, segments, and rays can transform students into geometric artists! Direct each child to use a pencil to draw a picture that includes as many objects as possible whose parts are made of segments and rays as she can. Next, instruct her to trade papers with a partner and use a crayon to trace the examples she finds. Then have her categorize the examples on the back of the paper. Impressive!

| line segments | rays |
|---|---|
| sails | light beams from lighthouse |
| lighthouse | |
| wharf | perpendicular line segments |
| | wire on fence |
| parallel line segments | post supporting sail and |
| fence posts | boat edge |
| horizontal bands on | |
| lighthouse | intersecting line segments |
| lines on posts | wire and fence post |
| supporting sails | |

**Find more student practice on pages 133–134.**

# Greg Makes the Grade!

Greg the alligator did well in school, and his teachers loved him. To find out why they loved him, match each set of words to the correct picture. Then write the letter for each answer in the matching blank below.

_____ 1. line AB

_____ 2. ray AB

_____ 3. segment AB

_____ 4. segment AB perpendicular to segment CD

_____ 5. segment AB parallel to segment CD

_____ 6. ray AB intersecting ray CD

_____ 7. 3 parallel rays

_____ 8. 3 intersecting rays

_____ 9. 3 segments perpendicular to segment AB

_____ 10. 3 segments parallel to segment AB

_____ 11. 3 intersecting segments

_____ 12. 3 intersecting lines

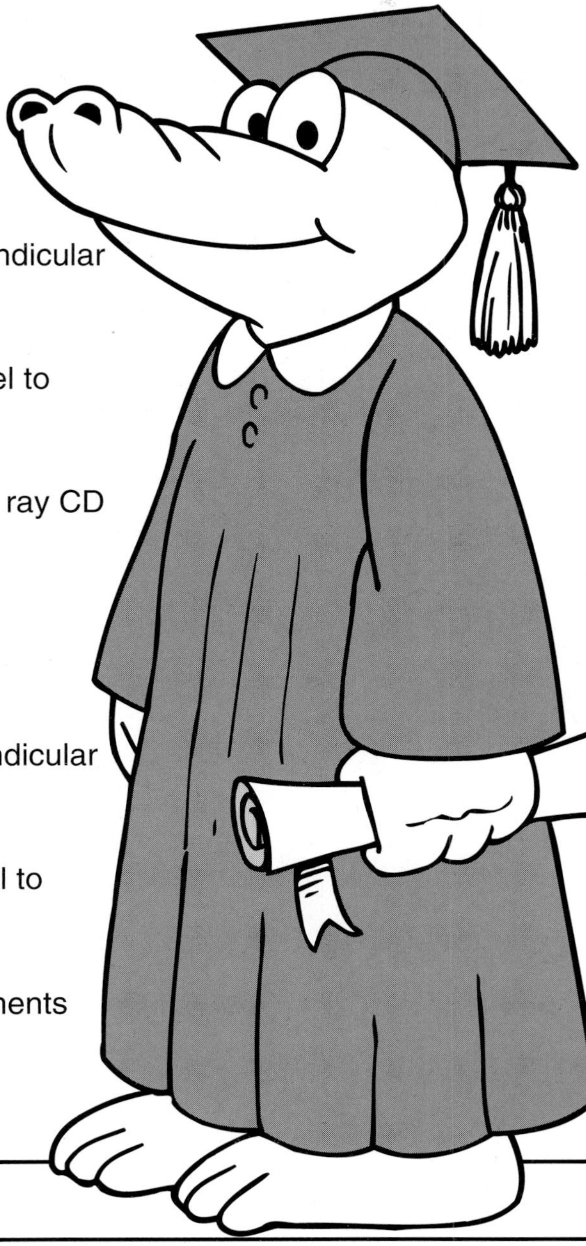

A.

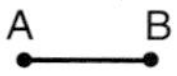

E.

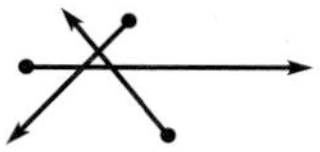

G.

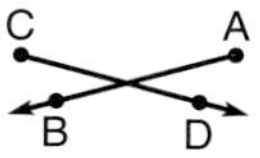

H.

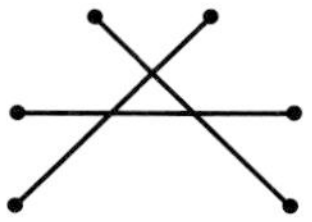

L.

N.

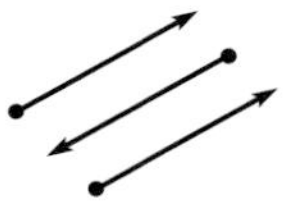

P.

R.

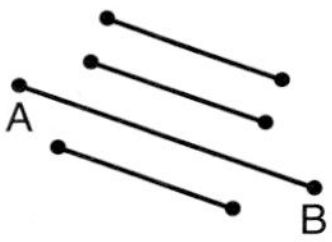

S.

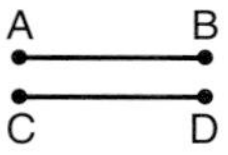

V.

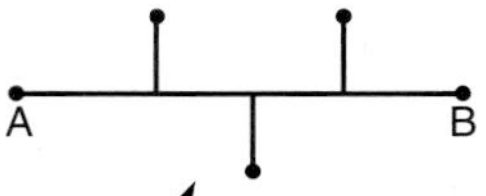

W.

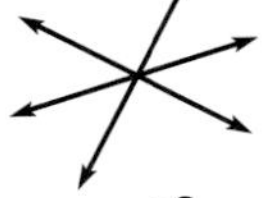

Y.

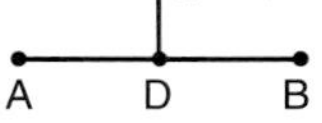

Greg's teachers loved him because ___ ___   ___ ___ ___ ___ ___ ___
                                    11  8    3  2  12  3  4  5

___ ___ ___ ___   ___ ___ ___ ___ ___ ___   ___ ___ ___ ___ ___ ___ ___!
 6  3  9  8      5  7  3  1  1  4      3  7  5  12  8  10  5

Name _____  Date _____

# Monkey See, Monkey Do!

Monte is a very smart monkey. He has been watching his sister sketch pictures of lines, segments, and rays. Now he wants to draw them too! Use a ruler to help him draw the pictures below.

1. Ray AB intersects and is perpendicular to segment CD.

2. Line EF is parallel to line GH. Segments FG and FH connect the two parallel lines.

3. Line MN is parallel to line OP. Another pair of parallel lines, QR and ST, intersect the first set but are not perpendicular to them.

4. Segment JK is perpendicular to segment KL. Adding segment JL forms triangle JKL.

5. Segment ST intersects line XY. Ray YZ starts at point Y and is perpendicular to line XY.

**Note to the teacher:** Each child will need a ruler to complete this page.

# Angles

## Designer Angles

Looking for a creative, hands-on way to introduce angles to your students? You've found it! Give each student eight craft sticks, a 12" x 18" sheet of construction paper, crayons or markers, and glue. Have each student fold her paper in half, greeting card style, and label the front "Angles." Next, allow students about ten minutes to color designs on their craft sticks. Then introduce the right angle and challenge each student to form this angle using a pair of her decorated craft sticks. After checking the angle's form, have her glue the sticks on the page and label the angle. Repeat with acute, obtuse, and straight angles. Encourage each student to keep her booklet as a handy reference while studying angles.

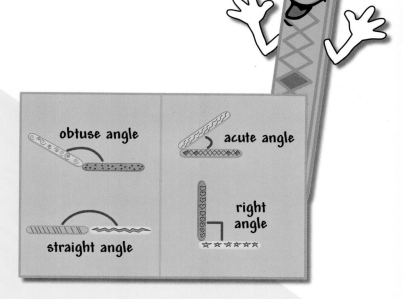

obtuse angle

acute angle

straight angle

right angle

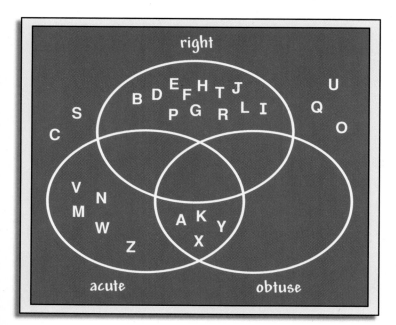

right

B D E F H T J
P G R L I
S
C
U
Q
O
V N
M
W
Z
A K Y
X

acute

obtuse

## ABC Challenge

Round up students for an activity in classifying angles that makes use of the letters of the alphabet. In advance, type each uppercase letter of the alphabet in a large font. Then draw a three-circle Venn diagram on the board and label it as shown. Pair students, giving each twosome a sheet of paper and a copy of the typed alphabet. Direct the pair to copy the Venn diagram on its paper. Next, challenge each pair to decide whether each letter has any right, acute, or obtuse angles. Have the pair write each letter in the appropriate section of the diagram. For an added challenge, have students repeat the activity with the alphabet typed in a different font to see whether they arrive at different answers.

# Straw Drop

Students review identifying types of angles with this fast-paced game! Give each group of four students ten drinking straws, scrap paper, and access to a clock with a second hand. Then guide students through the directions below to play the game.

## To play:

1. Each player signs the scrap paper to set up the group's scorecard as shown.
2. Player 1 holds the bundle of straws a foot above the playing surface and then drops them. He has 30 seconds to point out as many acute, obtuse, and right angles as he can find in the straw arrangement.
3. Player 2 counts the number of angles that Player 1 identifies and tallies them on the scorecard.
4. Player 2 takes a turn in the same manner with Player 3 counting for him.
5. Continue play for ten rounds. The player with the most points at the end is declared the winner.

# From Angles to Art

Practice measuring angles with this fun paper-folding activity. Give each student a sheet of paper, a ruler, crayons or colored pencils, and a protractor. Have each student randomly fold her paper four times, making large, irregular folds. Then have her open the paper and use the ruler to trace along each folded line. Next, direct the student to use her protractor to measure each angle created by a fold and to record its measurement. Finally, have the student identify each angle as acute, obtuse, or right and then color it according to a designated key (see the example). Display students' pages under the title "From Angles to Art."

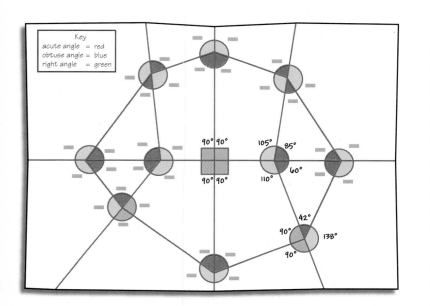

Name _____

Date _____

# Angling for Fun

Step right up! This carnival is full of angles! Decide whether each lettered angle is acute, obtuse, or right. Then write the angle's letter on the correct ticket booth.

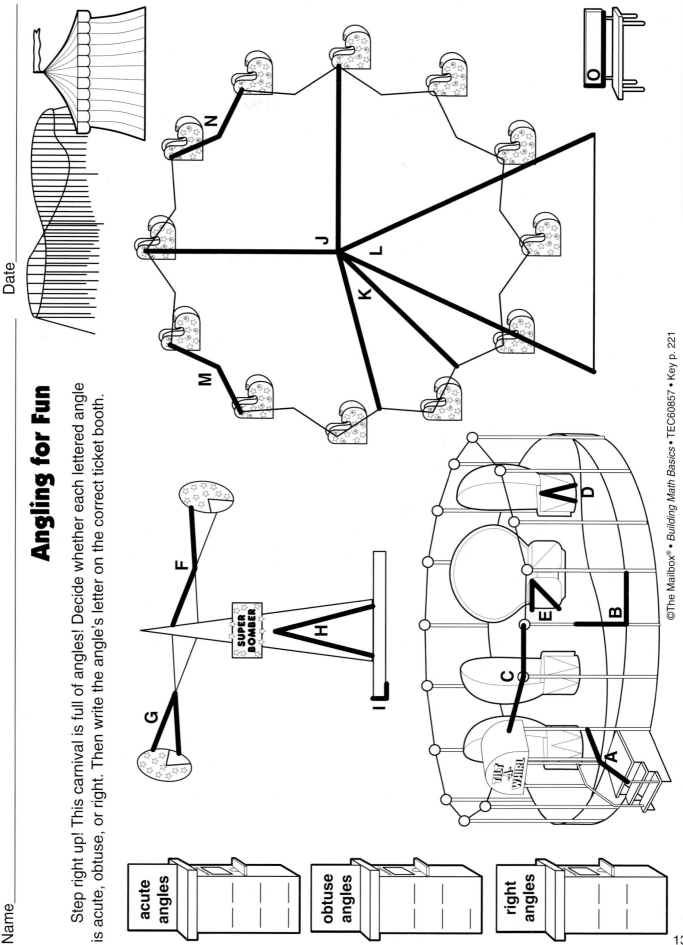

acute angles

obtuse angles

right angles

Name_____    Date _____

# Time to Measure

It's time to measure angles! For each time listed below, draw the hour hand on the clock. Then use a protractor to measure the angle you created. Write the measurement on the line below the time. Use the clock to answer the questions.

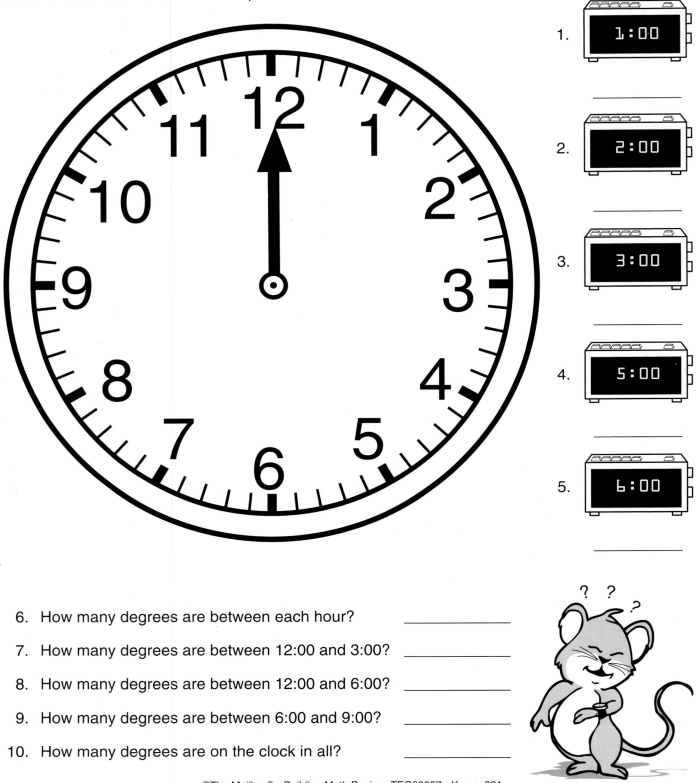

1. `1:00`
_____

2. `2:00`
_____

3. `3:00`
_____

4. `5:00`
_____

5. `6:00`
_____

6. How many degrees are between each hour?    _____

7. How many degrees are between 12:00 and 3:00?    _____

8. How many degrees are between 12:00 and 6:00?    _____

9. How many degrees are between 6:00 and 9:00?    _____

10. How many degrees are on the clock in all?    _____

**Note to the teacher:** Each student will need a protractor.

# Chords, Diameters, and Radii

## The Long and the Short of It

Drawing the longest and shortest sets of chords is the goal of this two-round partner challenge! Give each pair of students a ruler, a sheet of unlined paper, a circle cutout, and two colored pencils of different colors, such as red and blue. Direct the partners to trace the cutout on the paper. For Round 1, instruct each player to draw a short chord inside the circle, one player using the blue pencil and the other using the red pencil. Have the players take turns in this manner until each one has drawn three chords. Then have each player measure his three chords and total their lengths. Declare the player with the *lower* total the winner of that round. Direct the partners to play Round 2 in a similar way, but have them draw three long chords. (If desired, tell students not to draw chords that are also diameters.) Declare the player with the *higher* total the winner of this round.

### Short Chords
Red = 2.5 cm + 2.3 cm + 2 cm = 6.8 cm
Blue = 2.3 cm + 1.9 cm + 1.3 cm = (5.5 cm)
Winner!

### Long Chords
Blue = 7 cm + 6.9 cm + 8.1 cm = 22 cm
Red = 6.6 cm + 7.9 cm + 8.2 cm = (22.7 cm)
Winner!

## Misleading Measurements

Can your students be misled when it comes to measuring the length of a chord, diameter, or radius? Find out with an activity that involves a bit of intentional trickery! Give each child an unlined sheet of paper, a ruler, and a compass (or a round object to trace). Instruct her to draw at the top of her paper a circle with a radius, diameter, and chord. Below the circle, have her write the statements shown. Next, direct her to measure the three line segments and write their lengths in the answer blanks. Have her make sure that one or more of the measurements is incorrect. Explain that she could switch the measurements for two of the answers or even make all of the answers wrong. Then have each student trade papers with a partner and check the measurements. Conclude by having the partners circle and correct each sneaky answer.

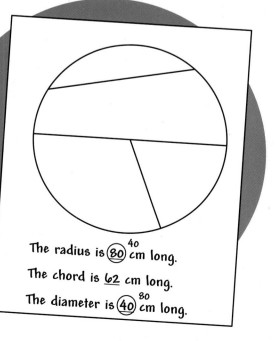

The radius is (80) 40 cm long.

The chord is 62 cm long.

The diameter is (40) 80 cm long.

# Stand Up; Sit Down!

Get students up and moving to review the properties of chords, diameters, and radii! Divide students into three groups and assign each group one of the following terms: *chord*, *diameter*, or *radius*. Announce that you will read aloud one statement at a time. Explain that whenever a statement describes a group's assigned term, its members should stand. Also explain that some statements will fit more than one term. Then read a statement from the list shown. Should a group stand when it shouldn't, stop and discuss why. By the time the last statement is read, students will have gained a better understanding of the terms *and* worked out all their wiggles!

1. It is a line segment. *(chord, diameter, radius)*
2. It has one endpoint at the center of a circle. *(radius)*
3. It always passes through the center of a circle. Its endpoints are on opposite sides of a circle. *(diameter)*
4. It is twice as long as a radius. *(diameter)*
5. It is a line segment that doesn't touch the center point of a circle. *(chord)*
6. It has at least one endpoint on a circle. *(chord, diameter, radius)*
7. It is half as long as the diameter. *(radius)*
8. In a particular circle, all of these will be exactly the same length. *(diameters, radii)*
9. In a particular circle, these may be many different lengths. *(chords)*
10. There can be an unlimited number of these in any circle. *(chords, diameters, radii)*

# Do the Shuffle!

Shuffle students around a circle with this activity that measures chords, diameters, and radii! Give each child an index card, a circle cutout, a ruler, and a marker. Direct her to trace the cutout on the card and then draw on the circle a colorful chord, diameter, or radius. At the bottom of the card, have her write "inches" or "centimeters." Collect the cutouts, markers, and cards and divide students into groups of three. Have each group member sit in a circle on the floor with her paper, pencil, and ruler. Next, shuffle and redistribute the cards. Assign each child a number (1, 2, or 3) to write on the card. Have her also write that number on her paper. Next to the number, have her identify the type of line segment shown on the circle and measure and record the segment's length in the unit requested. When each group mate is finished, have her leave the card on the floor in front of her, move to the next card at her right, and repeat the process. Continue in this manner until each child has measured all three cards in her group. Then have the group compare answers. If the answers do not agree, have the group remeasure the questionable segments.

**Find more student practice on pages 141–142.**

Name _____ Date _____

# Just "Bear-ly" Skating

Barnie and his friends are learning to ice-skate. Look at the marks their skates made on the ice. Use the code to color over the marks. Then answer the questions.

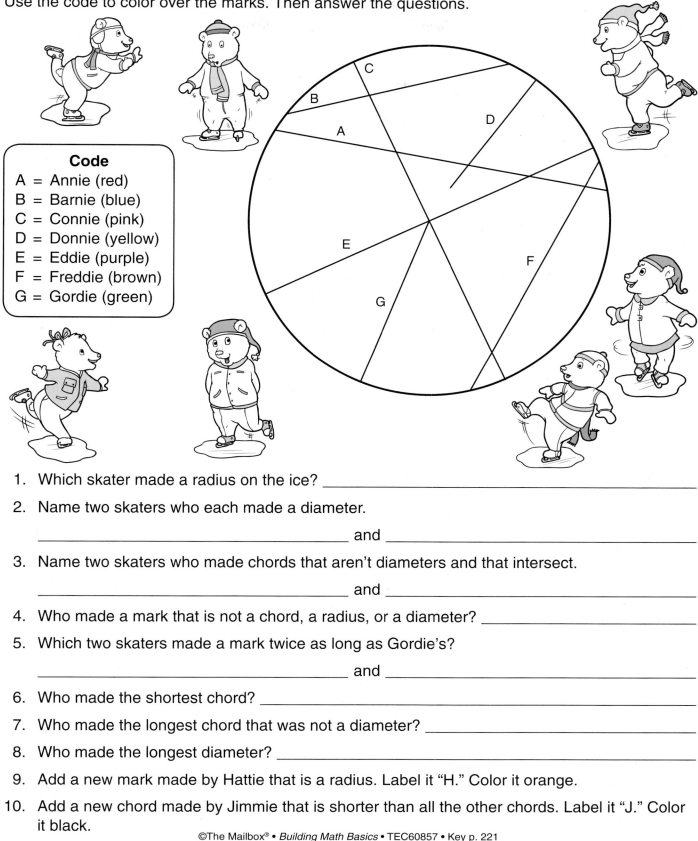

**Code**
A = Annie (red)
B = Barnie (blue)
C = Connie (pink)
D = Donnie (yellow)
E = Eddie (purple)
F = Freddie (brown)
G = Gordie (green)

1.  Which skater made a radius on the ice? _____

2.  Name two skaters who each made a diameter.

    _____ and _____

3.  Name two skaters who made chords that aren't diameters and that intersect.

    _____ and _____

4.  Who made a mark that is not a chord, a radius, or a diameter? _____

5.  Which two skaters made a mark twice as long as Gordie's?

    _____ and _____

6.  Who made the shortest chord? _____

7.  Who made the longest chord that was not a diameter? _____

8.  Who made the longest diameter? _____

9.  Add a new mark made by Hattie that is a radius. Label it "H." Color it orange.

10. Add a new chord made by Jimmie that is shorter than all the other chords. Label it "J." Color it black.

©The Mailbox® • *Building Math Basics* • TEC60857 • Key p. 221

# Thumbs-Up, Thumbs-Down!

Tom is all thumbs when it comes to drawing and measuring! Follow the directions to help him draw and measure the line segments he needs for his circle. Then decide whether each statement is true or false. If it is true, color the "Thumbs-Up" box. If it is false, color the "Thumbs-Down" box.

| Thumbs-Up | Thumbs-Down |
|---|---|
| 👍 | 👎 |
| 👍 | 👎 |
| 👍 | 👎 |
| 👍 | 👎 |
| 👍 | 👎 |
| 👍 | 👎 |
| 👍 | 👎 |
| 👍 | 👎 |
| 👍 | 👎 |
| 👍 | 👎 |

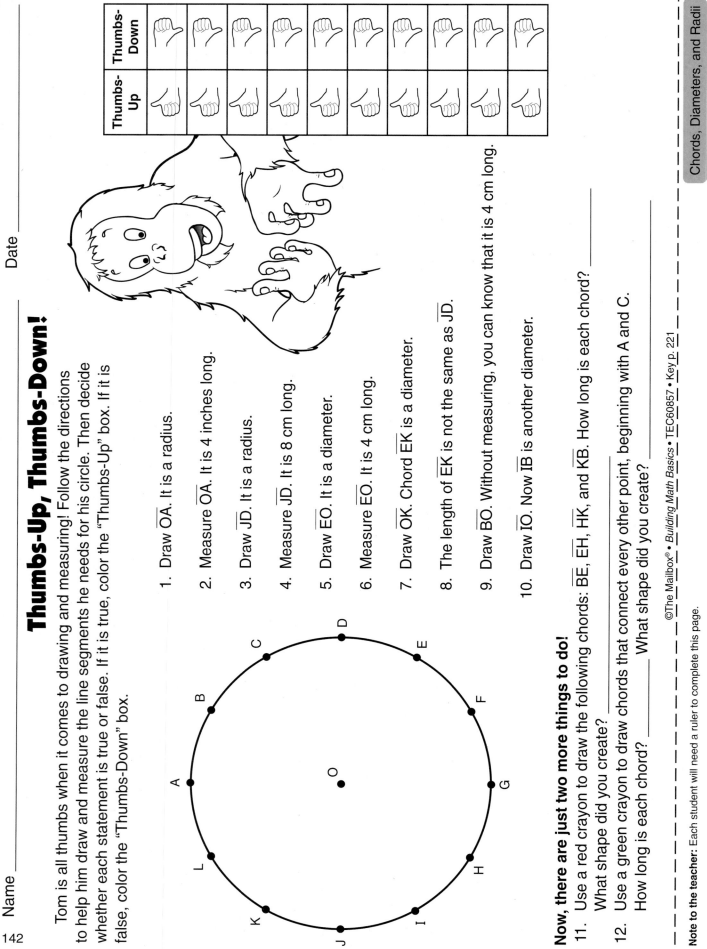

1. Draw $\overline{OA}$. It is a radius.

2. Measure $\overline{OA}$. It is 4 inches long.

3. Draw $\overline{JD}$. It is a radius.

4. Measure $\overline{JD}$. It is 8 cm long.

5. Draw $\overline{EO}$. It is a diameter.

6. Measure $\overline{EO}$. It is 4 cm long.

7. Draw $\overline{OK}$. Chord $\overline{EK}$ is a diameter.

8. The length of $\overline{EK}$ is not the same as $\overline{JD}$.

9. Draw $\overline{BO}$. Without measuring, you can know that it is 4 cm long.

10. Draw $\overline{IO}$. Now $\overline{IB}$ is another diameter.

## Now, there are just two more things to do!

11. Use a red crayon to draw the following chords: $\overline{BE}$, $\overline{EH}$, $\overline{HK}$, and $\overline{KB}$. How long is each chord? _____ What shape did you create? _____

12. Use a green crayon to draw chords that connect every other point, beginning with A and C. _____ What shape did you create? _____ How long is each chord? _____

©The Mailbox® • *Building Math Basics* • TEC60857 • Key p. 221

**Note to the teacher:** Each student will need a ruler to complete this page.

# 2-D Figures

## Shape Walk

Take a step in the right direction with this fun activity! Obtain a copy of *The Greedy Triangle* by Marilyn Burns. Read the book aloud and then, as a class, list on the board all the shapes mentioned in the story. Have each child copy the list onto a sheet of paper. Next, take students (with their paper and pencils) on a shape walk through the school. Have each student list each object he sees that matches a listed shape. After returning to the classroom, divide students into groups of three. Instruct each group to tally the number of objects of each shape that the students saw and then make a cooperative graph of the results. If desired, have each group create a shape mobile representing each shape observed.

## POLYGON COLLAGES

These cool collages help students identify the characteristics of 2-D figures! Gather a supply of magazines and catalogs. Begin the activity by reviewing with the class characteristics of different types of polygons, writing each on the board. Next, give each student a sheet of 12" x 18" construction paper, access to magazines or catalogs, scissors, and glue. To create a collage, each student divides her paper into four sections and labels each section with a different characteristic from the list. She then looks through the magazines for pictures of polygons matching those characteristics. When she finds a picture, she cuts it out and glues it in the appropriate section. Post the completed collages on a bulletin board titled "Picturing Polygons."

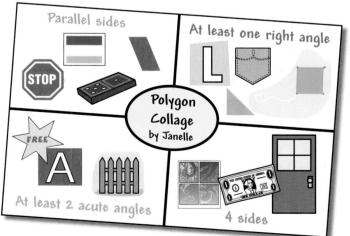

# Match 'em Up!

Your class will love this domino-type game for two that reviews classifying polygons! Give each child ten 3" x 5" index cards and then guide him through the steps below to make a set of game cards. After verifying the accuracy of the sets, have each student trade his card set with another student. Challenge each child to place the cards in the correct order by matching each polygon to its characteristics. To check his work, a student simply flips the cards over to see if the numbers are in the correct order.

**To prepare a set of game cards:**
1. Draw a vertical line dividing each index card in half.
2. Lay the cards down end to end. Label the left half of the first card "START" and the right half of the last card "FINISH."
3. Draw a different polygon on the left side of each of the remaining cards in the set.
4. Write the matching characteristics for each polygon on the right side of the previous card.
5. Flip the cards over and number them in order from 1 to 10. Then shuffle the cards.

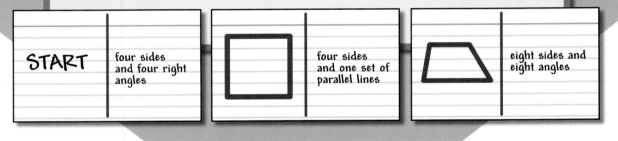

| START | four sides and four right angles |
| square | four sides and one set of parallel lines |
| trapezoid | eight sides and eight angles |

# GEOCREATURES

Challenge students to create geo-creatures to sharpen both their geometry and computation skills! Copy on the board the chart below and explain that students will use it to create a geocreature. Next, give students a price range for the creature's value, such as between $30 and $40. Then give each child a 9" x 12" sheet of white construction paper. Have the student draw her creature on the paper and then list on the back of her paper the shapes used in its construction, as well as the total cost. Allow students to share their creations before displaying them with the title "Geocreature Creations."

| Shape | Cost |
|---|---|
| Rhombus | $1.50 |
| Triangle | $2.00 |
| Square | $2.50 |
| Trapezoid | $3.00 |
| Pentagon | $3.50 |
| Hexagon | $4.00 |
| Octagon | $4.50 |
| Decagon | $5.00 |

**Find more student practice on pages 145 and 146.**

# Secret Stash

Skippy can't find his stashed acorns! Color the shape that matches each description. The colored shapes will show the path to the missing acorns.

1. an octagon

2. a polygon with parallel sides

3. a polygon with all right angles

4. a polygon that is not a quadrilateral

5. a rhombus

6. a polygon with no obtuse angles

7. a polygon with all obtuse angles

8. a hexagon

9. a polygon that is a parallelogram

10. a polygon that has 2 acute angles

11. a pentagon

12. a quadrilateral with 2 acute angles

13. a trapezoid

14. a quadrilateral with 2 obtuse angles

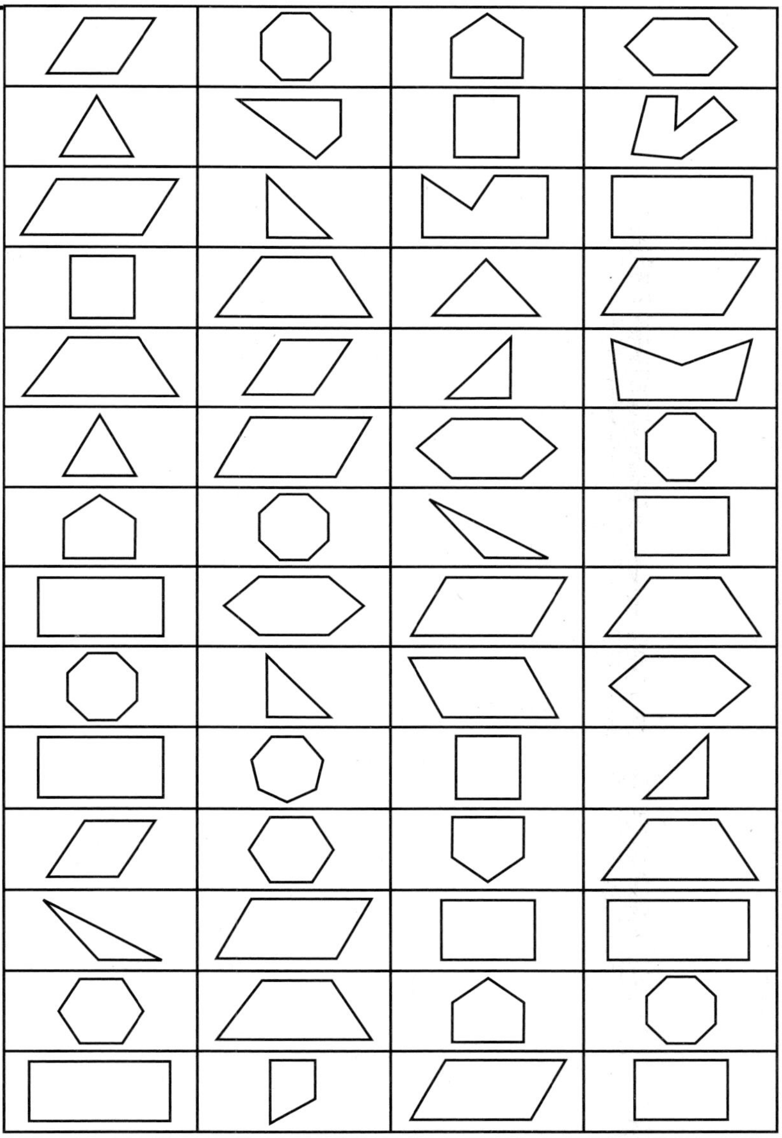

bushes          hollow tree          under bed          closet

Name _____     Date _____

# Polly's Polygon Parlor

Each flavor of ice cream below includes a quadrilateral in its name. List the features of each quadrilateral on the ice-cream box. Use the list at the bottom of the page. Each time you use a feature, color a matching ice-cream scoop.

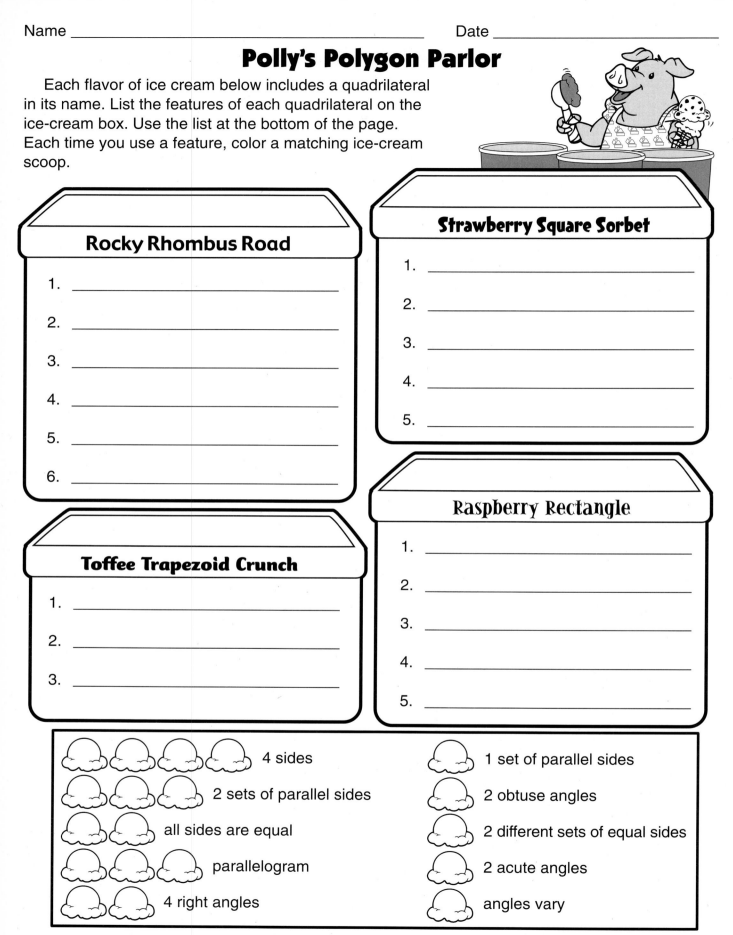

**Rocky Rhombus Road**

1. _____
2. _____
3. _____
4. _____
5. _____
6. _____

**Strawberry Square Sorbet**

1. _____
2. _____
3. _____
4. _____
5. _____

**Toffee Trapezoid Crunch**

1. _____
2. _____
3. _____

**Raspberry Rectangle**

1. _____
2. _____
3. _____
4. _____
5. _____

4 sides

2 sets of parallel sides

all sides are equal

parallelogram

4 right angles

1 set of parallel sides

2 obtuse angles

2 different sets of equal sides

2 acute angles

angles vary

©The Mailbox® • Building Math Basics • TEC60857 • Key p. 221

146   2-D Figures

# 3-D Figures

## Scavenging for Solids

Discover how fast your class can identify 3-D figures! Divide students into groups. Give each group ten minutes to list on paper as many classroom examples of solid figures as possible. Explain that the lists should include both the item's name and the type of figure it represents. For example, a filing cabinet represents a rectangular prism. When time is up, invite one group at a time to read its list aloud. Have members of the other groups raise their hands and place a check next to an item whenever their lists include an object found by another group. After all the groups have had a turn, have each group circle any items not named by other groups. Award each group one point for each checked item and two points for each circled item. Then declare the group with the most points the winner!

| Classroom Item | Points |
|---|---|
| ✓ vase—cylinder | 1 |
| ✓ basketball—sphere | 1 |
| plastic crate—rectangular prism | 2 |
| ✓ pencil holder—cylinder | 1 |
| ✓ globe—sphere | 1 |
| Total | 6 |

## Venn Comparisons

Examine the similarities and differences of 3-D figures with this "Venn-tastic" activity! On the board, draw a Venn diagram and two different figures such as the ones shown. Fill in the diagram, pointing out characteristics such as the following: number of faces, edges, and vertices; shapes of faces and bases; whether the bases are parallel; whether the faces are congruent; and whether the figures are prisms or pyramids. Discuss the attributes. Then pair students. Have each duo choose two different figures and work together to complete a similar diagram. For an extra challenge, have the partners compare three figures that share at least one common attribute!

For additional practice with faces, vertices, and edges, see the reproducible on page 149.

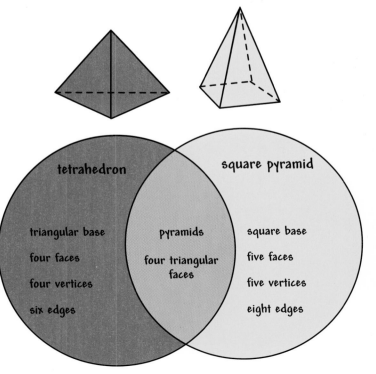

tetrahedron

triangular base

four faces

four vertices

six edges

pyramids

four triangular faces

square pyramid

square base

five faces

five vertices

eight edges

# Clued In to Construction

Teamwork is the name of the game with this 3-D construction activity! Obtain nine tubs of play dough. Next, write each clue for each figure below (omitting the italicized name) on a separate paper strip, using a different-colored strip for each figure. Place each set of strips in a different resealable plastic bag labeled with the corresponding figure number. To each bag, add more toothpicks than the number of edges. Then divide students into nine groups. Give each group a bag of clues and a tub of play dough. Direct the group to use the clues, toothpicks, and play dough to construct the figure and then identify it by number on a sheet of paper to note that it's been done. After checking each structure, instruct the groups to disassemble them and put the clues and toothpicks back in the bags. Then rotate the groups. Continue in this manner until each group has built all nine figures.

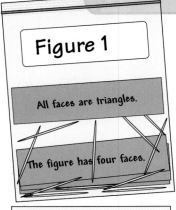

### Figure 1

All faces are triangles.

The figure has four faces.

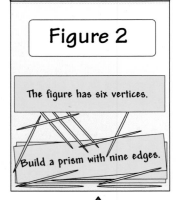

### Figure 2

The figure has six vertices.

Build a prism with nine edges.

## Clues

**Figure 1:** Build a pyramid with six edges. The figure has four faces. The pyramid has four vertices. All faces are triangles. *(tetrahedron)*

**Figure 2:** Build a prism with nine edges. The figure has five faces. The figure has six vertices. Some of the faces are rectangles and some are triangles. *(triangular prism)*

**Figure 3:** Build a figure with 12 edges. The figure has eight vertices. The figure has six faces. All faces are congruent. All faces are quadrilaterals. *(cube)*

**Figure 4:** Build a prism with six faces. The figure has 12 edges. The figure has eight vertices. Two faces are squares. Break four toothpicks in half and use these smaller pieces to construct the square faces. Four faces are rectangles. *(rectangular prism)*

**Figure 5:** Build a pyramid with six faces. The figure has ten edges. The pyramid has six vertices. One face has more than four edges. The figure has five triangular faces. *(pentagonal pyramid)*

**Figure 6:** Build a shape with eight faces. The figure has 12 edges. The figure has six vertices. All faces are congruent triangles. Two pyramids share the same base. *(octahedron)*

**Figure 7:** Build a prism with eight faces. The figure has 18 edges. The shape has 12 vertices. There are six rectangular faces on the figure. The total number of edges on the top and bottom bases is an even number that is a multiple of three. *(hexagonal prism)*

**Figure 8:** Build a pyramid with five faces. The shape has five vertices. The figure has eight edges. The base has four right angles. *(square pyramid)*

**Figure 9:** Build a prism with seven faces. The figure has 15 edges. The shape has ten vertices. The base has more sides than a quadrilateral but fewer than a hexagon. *(pentagonal prism)*

**Find more student practice on page 150.**

# Polly Hedra's Grand Opening

Polly is preparing for the grand opening of her brand-new store. To help her complete the signs, fill in the number of faces, edges, and vertices for each style of 3-D figure. Then use the pricing guide to find each one's cost.

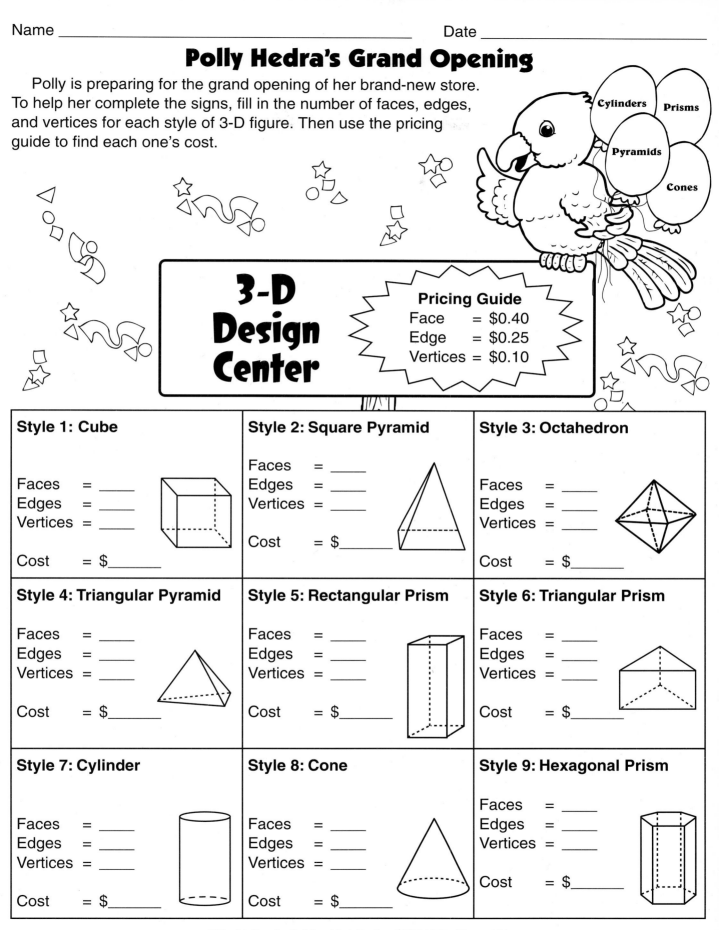

**3-D Design Center**

**Pricing Guide**
Face = $0.40
Edge = $0.25
Vertices = $0.10

**Style 1: Cube**

Faces = ____
Edges = ____
Vertices = ____

Cost = $_____

**Style 2: Square Pyramid**

Faces = ____
Edges = ____
Vertices = ____

Cost = $_____

**Style 3: Octahedron**

Faces = ____
Edges = ____
Vertices = ____

Cost = $_____

**Style 4: Triangular Pyramid**

Faces = ____
Edges = ____
Vertices = ____

Cost = $_____

**Style 5: Rectangular Prism**

Faces = ____
Edges = ____
Vertices = ____

Cost = $_____

**Style 6: Triangular Prism**

Faces = ____
Edges = ____
Vertices = ____

Cost = $_____

**Style 7: Cylinder**

Faces = ____
Edges = ____
Vertices = ____

Cost = $_____

**Style 8: Cone**

Faces = ____
Edges = ____
Vertices = ____

Cost = $_____

**Style 9: Hexagonal Prism**

Faces = ____
Edges = ____
Vertices = ____

Cost = $_____

# 3-D Dilemma

Rocky has all the pieces he needs to make eight new figures for his 3-D collection. But there are four extra shapes! On the pawprints, draw the shapes needed to make each figure. As you draw each shape, color it on the tree. Then draw the figure that can be made with the leftover shapes.

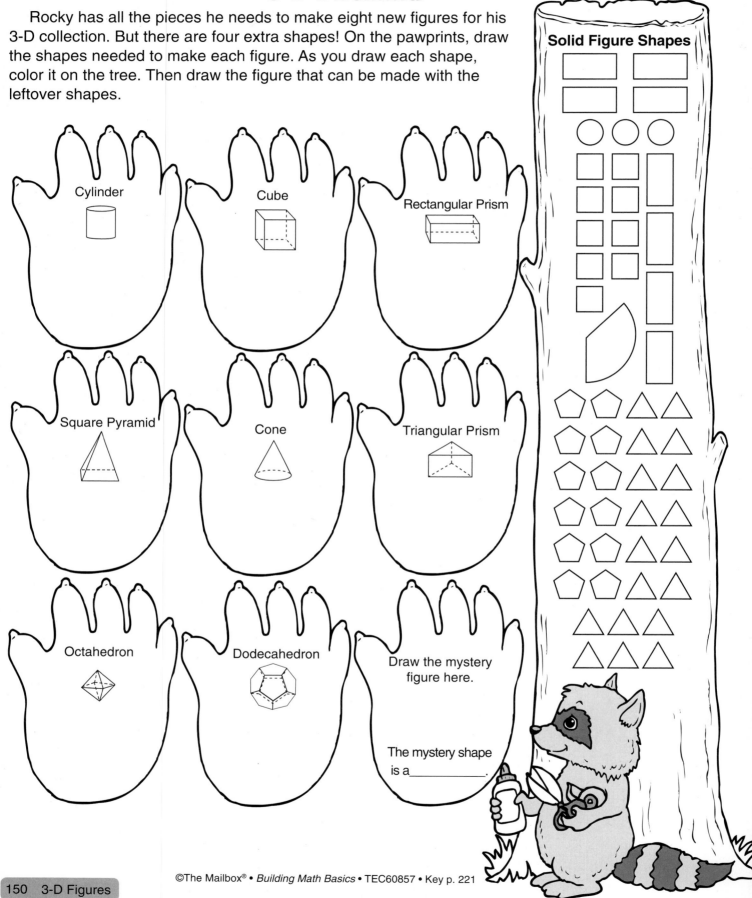

**Solid Figure Shapes**

Cylinder

Cube

Rectangular Prism

Square Pyramid

Cone

Triangular Prism

Octahedron

Dodecahedron

Draw the mystery figure here.

The mystery shape is a _____.

## Make It Similar

Combine art and math for this fun exercise in drawing similar figures. In advance, make one copy of the animal patterns on page 152 for every four students and cut apart the patterns. Give each student one pattern from the page, a sheet of one-inch graph paper, a sheet of one-centimeter graph paper, and a ruler. Instruct each student to draw a grid of half-inch squares over his pattern by connecting the tick marks on all sides. Then have the student use the grid to draw figures that are both larger and smaller than, but similar to, the original pattern. If desired, make additional copies and challenge early finishers to repeat the process with a different pattern.

# Congruency Quest

Strengthen students' skills at identifying congruent figures with this fun game. To prepare game cards, give each student two index cards and scissors. A student lays one card on top of the other and makes a cut through both cards, creating two pairs of congruent shapes. She then makes one more cut in one pair of cards, resulting in a total of three sets of congruent shapes. Finally, divide students into small groups and guide them through the steps below for playing the game.

## To play:
1. All players combine their shapes and lay them down on the playing surface.
2. Player 1 selects two shapes she thinks are congruent. She then tests their congruency by stacking the shapes, turning or flipping them as necessary.
3. If the shapes are congruent, she keeps them. If they are not congruent, she returns them to the playing surface.
4. The remaining players take turns in the same manner.
5. Play continues until all shapes have been matched. Declare the player with the most matches the winner.

# Animal Patterns

Use with "Make It Similar" on page 151.

Name_____  Date _____

# Spinning Similar Webs

Spud spins swell webs. Each web is made of similar shapes.
Finish each web below. Draw a line from the shape's center to
one centimeter past each corner. Then connect each line to
make a shape similar to the original. Repeat two more times for
each web. The first one has been started for you.

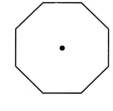

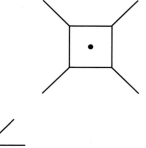
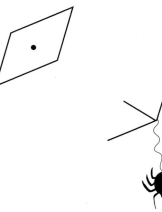

**Note to the teacher:** Students will need centimeter rulers to complete this page.

## Silly Sally!

Sally made Sammy a set of matching keys so he could get to the locked-up acorns. Now the keys are all mixed up! Cut out each key at the bottom of the page. Then glue it below its congruent match.

# Symmetry

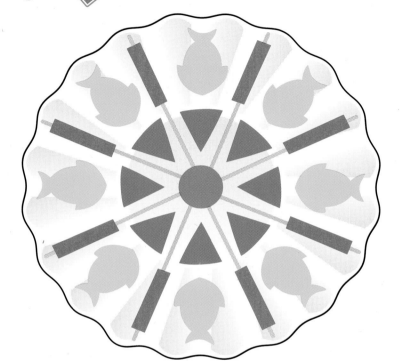

## Picture Pies

Show students that symmetry is as easy as pie! Gather a supply of stencils or templates. Also gather colored pencils and a large coffee filter for each child. After reviewing the concepts of line and rotational symmetry, give each child the materials gathered. Direct her to fold her coffee filter in half three times. Next, have her unfold the filter and trace the fold lines with colored pencils. Then challenge her to decorate the pie's sections with tracings of different shapes that represent line and rotational symmetry. When students are finished, invite them to share their work with the class and point out examples of each type of symmetry. Display the projects on a bulletin board titled "Symmetry Is As Easy As Pie!"

## Stackable Symmetry

For a symmetry activity that really stacks up, give each pair of students a sheet of ½-inch grid paper, a colorful marker, and a supply of gram unit cubes. Direct the students to place the grid on a flat surface between them and use the marker to divide the grid into two equal playing areas. Instruct Student A to place a cube in any square of his area. Challenge Student B to place in her area a cube that shows the reflection of Student A's cube. Once the players agree on the placement, have Student B either place a second cube on a different square in her area or stack one atop the existing cube. Have Student A duplicate the last move and then add another cube somewhere in his playing area. Continue play in this manner for about five minutes. Conclude by having each pair of players share with another pair how its 3-D model illustrates symmetry.

## "Sun-sational" Symmetry

Shed more light on symmetry with this "sun-sational" activity! Give each child a five-inch square of white paper, masking tape, and pattern blocks. Direct him to fold his paper in half twice and then unfold the paper. Have him identify its two fold lines as lines of symmetry. Next, have him arrange on the paper pattern pieces to create a symmetrical design and tape them in place. When he has finished, give him a five-inch square of transparency film and permanent markers in different colors. Instruct the student to tape the film atop the pattern-block design and trace it with a black marker. Then have him remove the film and color the design. Invite students to share the resulting symmetrical suncatchers with the class. As they do, guide them to sort the projects using questions such as "Which suncatchers have rotational symmetry?" and "Which have line symmetry?" Then display the groupings in a window!

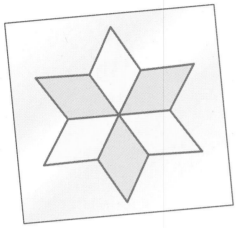

## Butterfly Kites

Send symmetry investigations sky-high! Gather templates or mini stickers with symmetrical designs. Next, give each child scissors, glue, and two colorful pieces of construction paper (6" x 9" and 12" x 18"). Direct the student to fold each paper in half lengthwise and to cut the larger piece into a kite shape and the smaller into a butterfly shape. Instruct her to open the shapes, align the fold lines, and glue the butterfly cutout to the kite shape. After she writes her name on the back, have her take her kite and sit in a circle with her classmates. Give each student in the circle a ruler, colored pencils, and templates (or stickers). Have her add two different simple symmetrical designs to her cutout: one to the butterfly and one to the kite. Then, at your signal, have her pass her kite to her left and add two similar designs to the kite she receives. Continue having students pass their kites and add designs until each kite has several different decorations. After students discuss the designs, have them add tails to their kites and display them on a bulletin board titled "High-Flying Symmetry!"

**Find more student practice on pages 157–158.**

# What a Gem!

Max has struck it rich! Find the four symmetrical designs on the gem. Each one is located on two triangular faces that share a line of symmetry. Color each pair of triangular faces a different color. Then cut out the gem, fold it along the dotted lines, and glue the tabs in place.

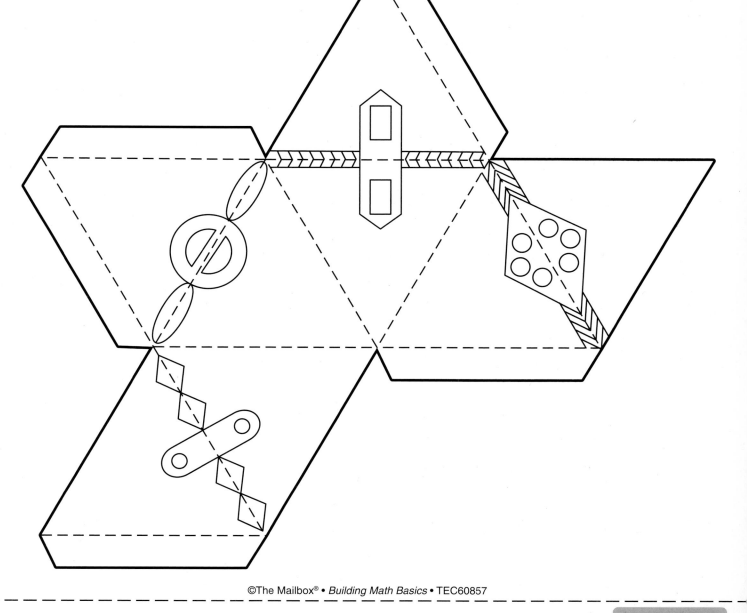

**Note to the teacher:** Each student will need scissors, glue, and crayons or markers to complete this page.

# Clowning Around With Symmetry

Clyde needs your help! Draw all the lines of symmetry for each figure and write the number on the line provided. The total lines of symmetry should be 38.

1. _____ line(s) of symmetry

2. _____ line(s) of symmetry

3. _____ line(s) of symmetry

4. _____ line(s) of symmetry

5. _____ line(s) of symmetry

6. _____ line(s) of symmetry

7. _____ line(s) of symmetry

8. _____ line(s) of symmetry

9. _____ line(s) of symmetry

10. _____ line(s) of symmetry

11. _____ line(s) of symmetry

12. _____ line(s) of symmetry

13. _____ line(s) of symmetry

14. _____ line(s) of symmetry

15. _____ line(s) of symmetry

16. _____ line(s) of symmetry

©The Mailbox® • Building Math Basics • TEC60857 • Key p. 221

# Translations, Rotations, and Reflections

## Transformed by Color

Introduce the concept of translations, rotations, and reflections with this colorful idea. At a craft store, purchase a package of paper that features one color on the front and another color on the back, such as origami paper. Then die-cut from the paper two identical asymmetrical shapes for each child in your class. Guide students to use the shapes to model the various transformations. They'll easily see that with translations and rotations the colors remain the same for both shapes. However, when modeling a reflection, the color changes after the flip, illustrating that the shape was physically turned over. The colors will help students visualize the different types of transformations and help you more easily assess their understanding.

## EVERYBODY...FLIP!

Head on over to a large open area for this kinesthetic review of transformations! Have students lie down on the floor facing the same direction. (Be sure they have enough room to move around without bumping into each other.) Then call out a transformation and challenge each student to make that movement with her body. After repeating several times with different movements, divide students into groups of three or four. Have each group create its own series of movements to perform for the class. As each group performs, the remaining groups try to identify its movements.

## Sliding Through Geometry

Combine math and music, and your students will be dancing with delight! After investigating geometric transformations with pencil and paper, teach your class the steps to the Electric Slide dance. Every time a child turns or slides while dancing, the concepts of rotation and translation are reinforced. Now that's a step in the right direction!

# BACK TO START

This whole-class game is sure to draw in your students! Make a copy of the game cards below and place them facedown in a stack at the front of the classroom. Then draw on the board an easy-to-copy asymmetrical shape. Divide the class into two teams and invite one student from Team 1 to the board. The student draws a card and then transforms the shape according to the directions, drawing the new image to the right of the original shape. If he is correct, award the team one point and have Team 2 take a turn. If incorrect, a student from Team 2 can attempt to earn the point for her team. Continue play in this manner until one team draws the shape in its original orientation. Award this team two points. Then draw a new shape on the board and repeat. The team with the most points at the end of the game is the winner.

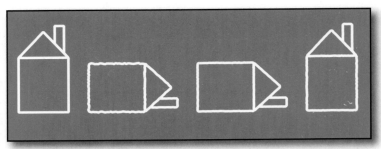

Find more student practice on pages 161–162.

## Game Cards
Use with "Back to Start" on this page.

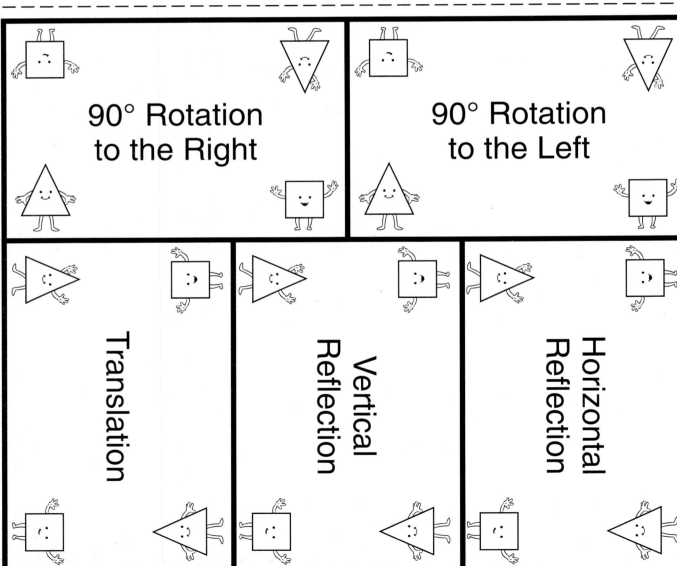

Name _____  Date _____

# Topsy Turvy

Identify whether each object in a box has been rotated or reflected. Color by the code.

**Color Code**
rotated 90° = yellow
reflected = red

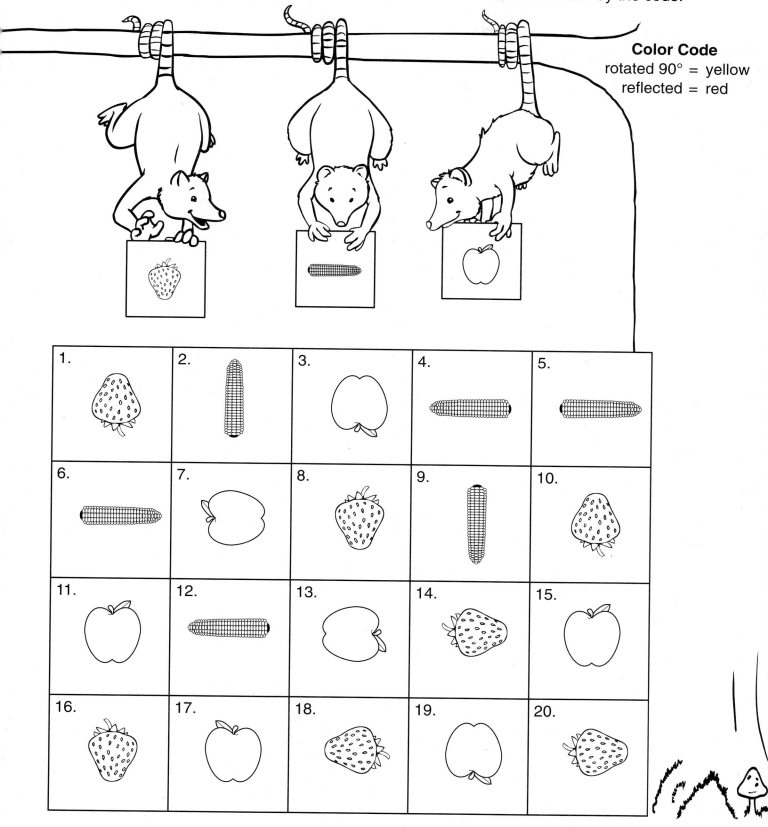

# Route to the Loot

Help Pete find the missing loot. Follow the clues on the treasure map to color a path that shows the way. Hint: You can move up, down, left, or right, but not diagonally.

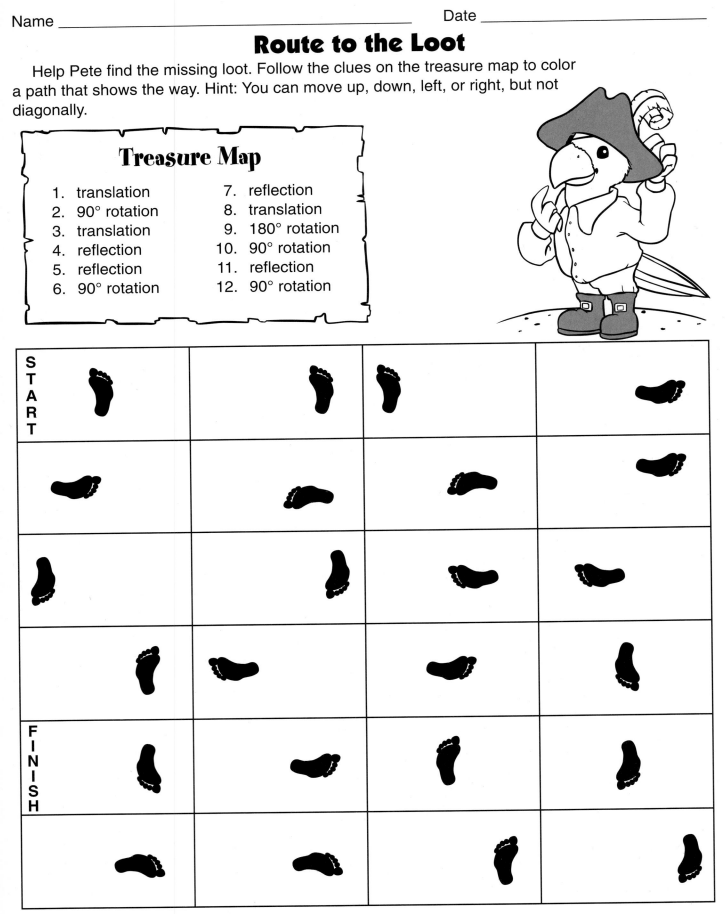

**Treasure Map**

1. translation
2. 90° rotation
3. translation
4. reflection
5. reflection
6. 90° rotation
7. reflection
8. translation
9. 180° rotation
10. 90° rotation
11. reflection
12. 90° rotation

# Tessellations

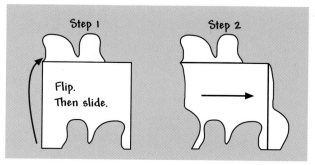

## Connected Cats and Puzzled Pooches

Create fabulous felines and delightful doggies with these top-notch tessellations! Give each child a three-inch square cut from an index card, scissors, tape, glue, markers, and two 9" x 12" sheets of construction paper (one white, one colored). Then guide him through the steps below to create either a cat or a dog tessellation. For a finishing touch, have him give his artwork a creative title!

*"Purr-fect" Design by Morris*

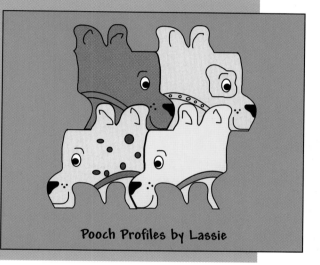

*Pooch Profiles by Lassie*

**Cat Tessellation:**

1. Draw ears along the bottom edge of the paper square. Cut out the ears in one piece, slide them to the square's top edge, and tape them in place.
2. Draw the outline of one side of a cat's head on the left edge of the paper square. Cut out this piece, slide it to the right edge of the square, and tape it in place.
3. Trace the cat's head onto the white paper to make two rows of tracings. Trace the heads so they fit next to each other without any gaps or overlaps.
4. Color the design and add details.
5. Cut out your entire design and glue it to the colored construction paper.

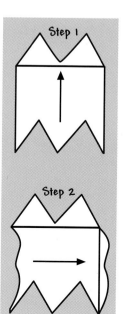

Step 1

Step 2

**Dog Tessellation:**

Follow the steps for the cat tessellation, but flip the ears before sliding them to make a profile. When drawing the outline of the head, give the dog a long snout. The second row of dogs will face the opposite direction of those in the first row.

Step 1

Step 2

Flip.
Then slide.

# Window Wonders

Decorate your windows with dazzling tessellation designs! Have each child trace a tessellation pattern several times on white paper and color it with colored pencils or markers. After he adds details, have him place his design facedown on a double layer of paper towels. Direct him to brush the back with just enough cooking oil to make the paper translucent to resemble stained glass. Allow the paper to dry for an hour. Then invite the student to fit his picture with a colorful paper frame and tape it to a window. On sunny days, your windows will come alive with color!

# Diminishing Designs

For an exciting project, create tessellated miniatures! Give each student a clean white foam tray from a local deli or meat department or a smooth lid from a foam takeout box. (Have extras on hand in case of shrinking accidents.) Instruct each child to trace a tessellation pattern onto the flat part of the tray and color it with permanent markers. After she outlines the design and adds details with a black marker, have her sign the back and cut out the design, keeping a narrow white border around the edge. Have her also punch a hole at one end if the artwork will be hung.

Next, preheat an oven to 350°F (or ask a parent volunteer to complete the shrinking step at home). Have each child wrap her design loosely in aluminum foil. Place several designs in the oven for about five minutes until the pieces shrink and curl. When they start to uncurl, quickly remove them from the oven and flatten each one with a spatula. Once the pieces are cool, invite each designer to tie a loop of yarn through the hole to create a key chain or a tree ornament. Or have her glue on a pin back for wearable art!

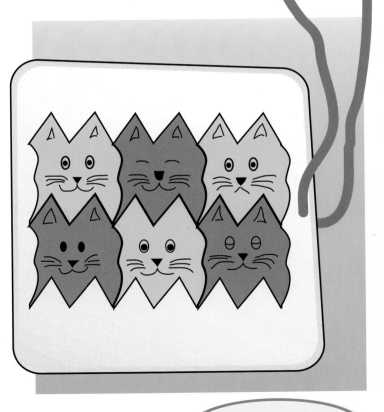

**Find more student practice on page 165.**

Name _____  Date _____

# Tessellated Tiles

Katie is Outback Tile Company's top designer. Help her create designs for her latest customers by cutting out the shapes below and tracing them in the rectangles. Then color and find the cost of each design. In places where only half a tile is needed, charge half price for it!

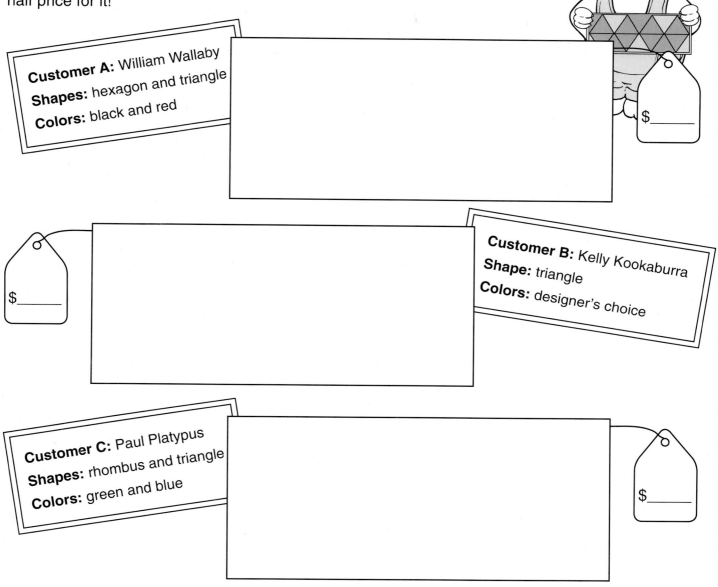

**Customer A:** William Wallaby
**Shapes:** hexagon and triangle
**Colors:** black and red

$ _____

$ _____

**Customer B:** Kelly Kookaburra
**Shape:** triangle
**Colors:** designer's choice

**Customer C:** Paul Platypus
**Shapes:** rhombus and triangle
**Colors:** green and blue

$ _____

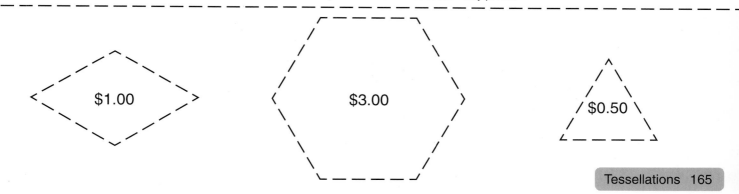

$1.00

$3.00

$0.50

# Ordered Pairs

## "En-chant-ing" Practice

Make ordered pairs something to cheer about with this activity, which gets students on their feet! Take your class outside to a large paved area (such as a safe area of the parking lot) and use sidewalk chalk to draw two 6 x 6 grids large enough for students to walk along. (Or, to complete the activity indoors, use masking tape to create grids on the floor.) Then teach your students the following chant to help them remember how to find ordered pairs: Don't get mixed up; move over, then up! As you recite the second part of the chant, model how to step to the right and then hop forward. Next, divide your class into two groups, lining up each group in front of a grid. Call out an ordered pair and have the first child in each line stand on that point on the grid. Encourage each group to recite the chant while its group mate moves to the point. After verifying each student's location, send him to the back of the line and call out another ordered pair for the next two students in line.

*Don't get mixed up; move over, then up!*

## Cereal Marks the Spot

This variation of the popular Battleship game really hits the mark! In advance, gather one more than a class supply of Geoboards and a box of colored O-shaped cereal. Cut pieces of blank labels or sticky notes to label a grid on each board as shown. To play, secretly place cereal pieces over several different pegs of one Geoboard. Then give each child a Geoboard and a handful of cereal. Invite students to take turns naming coordinate pairs to try to guess the placement of your cereal pieces. Have students use their cereal pieces to mark your response to each guess, using one color to indicate hits and the remaining colors to indicate misses. After each hidden cereal piece is revealed, have students clear their boards to play another round, or challenge students to play against a partner.

*"(1, 4); that's a hit!"*

**Find more student practice on page 167–168.**

Name _____

# Trotting and Plotting

Henry just ran out of the stable! Plot the ordered pairs below to reveal what Henry is looking for.

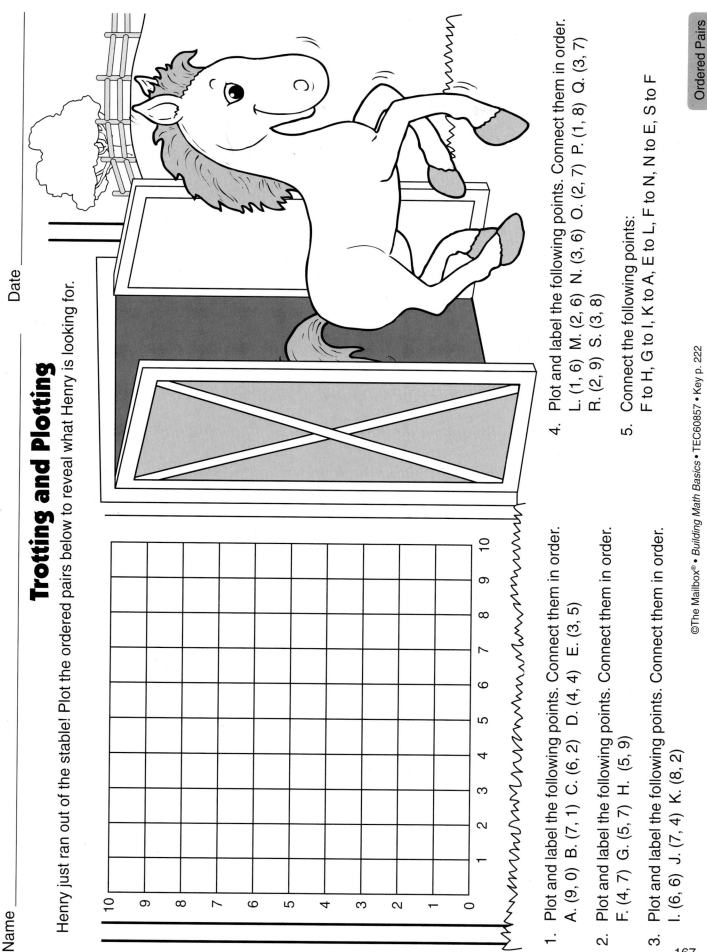

1. Plot and label the following points. Connect them in order.
   A. (9, 0)  B. (7, 1)  C. (6, 2)  D. (4, 4)  E. (3, 5)

2. Plot and label the following points. Connect them in order.
   F. (4, 7)  G. (5, 7)  H. (5, 9)

3. Plot and label the following points. Connect them in order.
   I. (6, 6)  J. (7, 4)  K. (8, 2)

4. Plot and label the following points. Connect them in order.
   L. (1, 6)  M. (2, 6)  N. (3, 6)  O. (2, 7)  P. (1, 8)  Q. (3, 7)
   R. (2, 9)  S. (3, 8)

5. Connect the following points:
   F to H, G to I, K to A, E to L, F to N, N to E, S to F

©The Mailbox® • *Building Math Basics* • TEC60857 • Key p. 222

167

Name _____  Date _____

# Hysterical Hare

Find each ordered pair on the grid. Write the matching letter in the blank to solve the riddles below.

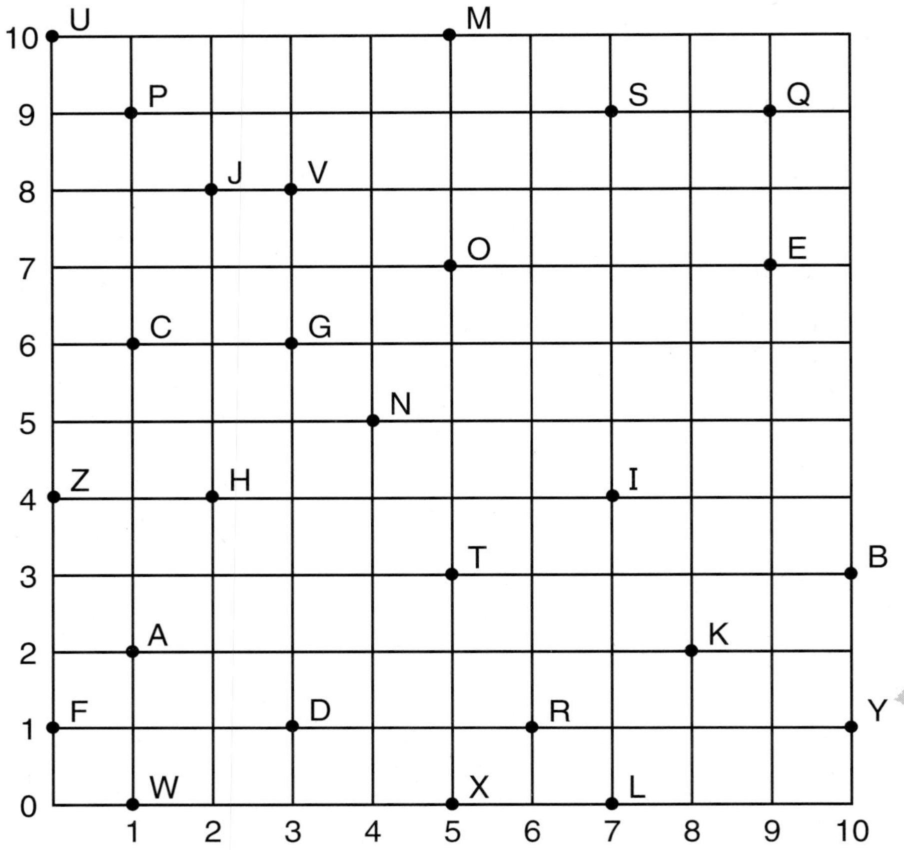

HA HA HA HA HA HA HA

**1. What do hares put in their computers?**

" _____ _____ _____ _____ _____ "   _____ _____ _____ _____ _____ !
(2, 4)  (5, 7)  (1, 9)  (1, 9)  (10, 1)    (3, 1)  (7, 4)  (7, 9)  (1, 6)  (7, 9)

**2. What's a hare's favorite thing to do at recess?**

_____ _____ _____ _____    _____ _____ _____ _____ _____ _____ _____ _____ _____ !
(1, 9)  (7, 0)  (1, 2)  (10, 1)    (2, 4)  (5, 7)  (1, 9)  (7, 9 )  (1, 6)  (5, 7)  (5, 3)  (1, 6)  (2, 4)

**3. Why don't hares get hot in the summer?**

_____ _____ _____ _____    _____ _____ _____ _____    " _____ _____ _____ _____ "
(5, 3)  (2, 4)  (9, 7)  (10, 1)    (2, 4)  (1, 2)  (3, 8)  (9, 7)    (2, 4)  (1, 2)  (6, 1)  (9, 7)

_____ _____ _____ _____ _____ _____ _____ _____ _____ _____ _____ !
(1, 6)  (5, 7)  (4, 5)  (3, 1)  (7, 4)  (5, 3)  (7, 4)  (5, 7)  (4, 5)  (9, 7)  (6, 1)  (7, 9)

## On the Hunt

Strengthen students' measuring skills with this class game! Divide students into groups of four and give each group a meterstick. Announce a target length for Round 1, such as 6 cm. Challenge each group to look around the classroom for an object that it thinks would measure 6 cm in length. Next, write on the board a chart similar to the one shown; record each group's chosen object. Then have each group, in turn, measure its object and then record its length on the class chart. Award one point to the team whose object is closest to the target length. Continue play, announcing a new target length for each round of play. The group with the most points at the end of the game is the winner.

|  | Group | Object | Length |
|---|---|---|---|
| Target 1: 6 cm | 1 | marker | 13 cm |
|  | 2 |  |  |
|  | 3 |  |  |
|  | 4 |  |  |
| Target 2: |  |  |  |
|  |  |  |  |
|  |  |  |  |

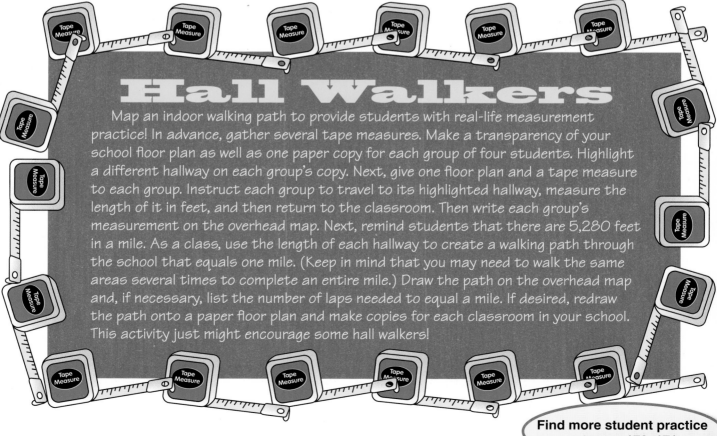

## Hall Walkers

Map an indoor walking path to provide students with real-life measurement practice! In advance, gather several tape measures. Make a transparency of your school floor plan as well as one paper copy for each group of four students. Highlight a different hallway on each group's copy. Next, give one floor plan and a tape measure to each group. Instruct each group to travel to its highlighted hallway, measure the length of it in feet, and then return to the classroom. Then write each group's measurement on the overhead map. Next, remind students that there are 5,280 feet in a mile. As a class, use the length of each hallway to create a walking path through the school that equals one mile. (Keep in mind that you may need to walk the same areas several times to complete an entire mile.) Draw the path on the overhead map and, if necessary, list the number of laps needed to equal a mile. If desired, redraw the path onto a paper floor plan and make copies for each classroom in your school. This activity just might encourage some hall walkers!

**Find more student practice on pages 170–171.**

Name_____    Date _____

# Ruby's Ribbons

Ruby sells ribbons by the inch, foot, and yard. Convert the units on the chart below. Then solve the problems.

| Ribbon | Inches | Feet | Yards |
|--------|--------|------|-------|
| Golden Goose | | | 1 |
| Robin Red | | 6 | |
| Bluebird Blue | | | 7 |
| Poodle Pink | 108 | | |
| Peacock Purple | | 27 | |
| Osprey Orange | 144 | | |

1. Robbie needs 6 feet of ribbon. He buys a piece that is 60 inches long. Does Robbie have enough ribbon? _____

2. Rhonda wants to order 48 inches of orange ribbon. The ribbon is only sold in yards. If she buys 2 yards, how much extra ribbon will she have? _____ inches

3. Ron is buying 3 yards of red ribbon and 4 feet of purple ribbon. How many inches of ribbon is Ron buying in all? _____ inches

4. Rachel needs 144 inches of gold ribbon and 24 inches of pink ribbon. Both colors are sold by the yard. How many yards will she need to buy of each? yellow: _____ yard(s)    pink: _____ yard(s)

5. Ryan is buying 3 feet of gold ribbon, 72 inches of purple ribbon, and 6 yards of blue ribbon. How many feet of ribbon is Ryan buying in all? _____ feet

# "Sssuper" Long Snake

Color by the code. If the equation is incorrect, cross out the underlined number and write the correct answer above it.

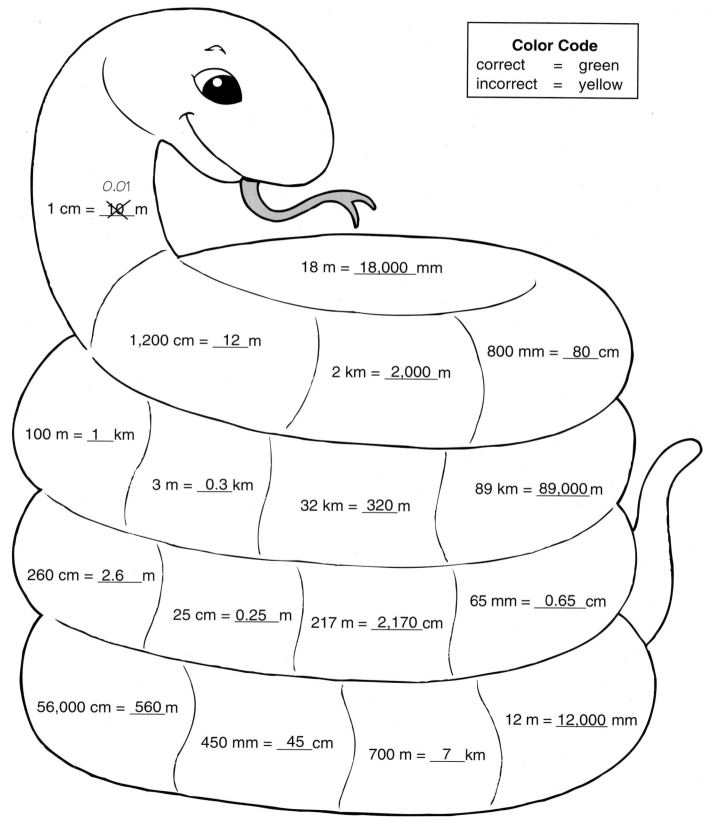

**Color Code**
correct   = green
incorrect = yellow

*0.01*
1 cm = ~~10~~ m

18 m = _18,000_ mm

1,200 cm = _12_ m

800 mm = _80_ cm

2 km = _2,000_ m

100 m = _1_ km

3 m = _0.3_ km

32 km = _320_ m

89 km = _89,000_ m

260 cm = _2.6_ m

25 cm = _0.25_ m

217 m = _2,170_ cm

65 mm = _0.65_ cm

56,000 cm = _560_ m

450 mm = _45_ cm

700 m = _7_ km

12 m = _12,000_ mm

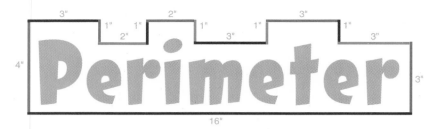

### Quick Draw

Provide perimeter practice with this fun center game! Write a different perimeter in centimeters on each of a supply of index cards. Place the cards in a center along with a supply of centimeter graph paper. Invite groups of three students to follow the directions below to play.

**To play:**

1. Place the cards facedown in a stack. Designate one player as the judge.
2. The judge turns a card faceup. On separate sheets of graph paper, Players 1 and 2 each draw a figure with a perimeter matching the displayed card.
3. The first player to finish calls, "Done!" and the judge checks his work. If correct, the student takes the card. If incorrect, the other player finishes his drawing and is judged for the card. If neither player is correct, the card is placed at the bottom of the pile.
4. The judge draws another card and Players 1 and 2 repeat the process.
5. The first player to collect five cards is the winner and plays against the judge in the next game. The losing player becomes the judge.

18 cm

### All About Adding!

Reinforce the difference between perimeter and area with this quick tip! Have each student write "PERIME+ER" on the top of his paper, substituting an addition sign in place of the T. Students won't forget to use addition when calculating perimeter!

### Perimeter at Your Feet

Look no further than the floor tiles beneath your feet for this perimeter activity! To begin, divide students into pairs. Give each twosome a ruler and two different lengths of yarn. Then take students to an area of your school that has square floor tiles. Have the pair use one piece of yarn to create a polygon on the floor. Explain that the polygon does not need to take up the entire length of yarn. Next, direct the pair to find the perimeter of the polygon using the length of a tile as the unit. Then have the duo use the ruler to find the perimeter in inches. Direct the pair to repeat the process with the second length of yarn. Finally, invite pairs to share their results with the class.

**Find more student practice on pages 173–174.**

Name _____ Date _____

# Fence Defense

Farmer Ron wants to put a fence around each of his carrot patches. For each patch, color the carrot if the perimeter of the patch is correct. If the perimeter is incorrect, cross it out and write the correct answer next to it.

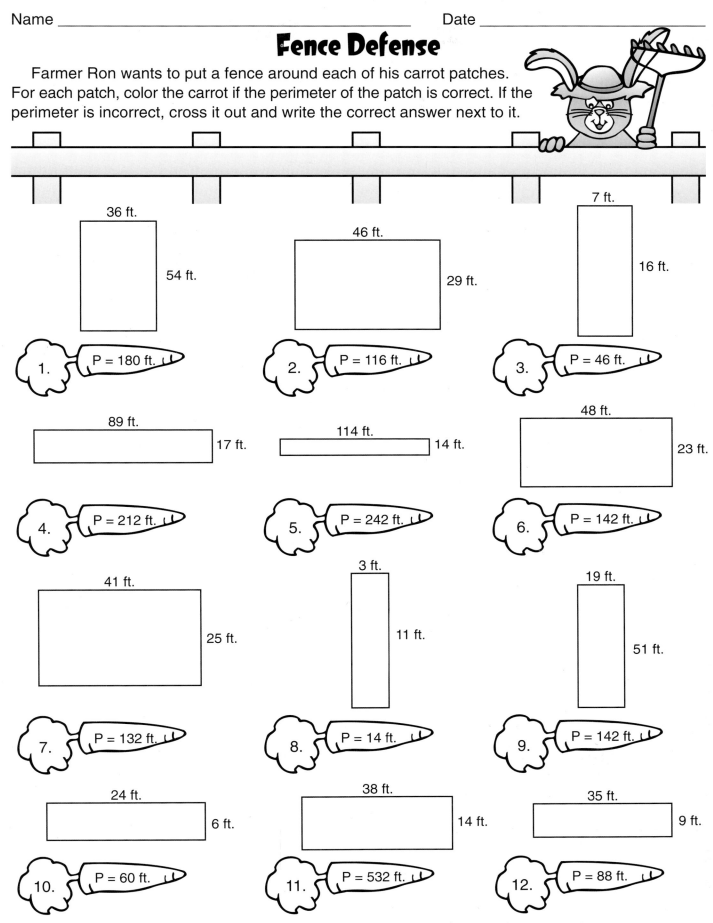

36 ft.
54 ft.

1. P = 180 ft.

46 ft.
29 ft.

2. P = 116 ft.

7 ft.
16 ft.

3. P = 46 ft.

89 ft.
17 ft.

4. P = 212 ft.

114 ft.
14 ft.

5. P = 242 ft.

48 ft.
23 ft.

6. P = 142 ft.

41 ft.
25 ft.

7. P = 132 ft.

3 ft.
11 ft.

8. P = 14 ft.

19 ft.
51 ft.

9. P = 142 ft.

24 ft.
6 ft.

10. P = 60 ft.

38 ft.
14 ft.

11. P = 532 ft.

35 ft.
9 ft.

12. P = 88 ft.

Name _____ Date _____

# Dragon Designer

Use a ruler to measure the sides of each room below. Write your measurements on the diagram. The first one has been started for you.

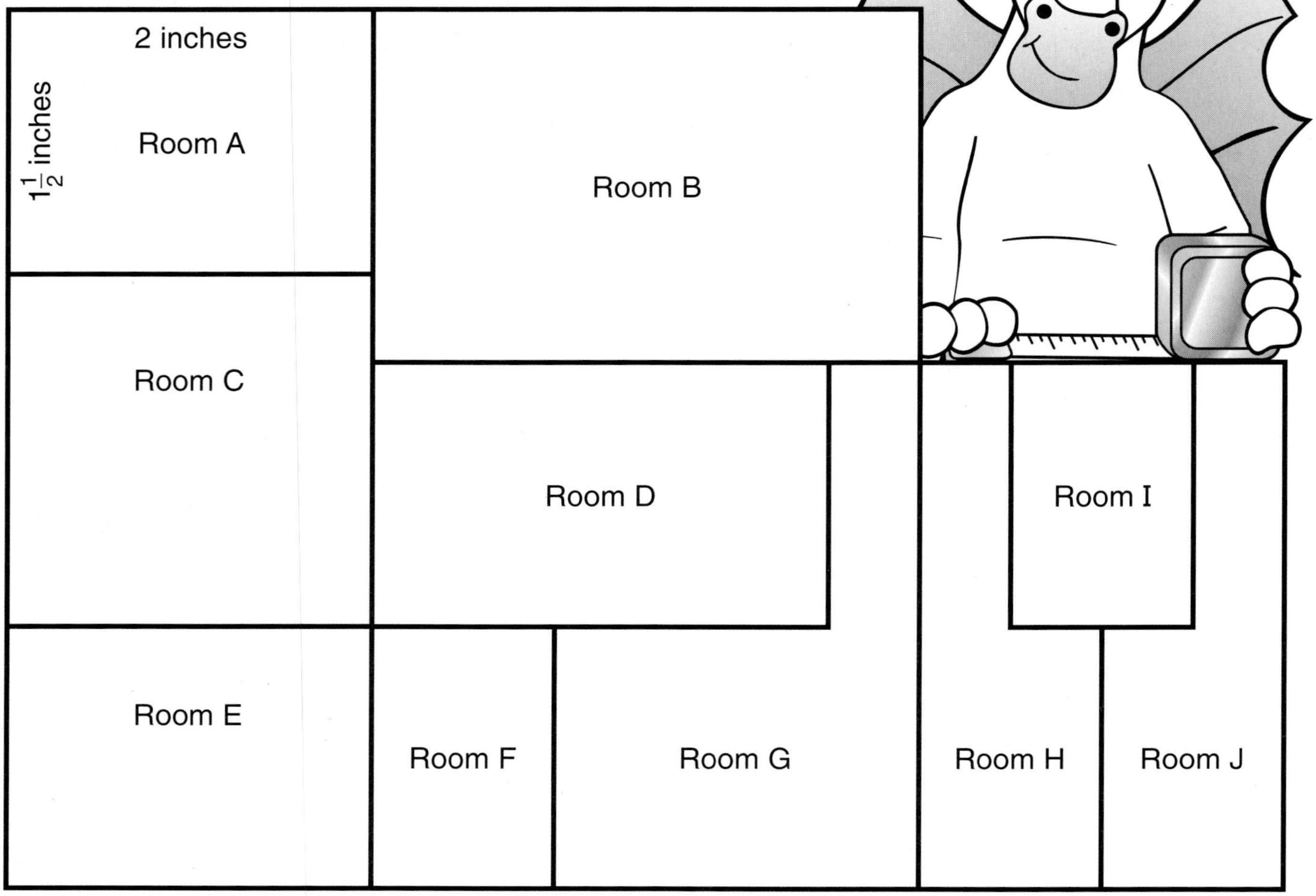

2 inches

$1\frac{1}{2}$ inches

Room A

Room B

Room C

Room D

Room I

Room E

Room F

Room G

Room H

Room J

Find the perimeter of each room.

Room A: _____          Room F: _____

Room B: _____          Room G: _____

Room C: _____          Room H: _____

Room D: _____          Room I: _____

Room E: _____          Room J: _____

**Note to the teacher:** Students will need rulers to complete this page.

# Area

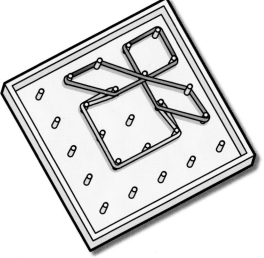

## Pass the Picture

This finding-area activity turns your classroom into a rotating art gallery! Give each student a Geoboard, a supply of colorful rubber bands, and a small sticky note. To start, each student makes a design on his board using as many rubber bands as desired. He then counts the number of square units contained within the rubber bands to calculate the area, writes the answer on his sticky note, and sticks it to the back of the board. On your signal, each student passes his picture to another student and calculates the area of the picture he receives, turning the board over to check his answer. After two minutes, say, "Pass the picture," as the signal for students to again pass their Geoboards. Continue until each student has calculated the area of each picture.

## Triangular Exploration

Students explore areas of triangles with this colorful activity. Give each student graph paper, a ruler, and crayons or colored pencils. Instruct the student to use her ruler to help her draw any size triangle on the paper and then color each complete square contained inside the same color. Next, have each youngster study the uncolored areas of the triangle, looking for sections that when pieced together might equal one square unit. Have the student color each set of these pieces a different color (see the example). Finally, have her count the total number of square units (both whole and combined) to find her triangle's area. Next, introduce the formula for finding the area of a triangle: Area = ½(base x height). Guide each student to again calculate her triangle's area, this time using the formula. Instruct each student to compare this answer with her first calculation. (The answers should be almost identical.) Repeat this process, having students draw several more triangles and then calculate their areas using both methods.

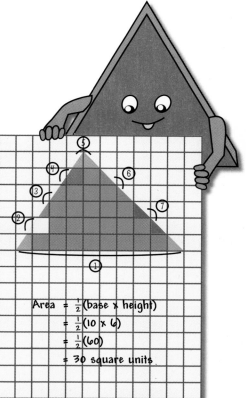

$$Area = \frac{1}{2}(\text{base} \times \text{height})$$
$$= \frac{1}{2}(10 \times 6)$$
$$= \frac{1}{2}(60)$$
$$= 30 \text{ square units}$$

## Supersize Practice

Supersize your practice of calculating area! Grab some sidewalk chalk and yardsticks and take your class to a large paved area outside. Divide students into groups and have each group draw three rectangles on the ground, writing the area under each shape. Then have groups switch places and check each other's work. Super fun!

**Find more student practice on pages 176–177.**

Name _____

Date _____

# Gracie's Golf Course

Gracie is building a new golf course. Help her find the area of the first eight holes. Then draw the ninth hole so that it has an area of 15 square units.

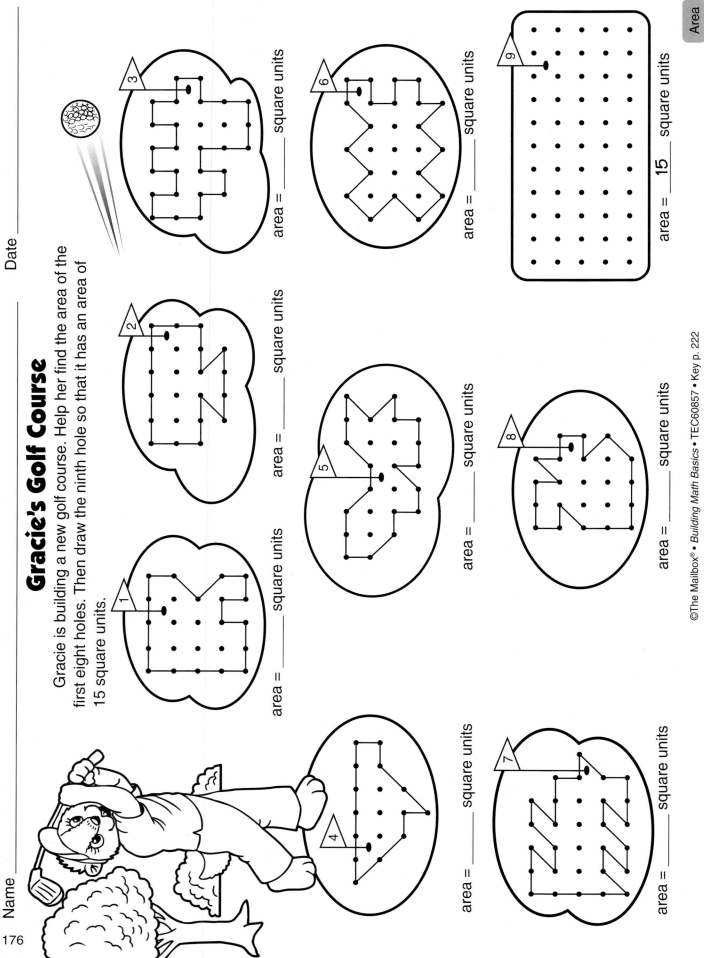

1   area = _____ square units

2   area = _____ square units

3   area = _____ square units

4   area = _____ square units

5   area = _____ square units

6   area = _____ square units

7   area = _____ square units

8   area = _____ square units

9   area = __15__ square units

176

©The Mailbox® • *Building Math Basics* • TEC60857 • Key p. 222

Name _____ Date _____

# Wall-to-Wall Area

Mel, the mall manager, wants to put new carpet in each mall store. He got a great deal on 700 square yards of carpet. Find each store's area below. Then find the total square yards to see whether Mel got enough carpet.

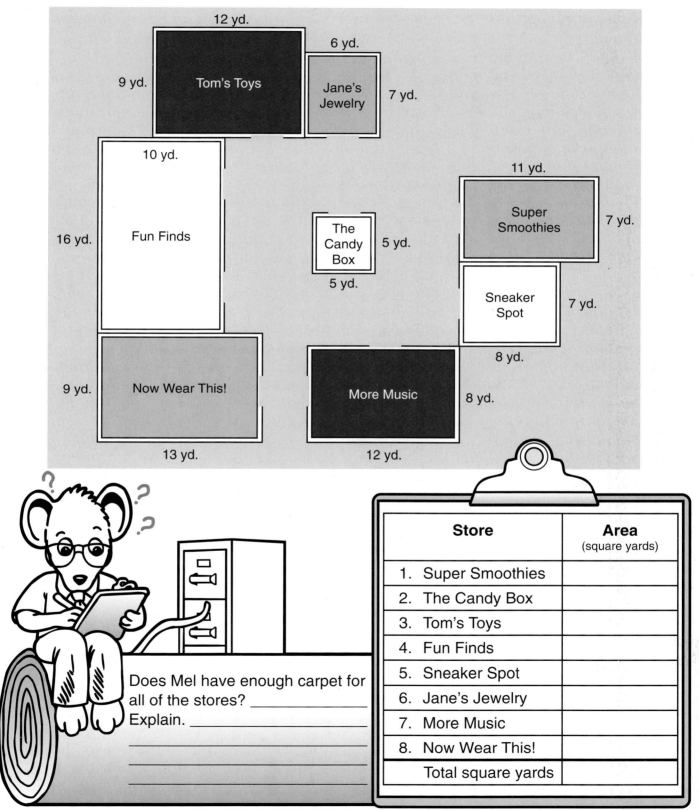

Does Mel have enough carpet for all of the stores? _____
Explain. _____
_____
_____
_____

| Store | Area (square yards) |
|---|---|
| 1.  Super Smoothies | |
| 2.  The Candy Box | |
| 3.  Tom's Toys | |
| 4.  Fun Finds | |
| 5.  Sneaker Spot | |
| 6.  Jane's Jewelry | |
| 7.  More Music | |
| 8.  Now Wear This! | |
| Total square yards | |

# Circumference

## Racing Round the Track

Here's a fun way to have students review drawing circles and finding circumference. First, give each student paper, a ruler, and a compass. Then guide students through the steps below to draw a racetrack constructed of concentric circles.

**Steps:**
1. Draw point C in the middle of the page. Point C will be the center of each circle you create.
2. Draw a circle with a one-inch radius.
3. Draw a circle with a 1½-inch radius.
4. Draw a circle with a two-inch radius.
5. Draw a circle with a five-inch diameter.
6. Draw a circle with a six-inch diameter.
7. Draw a circle with a 3½-inch radius.
8. Calculate each circle's circumference and then add details to your four-lane racecourse.

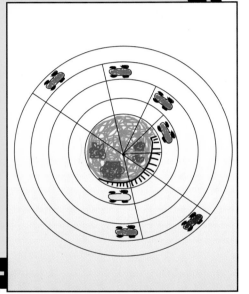

## Easy as Pi

Want to help students easily learn the formula for finding circumference? Try using the mnemonic device, **C**herry **P**ie **D**elight to remind students that circumference equals pi times diameter!

## Spinning in Circles

Students can spin their way to calculating circumference with this partner game. Pair students and give each pair a compass, a ruler, paper, a paper clip, and a copy of the spinner pattern on page 179. To play, Player 1 spins the spinner, draws a circle as directed, and then finds its circumference. Player 2 verifies Player 1's answer. If correct, Player 1 earns a point. Player 2 takes a turn in the same manner. Players alternate play for ten rounds. If a player's spin directs her to draw a circle she's already drawn, she skips a turn. The player who has more points at the end of the game is the winner.

**Find more student practice on pages 179–180.**

Name _____    Date _____

# Circle City

Use a ruler to measure Circle City's downtown buildings. Write the measurements in the table below. The first one has been started for you.

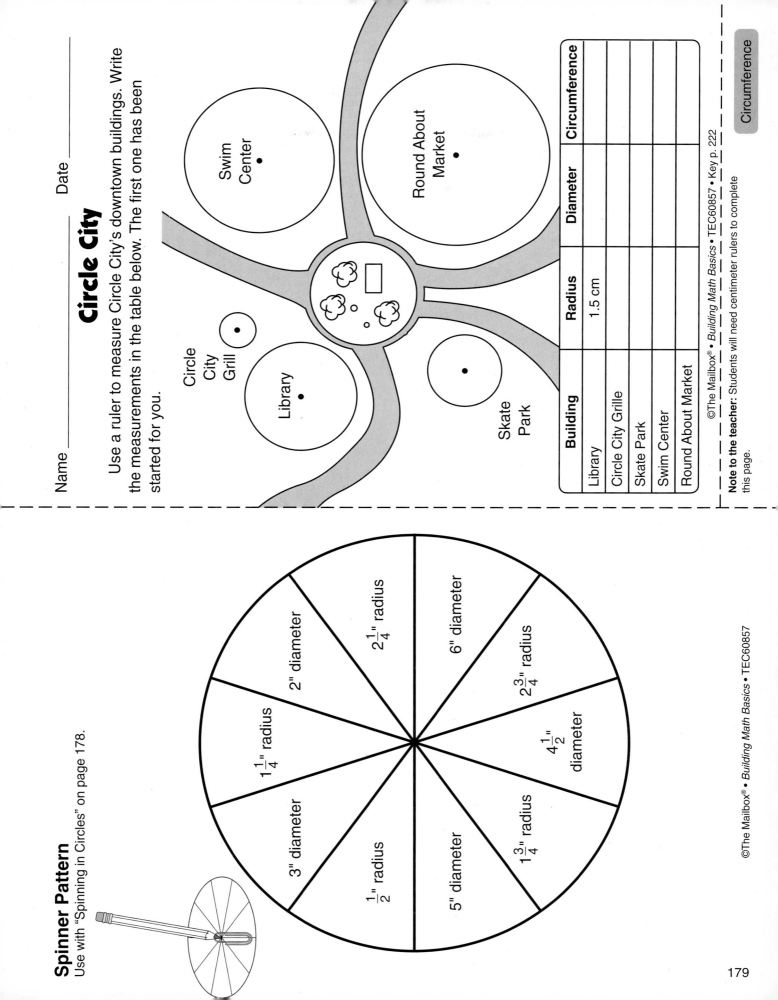

| Building | Radius | Diameter | Circumference |
|----------|--------|----------|---------------|
| Library | 1.5 cm | | |
| Circle City Grille | | | |
| Skate Park | | | |
| Swim Center | | | |
| Round About Market | | | |

©The Mailbox® • *Building Math Basics* • TEC60857 • Key p. 222

**Note to the teacher:** Students will need centimeter rulers to complete this page.

Circumference

---

## Spinner Pattern

Use with "Spinning in Circles" on page 178.

©The Mailbox® • *Building Math Basics* • TEC60857

179

Name _____ Date _____

# Gary's Garden

Read and solve each problem below about Gary
and his circular garden.

1. Gary put in a border around the daisy
   garden. The garden is 26 meters
   in diameter. What is the distance
   around the garden?

   _____ meters

2. Gary's goldfish pond has a radius
   of 15 meters. What is the pond's
   circumference?

   _____ meters

3. Gary wants to plant a tulip border
   around his rock garden. The rock
   garden's diameter is 12 meters. How
   many meters will the border be?

   _____ meters

4. Gary set up a fountain in the center
   of his garden. The fountain's
   circumference is 40.82 meters.
   What is the fountain's diameter?

   _____ meters

5. The distance around Gary's rose
   garden is 23.55 meters. What is the
   distance across the rose garden?

   _____ meters

6. Gary is proud of his homemade
   sundial. If the distance around it
   is 9.42 meters, what is the radius?

   _____ meters

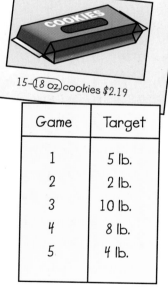

# Weight

## Targeting Weight

This center game for two or three players adds up to lots of fun with conversions! To create game cards, cut out pictures of 24 items from a grocery store circular (each item's weight should be included). Circle the weights and then glue each picture to a separate index card. (If a weight span is listed, just circle one measurement.) Place the cards in a center along with an index card programmed with target weights as shown. Then guide students through the steps below to play.

**Object of the game:** to collect cards with weights totaling closest to the target weight

**To play:**
1. One player deals three cards to each partner. He then places the remaining cards facedown in a stack, turning one card over in a discard pile.
2. Player 1 finds the total weight of his cards, converting units if necessary. He then compares his weight to the target weight listed for Game 1.
3. Player 1 either picks up the card in the discard pile or draws one from the stack. He then recalculates his total and discards one of his cards faceup in the discard pile.
4. Players 2 and 3 take turns in the same manner.
5. Play continues for three rounds. The player whose cards' total weight is closest to the target weight is the winner.
6. To play again, one player collects and shuffles all the cards. Players repeat Steps 1–5, this time targeting the weight listed for Game 2.

13 oz. coffee $2.50

15–18 oz. cookies $2.19

| Game | Target |
|------|--------|
| 1 | 5 lb. |
| 2 | 2 lb. |
| 3 | 10 lb. |
| 4 | 8 lb. |
| 5 | 4 lb. |

## Two Scoops of Practice

Give your students a taste of comparing weights with this whole-class game. Program a supply of plastic spoons each with a different metric weight, making sure to vary the units. Place the spoons in a cup and divide students into teams. Pull two spoons from the cup and read aloud the weights. Challenge each team to compare the two weights, converting units if necessary, to determine which is heavier. Award the first team to answer correctly one point. Return the spoons to the cup and continue play in the same manner. The team with the most points at the end of play is the winner.

6.7 kg

438 g

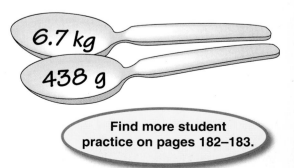

**Find more student practice on pages 182–183.**

Name _____ Date _____

# Mightiest Ant

Convert the weight on each barbell. Then compare each weight in grams to find the heaviest and the lightest barbell. Color the heaviest barbell red and the lightest barbell blue.

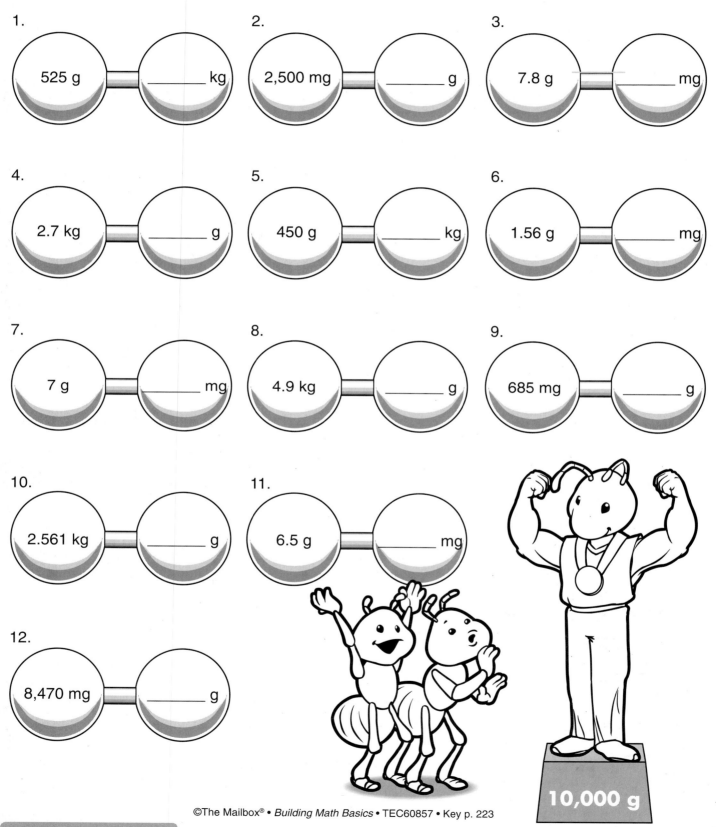

1. 525 g _____ kg

2. 2,500 mg _____ g

3. 7.8 g _____ mg

4. 2.7 kg _____ g

5. 450 g _____ kg

6. 1.56 g _____ mg

7. 7 g _____ mg

8. 4.9 kg _____ g

9. 685 mg _____ g

10. 2.561 kg _____ g

11. 6.5 g _____ mg

12. 8,470 mg _____ g

10,000 g

# Weighing In

Convert the weight on each basket. Then write the missing weight on the blank apple so that the sum of all the apples matches the weight on the basket. The first one has been started for you.

1. 4 oz. 6 oz. _____
   1 lb. = __16__ oz.

2. 9 oz. 7 oz. _____
   24 oz. = _____ lb.

3. 24 oz. 20 oz. _____
   4 lb. = _____ oz.

4. 54 oz. 16 oz. _____
   96 oz. = _____ lb.

5. 12 oz. 9 oz. 17 oz. _____
   5 lb. = _____ oz.

6. 552 lb. 279 lb. 459 lb. _____
   1 T = _____ lb.

7. 12 oz. 8 oz. 4 oz. _____
   $2\frac{1}{2}$ lb. = _____ oz.

8. 20 oz. 14 oz. _____
   48 oz. = _____ lb.

9. 12 oz. 12 oz. _____
   2 lb. = _____ oz.

10. 89 lb. 411 lb. 2,500 lb. _____
    4,000 lb. = _____ T

SCALE

## An Eye on Volume

Help students develop visual-estimation skills while they practice finding volume! Give each student an index card and have him label it as shown. Explain that his assignment is to find an empty box at home and calculate the volume. The student measures the box's length, width, and height (each rounded to the nearest whole number) and records the measurements on the card. He then brings his box and card to school the next day. Collect the cards and matching boxes. Then divide students into four teams, giving each team a yardstick and a set of four cards and matching boxes. (Be sure no team member receives his own box.) Instruct the team to match each card to a box by estimating each box's volume. Finally, have teams check their work by measuring each box and finding its actual volume.

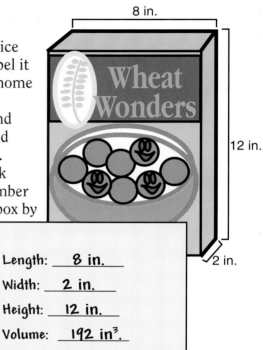

Length: __8 in.__

Width: __2 in.__

Height: __12 in.__

Volume: __192 in³.__

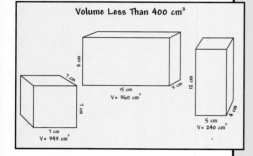

Volume Less Than 400 cm³

8 cm
7 cm
7 cm
7 cm
V= 343 cm³

15 cm
V= 360 cm³

12 cm
3 cm
5 cm
4 cm
V= 240 cm³

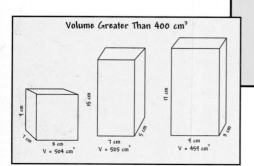

Volume Greater Than 400 cm³

9 cm
7 cm
8 cm
V = 504 cm³

15 cm
7 cm
5 cm
V = 525 cm³

17 cm
9 cm
3 cm
V = 459 cm³

## Container Creations

Practice finding volume with this creative challenge! Divide students into groups of four, giving each team two 12" x 18" sheets of light-colored construction paper and a few centimeter rulers. Challenge each team to design six different-size boxes. Explain that three boxes should be smaller than 400 cm³ and three should be larger than 400 cm³. Have each team first sketch its boxes on scrap paper to check the dimensions. Then direct the team to draw its final box designs (actual size) on the construction paper, labeling each length, width, height, and volume. Invite groups to share their boxes with the class before displaying the designs with the title "Container Creations."

**Find more student practice on pages 185–186.**

Name _Ava Croce_   Date _____

# A "Pop-ular" Place

Find the volume of each box below. Then shade the matching popcorn piece. The shaded pieces will reveal the answer to the riddle below.

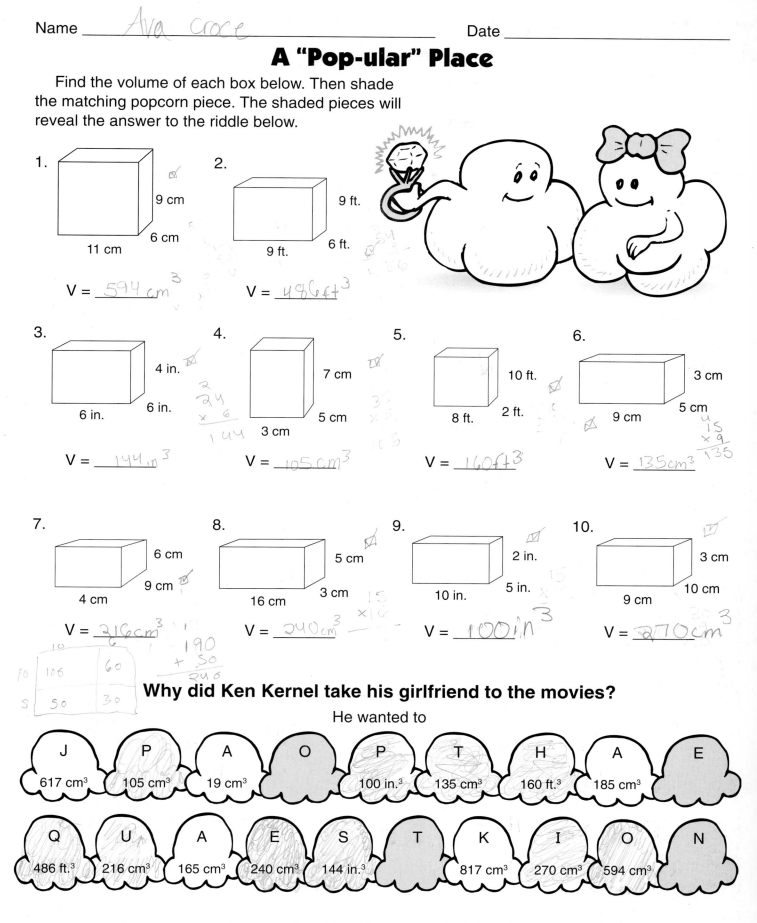

1.
9 cm
6 cm
11 cm
V = _594 cm³_

2.
9 ft.
9 ft.
6 ft.
V = _486ft³_

3.
4 in.
6 in.
6 in.
V = _144 in³_

4.
7 cm
5 cm
3 cm
V = _105 cm³_

5.
10 ft.
8 ft.
2 ft.
V = _160ft³_

6.
3 cm
5 cm
9 cm
V = _135cm³_

7.
6 cm
9 cm
4 cm
V = _216cm³_

8.
5 cm
3 cm
16 cm
V = _240cm³_

9.
2 in.
5 in.
10 in.
V = _100in³_

10.
3 cm
10 cm
9 cm
V = _270cm³_

## Why did Ken Kernel take his girlfriend to the movies?

He wanted to

J 617 cm³   P 105 cm³   A 19 cm³   O 100 in.³   P 100 in.³   T 135 cm³   H 160 ft.³   A 185 cm³   E

Q 486 ft.³   U 216 cm³   A 165 cm³   E 240 cm³   S 144 in.³   T 817 cm³   K 270 cm³   I 594 cm³   O   N

Name _Ava Croce_  Date _____

# Greta's Great Grains

Greta works at the Great Grains store. She needs your help finding the four boxes that are labeled with the wrong volume. Find the volume of each box. Color the card on the box if it is correct. If it's incorrect, write the correct volume on a new card at the bottom of the page.

**Box A**  
V = 312 in.³  
13 in. 2 in. 12 in.

**Box E**  
V = 214 in.³  
7 in. 6 in. 7 in.

**Box I**  
V = 148 in.³  
6 in. 2 in. 13 in.

**Box B**  
V = 562 in.³  
11 in. 3 in. 15 in.

**Box F**  
V = 1,152 in.³  
12 in. 8 in. 12 in.

**Box J**  
V = 504 in.³  
12 in. 3 in. 14 in.

**Box C**  
V = 144 in.³  
6 in. 4 in. 6 in.

**Box G**  
V = 476 in.³  
14 in. 2 in. 17 in.

**Box D**  
V = 324 in.³  
6 in. 6 in. 9 in.

**Box H**  
V = 675 in.³  
11 in. 4 in. 15 in.

Box _E_  
V = _294_ in.³

Box _H_  
V = _660_ in.³

Box _B_  
V = _495_ in.³

Box _I_  
V = _156_ in.³

©The Mailbox® • *Building Math Basics* • TEC60857 • Key p. 223

# Capacity

## Metric Conversions Made Easy

This nifty mnemonic device is helpful when converting metric units of capacity. Teach students the following sentence to help them remember the order of the units: King (kilo-) Henry (hecto-) doesn't (deka-) bother (base unit) drinking (deci-) chocolate (centi-) milk (milli-). Then encourage students to write this helper, as shown, atop their papers when converting metric units. To use the aid, a child puts his finger on the current metric unit and counts the number of words it takes to get to the desired unit. For example, to convert 2.5 liters to milliliters, a student starts with his finger on the base unit, liter (bother), and counts three words to the right, landing on milliliter (milk). He then moves his decimal point the same number of places to the right, converting 2.5 liters to 2500 milliliters. If while counting he moves his finger to the left, he then moves the decimal to the left. This also works when converting units of length or weight. Students simply use meters or grams as the base unit.

| King | Henry | doesn't | bother | drinking | chocolate | milk. |
|------|-------|---------|--------|----------|-----------|-------|
| i | e | e | a | e | e | i |
| l | c | k | s | c | n | l |
| o | t | a | e | i | t | l |
| | o | | u | | i | i |
| | | | n | | | |
| | | | i | | | |
| | | | t | | | |

## How Many?

Reinforce students' understanding of capacity with this hands-on activity. In advance, gather a set of cup, pint, quart, and gallon containers for each group of students. (Ask your local ice-cream parlor to donate containers for pint, quart, and gallon sizes.) Give each group a set of containers and access to water. Challenge the groups to determine how many cups are in a pint by filling the cup container with water and then pouring it into the pint container. Have them repeat this process until the pint container is full, counting each cup as it is poured. Then direct groups to dump the water out and use the containers to answer the remaining questions from the list on this page. If desired, place one set of containers in a center for further exploration.

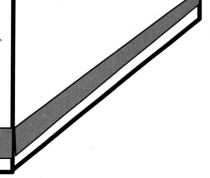

**Questions**

How many cups are in a pint? — 2
How many pints are in a quart? — 2
How many quarts are in a gallon? — 4
How many cups are in a quart? — 4
How many pints are in a gallon? — 8
How many cups are in a gallon? — 16

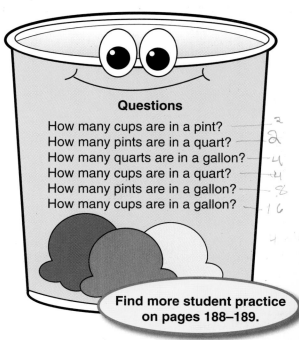

**Find more student practice on pages 188–189.**

# Powerful Thirst

If the capacity listed is a reasonable estimate, color the container.

1. bottle of water
   750 mL

2. sink full of water
   8 L

3. jug of lemonade
   250 L

4. can of soda
   34 mL

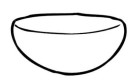

5. large bowl of water
   2 L

6. pitcher of tea
   20 L

7. pot of coffee
   1 L

8. glass of water
   5 mL

9. mug of coffee
   250 L

10. bottle of apple juice
    2 L

Circle the best estimate.

| 11. | large can of pineapple juice | 35 L | 350 mL | 35 mL |
|---|---|---|---|---|
| 12. | single serving of milk | 1 L | 10 mL | 100 mL |
| 13. | pitcher of Kool-Aid drink | 20 L | 2 L | 200 mL |
| 14. | spoonful of lemonade | 5 mL | 500 mL | 1 L |
| 15. | mug of cocoa | 30 mL | 3 L | 300 mL |

Name_____  Date_____

# It's Raining! It's Pouring!

Soggy Sam is collecting buckets of rain. Convert the units of measure shown on each bucket.

1. 8 gal. = _____ qt.

2. 32 oz. = _____ pt.

3. 8 c. = _____ qt.

4. 4 gal. = _____ c.

5. 9 qt. = _____ c.

6. 1 gal. = _____ c.

7. 20 c. = _____ pt.

8. 5 qt. = _____ pt.

9. 16 oz. = _____ pt.

10. 13 pt. = _____ oz.

11. 4 gal. = _____ pt.

12. 24 c. = _____ qt.

13. 32 oz. = _____ qt.

14. 8 qt. = _____ gal.

15. 3 gal. = _____ qt.

# Temperature

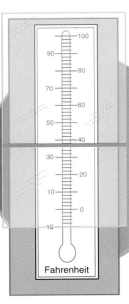

Fahrenheit

## Sliding Thermometers

These easy-to-make thermometers will help students practice reading temperatures correctly! Gather a supply of pin-style name badges and remove the pin from each one. To make a sliding thermometer, glue a copy of the thermometer pattern below onto a small index card cut to fit inside the plastic sleeve as shown. Finally, use a red permanent marker to draw a horizontal line on the plastic about one-fourth of the way from the bottom of the badge. To use the thermometer, simply slip the card inside the plastic and slide it up or down, lining up the red line at the desired temperature.

# Tracking Temperature

Have students make line graphs to track your town's daily temperatures! Remind students that a line graph is used for tracking change over time. Next, give each child a sheet of centimeter graph paper, a red crayon, and a blue crayon. Explain that they will track the daily high and low temperatures in their town for one week. Have the student title the graph, label its *x*-axis with dates, and label its *y*-axis with your town's normal temperature range. Each day, have the child locate the day's high and low temperatures in a newspaper or on the Internet and mark a blue dot on the graph for the low temperature and a red dot for the high temperature. At the end of the week, have students connect the dots for each color and then analyze the graphs and discuss any observations with the class.

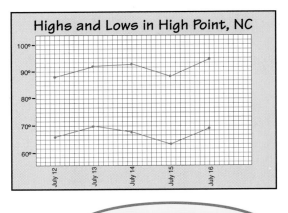

Highs and Lows in High Point, NC

**Find more student practice on pages 191–192.**

## Thermometer Patterns
Use with "Sliding Thermometers" on this page.

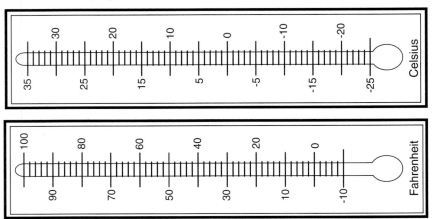

# Tuning In to Temperature

The Hoot Owls Band measured the daily temperature of each city on their 12-day concert tour. Read each thermometer below and write the temperature on the line. Then decide whether the temperature is higher or lower than on the previous day. Circle "up" or "down" and write the difference on the line.

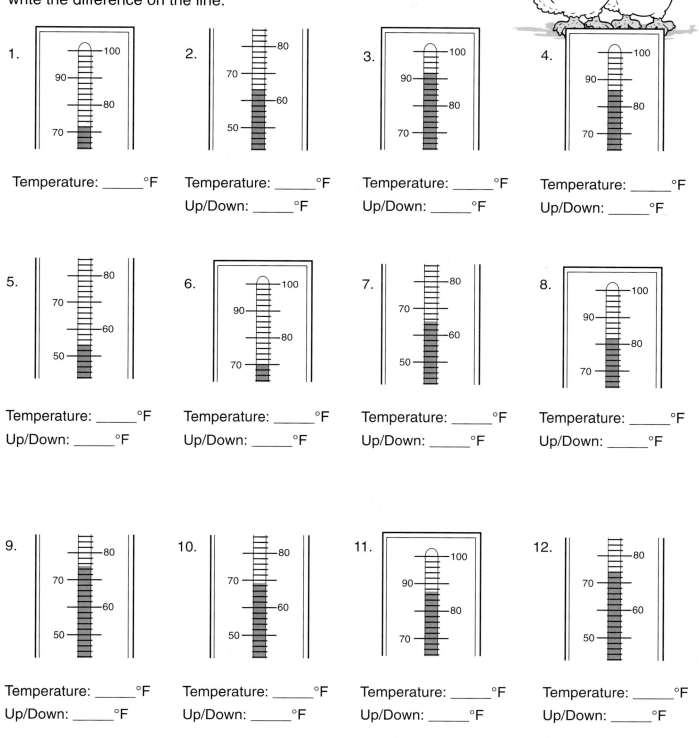

1. Temperature: _____°F

2. Temperature: _____°F
   Up/Down: _____°F

3. Temperature: _____°F
   Up/Down: _____°F

4. Temperature: _____°F
   Up/Down: _____°F

5. Temperature: _____°F
   Up/Down: _____°F

6. Temperature: _____°F
   Up/Down: _____°F

7. Temperature: _____°F
   Up/Down: _____°F

8. Temperature: _____°F
   Up/Down: _____°F

9. Temperature: _____°F
   Up/Down: _____°F

10. Temperature: _____°F
    Up/Down: _____°F

11. Temperature: _____°F
    Up/Down: _____°F

12. Temperature: _____°F
    Up/Down: _____°F

# Weather Wardrobe

Holly needs help packing for her vacation. Read each thermometer and write the temperature on the line. Then circle the best choice of clothing for the weather that day.

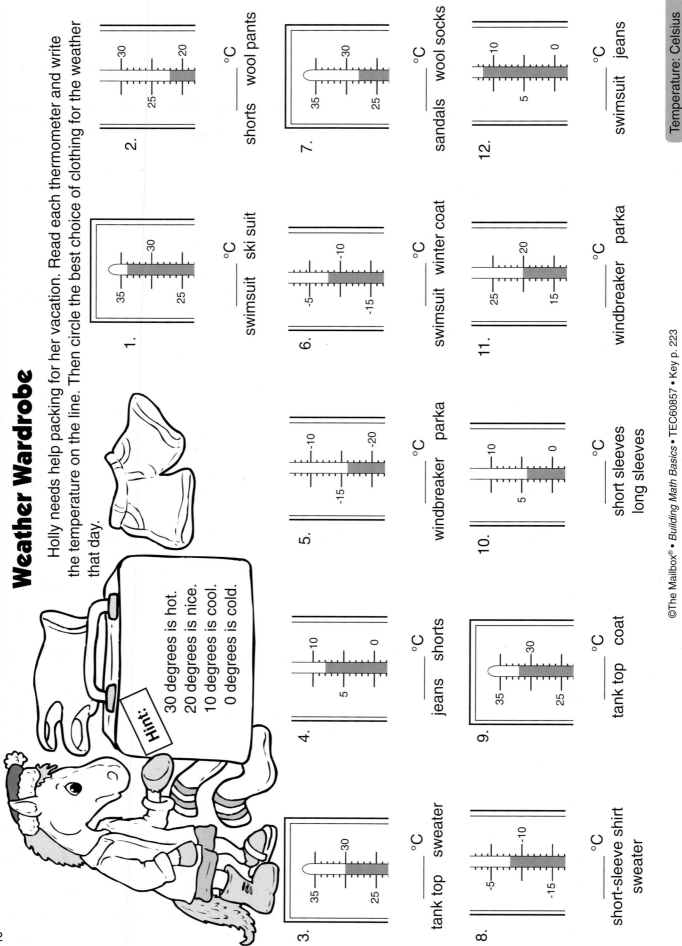

**Hint:**
30 degrees is hot.
20 degrees is nice.
10 degrees is cool.
0 degrees is cold.

1. _____ °C    swimsuit    ski suit

2. _____ °C    shorts    wool pants

3. _____ °C    tank top    sweater

4. _____ °C    jeans    shorts

5. _____ °C    windbreaker    parka

6. _____ °C    swimsuit    winter coat

7. _____ °C    sandals    wool socks

8. _____ °C    short-sleeve shirt    sweater

9. _____ °C    tank top    coat

10. _____ °C    short sleeves    long sleeves

11. _____ °C    windbreaker    parka

12. _____ °C    swimsuit    jeans

Temperature: Celsius

# Elapsed Time

## Daily Time Tracking

**Tuesday**

| | |
|---|---|
| Early Bird Work | 8:00—8:22 (elapsed time: 22 min.) |
| Math | 8:22—9:28 (elapsed time: 1 hr. 6 min.) |
| Language Arts | 9:30— |

Use your daily schedule to improve students' understanding of elapsed time. First, write your schedule of activities for the day on the board. Then, as you begin each activity, note the actual start time on the schedule. As you complete the activity, write the end time and challenge the class to find the elapsed time for the activity. At the end of the day, if desired, create a pie graph showing the amount of time spent on each subject that day. What a quick and easy way to reinforce elapsed time!

## That's My Time!

Watch students' elapsed-time skills come full circle with this whole-class game! In advance, make a copy of the game cards on page 194. Laminate the cards and cut them apart. Next, give each child one card and then select a student to begin the game by reading his card aloud. The student with the matching time on his card calls out, "That's my time!" and reads the time on his card. If correct, the student then reads his entire card aloud. Play continues in this manner until all cards have been read aloud and the student who started the game hears the question that matches the time shown on his card. Time for another round? Collect the cards and redistribute them to play again.

My time is 6:30 A.M. What time is 2 hours later?

My time is 8:30 A.M. What time is 3 hours and 40 minutes later?

**Find more student practice on page 195.**

# Game Cards

Use with "That's My Time!" on page 193.

| | | | | |
|---|---|---|---|---|
| My time is 6:30 A.M. What time is 2 hours later? | My time is 8:30 A.M. What time is 3 hours and 40 minutes later? | My time is 12:10 P.M. What time is 60 minutes earlier? | My time is 11:10 A.M. What time is 2 hours and 20 minutes later? | My time is 1:30 P.M. What time is 45 minutes later? |
| My time is 2:15 P.M. What time is 4 hours earlier? | My time is 10:15 A.M. What time is 1 hour and 5 minutes later? | My time is 11:20 A.M. What time is 4 hours 30 minutes later? | My time is 3:50 P.M. What time is 5 hours earlier? | My time is 10:50 A.M. What time is 3 hours and 15 minutes earlier? |
| My time is 7:35 A.M. What time is 35 minutes later? | My time is 8:10 A.M. What time is 2 hours and 50 minutes later? | My time is 11:00 A.M. What time is 4 hours and 40 minutes earlier? | My time 6:20 A.M. What time is 2 hours and 50 minutes later? | My time is 9:10 A.M. What time is 3 hours and 10 minutes later? |
| My time is 12:20 P.M. What time is 1 hour and 30 minutes earlier? | My time is 10:50 A.M. What time is 55 minutes earlier? | My time is 9:55 A.M. What time is 2 hours and 10 minutes later? | My time is 12:05 P.M. What time is 3 hours and 30 minutes later? | My time is 3:35 P.M. What time is 6 hours earlier? |
| My time is 9:35 A.M. What time is 4 hours and 50 minutes later? | My time is 2:25 P.M. What time is 30 minutes earlier? | My time is 1:55 P.M. What time is 1 hour and 10 minutes later? | My time is 3:05 P.M. What time is 3 hours and 50 minutes earlier? | My time is 11:15 A.M. What time is 4 hours and 45 minutes earlier? |

Name _Ava Croce_       Date _____

# At the "Moo-vies"

Cal loves going to the movies, but he needs help figuring out the schedule. Solve the problems below.

**NOW SHOWING**

| *Make Mine Milk* | | | |
| 10:15 A.M. | 12:50 P.M. | 3:55 P.M. | 7:00 P.M. |
| *The Green, Green Grass* | | | |
| 10:40 A.M. | 12:10 P.M. | 4:50 P.M. | 7:15 P.M. |
| *The Great Adventure* | | | |
| 11:00 A.M. | 1:20 P.M. | 3:30 P.M. | 6:50 P.M. |

| *Cow Capers* | | | |
| 1:00 P.M. | 3:15 P.M. | 6:00 P.M. | 8:05 P.M. |
| *Lost on the Prairie* | | | |
| 11:25 A.M. | 2:00 P.M. | 5:40 P.M. | 7:55 P.M. |
| *The Bravest Bull* | | | |
| 10:35 A.M. | 1:05 P.M. | 4:00 P.M. | 6:35 P.M. |

1. Cal arrived at the movie theater at 12:25 P.M. How long must he wait to see the first showing of *Cow Capers*? __35 mins__

2. How much time passes between the start of the third and fourth showings of *Make Mine Milk*? __3 hours and 5 mins__

3. Cal missed the second showing of *Lost on the Prairie*. It is now 2:15 P.M. How long must he wait until the third showing? __2 hours and 25 mins__  2:15 p.m.  5:40 p.m.

4. Which movie's last showing begins 1 hour and 30 minutes after the last showing of the *The Bravest Bull*? __Cow Capers__  6:35  + 1:30

5. How much time separates the first showing of *Cow Capers* and the last showing of *Lost on the Prairie*? __6 hours and 55 mins__  1:00 P.M.  7:05  7:55 p.m.

6. How much time separates the first and second showings of *The Green, Green Grass*? __1 hour and 30 mins__  10:40 A.M.  12:10 p.m.

7. *The Great Adventure* runs for 1 hour and 55 minutes. If Cal goes to the 1:20 P.M. show, when will the movie end? __3:15 p.m.__

8. How much time separates the first showing of *Make Mine Milk* and the second showing of *Cow Capers*? __4 hours and __  3:15 p.m.  10:15 A.M.  15

9. Which movie's third showing begins 3 hours and 30 minutes after the second showing of *The Great Adventure*? __The green, green grass__  1:20 p.m.

10. Cal's friend Carrie ushers from 1:00 until the beginning of the last movie's showing. How long does she work? _____  4:50 p.m.

# Graphs

## Great Graphing

Have students explore the uses of different types of graphs with this hands-on activity! In advance, gather the following items: a compact disc, a piece of candy, a book, a picture of a pet, and a toy. Next, review with students the different types of graphs. Divide students into groups of four or five, giving each group one of the gathered items. Allow five to ten minutes for each group to list possible graphing topics for its item and then identify the best graph type to display each topic. On your signal, have groups switch items and repeat the process. Continue in this manner until each group has received each item. Then allow groups to share their lists with the class. As a follow-up, have students complete the reproducible on page 199.

| Topic | Type of Graph |
|---|---|
| favorite types of music | pictograph |
| students' favorite CD titles | bar graph |
| boys' and girls' favorite CDs | double-bar graph |
| number of CDs students listened to each day for a week | line graph |

## You Ought to Be in Pictures!

Reel in students with this pictograph activity! In advance, create a poster like the one shown on a piece of tagboard. Then laminate the poster. Next, have students suggest favorite book titles they would like to see made into movies, and record each title on the chart. Give each child a 3" x 5" index card. Have him draw a picture of himself on the blank side and write his name at the bottom. Next, invite him to tape his picture on the chart next to the book he would most like to see made into a movie. Finally, post the graph on a display titled "You Ought to Be in Pictures!" and pose questions to the class about the completed graph. If desired, periodically update the graph using new book titles.

| | |
|---|---|
| The BFG | 👤 👤 |
| Maniac Magee | 👤 👤 👤 👤 👤 |
| Bud, Not Buddy | 👤 👤 👤 👤 |
| Walk Two Moons | 👤 👤 👤 |
| The Cay | 👤 👤 👤 👤 |

## Super Savers

Investigate coupon savings with this real-world graphing activity! In advance, cut out a supply of coupons from magazines and newspapers. Next, divide students into groups of four or five, giving each group 20–25 coupons. Each group sorts its coupons into categories similar to the ones shown. Then the group tallies the total savings in each category and creates a bar graph displaying the data. Invite each group to share its graph with the class. If desired, create a class graph to show which category offered the most savings.

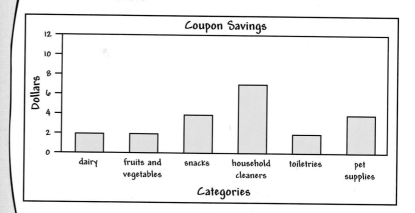

## It Takes Heart

Students will really put their hearts into this line graph activity. On a Monday, pair students and have each pair draw a frequency table like the one shown. Next, give the pair a jump rope and a stopwatch or access to a clock with a second hand. One partner jumps rope for a minute while her partner counts the number of successful jumps she completes in one minute. The student who jumped takes her pulse for six seconds and multiplies the number by ten to find her heart rate. She records her number of jumps and her heart rate on the frequency table and then the partners switch roles. Have students repeat the activity each day for the remainder of the week. On the last day, each student creates two line graphs, one displaying her jump rope data and one displaying her heart rate data. Invite student pairs to share their graphs to compare their results with other students.

| Day | Student 1 | | Student 2 | |
|---|---|---|---|---|
| | Jumps per Minute | Heart Rate | Jumps per Minute | Heart Rate |
| | | | | |
| | | | | |
| | | | | |
| | | | | |
| | | | | |

# Dream Day in the Sun

Tap into students' imaginations with this dreamy circle graph activity! In advance, make a class supply of the circle graph pattern below. Next, have students imagine that for one day the sun will shine for 24 hours. Have each child list on a sheet of paper how he would spend each hour of this special day. Explain that the sky's the limit and money is no object. Give each child a copy of the pattern and a sheet of yellow construction paper. Have him use the pattern to create a circle graph showing how he would spend his day. Then have him cut out his graph and glue it to a sun shape cut from the construction paper. Post students' completed graphs on a board titled "My Dream Day in the Sun."

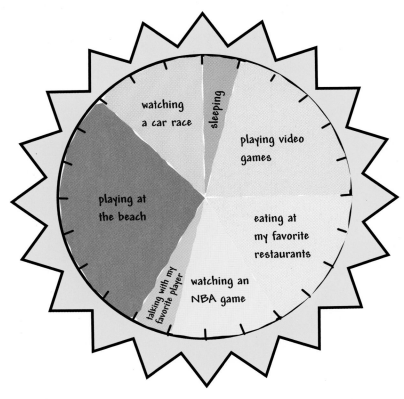

## Circle Graph Pattern
Use with "Dream Day in the Sun" above.

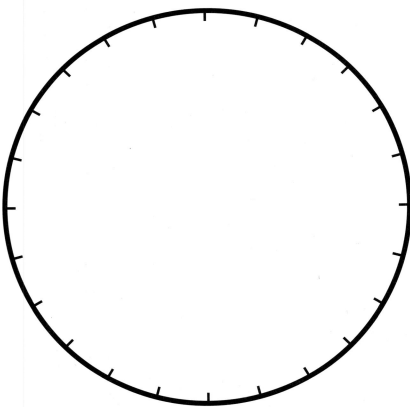

Name _____

Date _____

# Super Sale

Tammy and Trent had a yard sale to earn money for a family trip. The results of their sale are listed below. Decide which graph would best display each set of data. Then create the graph in the space given. Don't forget to title each graph and add labels.

| Sales | |
|---|---|
| **Type** | **Number Sold** |
| toys | 13 |
| books | 17 |
| CDs | 7 |
| arts and crafts | 12 |
| sports equipment | 10 |

| Customers | |
|---|---|
| **Day** | **Number** |
| Monday | 5 |
| Tuesday | 7 |
| Wednesday | 12 |
| Thursday | 10 |
| Friday | 18 |

| Hours Worked | |
|---|---|
| **Day** | **Time** |
| 1 | 1:30 |
| 2 | 2:00 |
| 3 | 1:00 |
| 4 | 2:00 |
| 5 | 2:30 |

Line graph title: _____

Bar graph title: _____

Pictograph title: _____

# Mean, Median, Mode, and Range

## "Graph-ic" Introduction

This hands-on line plot models how to find the mean, median, mode, and range. Divide your class into groups of four, giving each group a cup three-fourths full of O-shaped cereal, a large spoon, and four sticky notes. Instruct each group member, in turn, to scoop out a spoonful of cereal, count the number of pieces on the spoon, and record the number on a sticky note.

Next, draw a line on the board and have the student with the lowest recorded number place his note on the left end of the line and the student with the highest recorded number place his note on the right end of the line. Explain that these two numbers represent the *range* in the data. Have the remaining students plot their notes along the line in order, stacking repeated numbers as shown. Point out that the *mode* is the number in the tallest column. Then show students how to count in from each end to find the middle, or *median*, number. Finally, guide students to add all the numbers and divide the sum by the total number of sticky notes to find the average, or *mean*, number of pieces in a spoonful of cereal.

For even more practice, give each group a supply of sticky notes and have them repeat the exercise, scooping a predetermined number of spoonfuls and plotting the results on their own graphs. Allow each group to share its findings with the class.

range = 10
mode = 8
median = 11.5
mean = 10.7

| | | | | | | | | | | | |
|---|---|---|---|---|---|---|---|---|---|---|---|
| | 8 | | | | | | | | | | |
| | 8 | | 10 | | | | | | | | |
| | 8 | 9 | 10 | 11 | | | | | | | |
| | 8 | 9 | 10 | 11 | 11.5 | | | 13 | 14 | | |
| 7 | 8 | 9 | 10 | 11 | 11.5 | 12 | 13 | 14 | 14.5 | 17 | |

# Not Your Average Relay

All your students need to play this averaging relay race is the classroom board. Divide students into groups of four. Assign each group a section of the board and instruct its members to line up, one behind the other, in front of it. As you read aloud a series of four to eight numbers, have the first child in each line record the numbers in a column in her group's section of the board. When she is finished, she passes her chalk to the second person in line. This child adds the numbers and passes her chalk to the third child, who divides the sum by the number of numbers in the column to find the average. The chalk is then passed to the last child in line, who checks the division by multiplying. The first team to arrive at the correct answer earns a point. Repeat for ten rounds, having students rotate through the tasks. The group with the most points at the end of the game is the winner. For even more fun, try making it a silent relay. That's right, no talking!

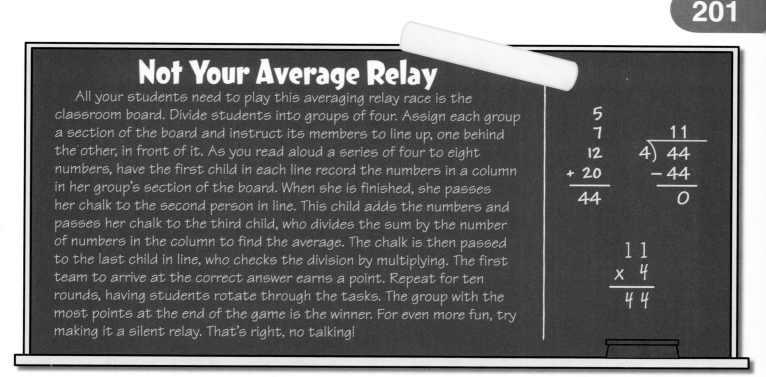

$$
\begin{array}{r}
5 \\
7 \\
12 \\
+\ 20 \\
\hline
44
\end{array}
\qquad
\begin{array}{r}
11 \\
4\overline{)\ 44} \\
-\ 44 \\
\hline
0
\end{array}
$$

$$
\begin{array}{r}
11 \\
\times\ 4 \\
\hline
44
\end{array}
$$

## Sweet Stem-and-Leaf Plots

Sweeten your study of mean, median, mode, and range with this fun stem-and-leaf plot. Fill a clean baby food jar with small candies. (Be sure to count and secretly record the number of pieces the jar holds.) Allow each child to get a good view of the jar; then distribute blank slips of paper. Have each child estimate how many candies are in the jar and then write his estimate and name on the paper slip. Collect the slips and write each estimate on the board. Then, as a class, use the information to create a stem-and-leaf plot. Next, have each student find the mean, median, mode, and range of the graph's data. Verify students' answers before revealing the actual number of candies in the jar and naming which student made the best estimate. If desired, divide the jar of candies among your students, giving the best estimator any leftovers. Repeat for several days using different candies or jars.

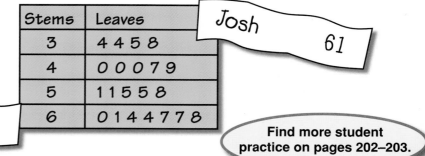

Josh 61

Cory 35

Sarah 47

| Stems | Leaves |
|-------|---------|
| 3 | 4 4 5 8 |
| 4 | 0 0 0 7 9 |
| 5 | 1 1 5 5 8 |
| 6 | 0 1 4 4 7 7 8 |

**Find more student practice on pages 202–203.**

Name _____

Date _____

202

## Looking for Clues

Detective Guess N. Check has a new mystery to solve! Help him by filling in the numbers below. Show your work in the notebook.

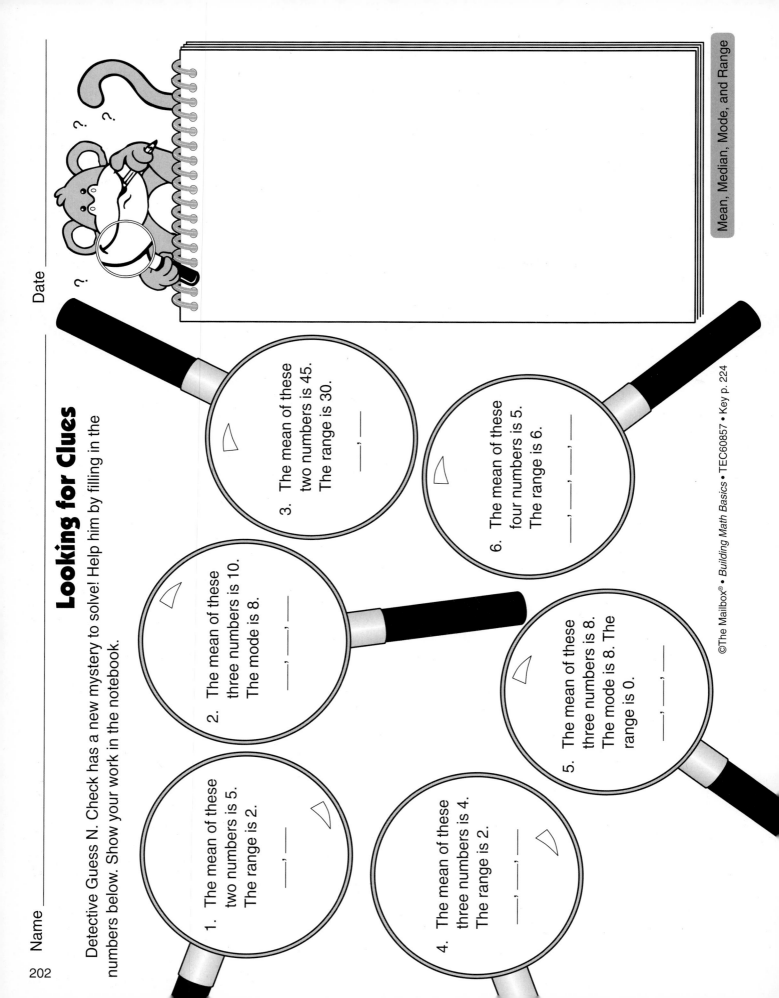

1. The mean of these two numbers is 5. The range is 2.

   ____, ____

2. The mean of these three numbers is 10. The mode is 8.

   ____, ____, ____

3. The mean of these two numbers is 45. The range is 30.

   ____, ____

4. The mean of these three numbers is 4. The range is 2.

   ____, ____, ____

5. The mean of these three numbers is 8. The mode is 8. The range is 0.

   ____, ____, ____

6. The mean of these four numbers is 5. The range is 6.

   ____, ____, ____, ____

©The Mailbox® • *Building Math Basics* • TEC60857 • Key p. 224

Mean, Median, Mode, and Range

Name _____  Date _____

# Winged Statistics

Find the mean, median, mode, and range of each butterfly's set of numbers below.

10  6  6  8  6  9

1. mean   = _____
   mode   = _____
   median = _____
   range  = _____

25  22  15  13  10  7  13

2. mean   = _____
   mode   = _____
   median = _____
   range  = _____

46  44  39  40  44  61  58  56

3. mean   = _____
   mode   = _____
   median = _____
   range  = _____

104  111  119  106  104  104

4. mean   = _____
   mode   = _____
   median = _____
   range  = _____

316  291  316  276  311  315  275

5. mean   = _____
   mode   = _____
   median = _____
   range  = _____

# Probability

## Probable Rewards

Explore probability with an activity that doubles as a student motivational tool. Fill a container with 60 jelly beans (or pom-poms) of one color, 20 of a second color, 15 of a third color, and 5 of a fourth color. Tell students that each color represents a prize, such as a sticker, popcorn, candy, or free time. Further explain that each student will choose a jelly bean and get the matching prize. Next, lead students to identify the possible outcomes and determine which ones are most likely and least likely to happen. Have each student predict the color he will choose and record students' predictions in a frequency table. Then shake the container and have each student draw a jelly bean without peeking. Record the results in another row of the frequency table and then discuss the findings. Finally, give each student his prize. Afterward, refill the jelly bean container and use it as a motivational tool by allowing well-behaved students to pick a prize!

## Counting the Combinations

Introduce some tasty combinations with this hands-on group activity. Divide students into groups, giving each group scissors, lined paper, and an old magazine containing pictures of food. Direct each group to cut out three pictures each of main dishes, side dishes, and desserts. Ask each group to predict how many different meal combinations it can make, with each meal including only one item from each category *(27)*. Next, instruct each group to arrange and rearrange its pictures to find all the possible combinations. Instruct the group to record its combinations in an organized list and count the total number. Follow up by modeling how to determine the total number of combinations by simply multiplying the number of items in each set *(3 x 3 x 3 = 27)*.

| Main Dish | Side Dish | Dessert |
|-----------|-----------|---------|
| hamburger | corn | pie |
| hamburger | corn | strawberries |
| hamburger | corn | ice cream |
| hamburger | pasta | pie |
| hamburger | pasta | strawberries |
| hamburger | pasta | ice cream |
| hamburger | fries | pie |
| hamburger | fries | strawberries |
| hamburger | fries | ice cream |
| fish | corn | pie |
| fish | corn | strawberries |

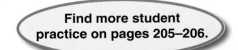

**Find more student practice on pages 205–206.**

Name _____

Date _____

# What a Catch!

Follow the directions in the net. Then answer the questions.

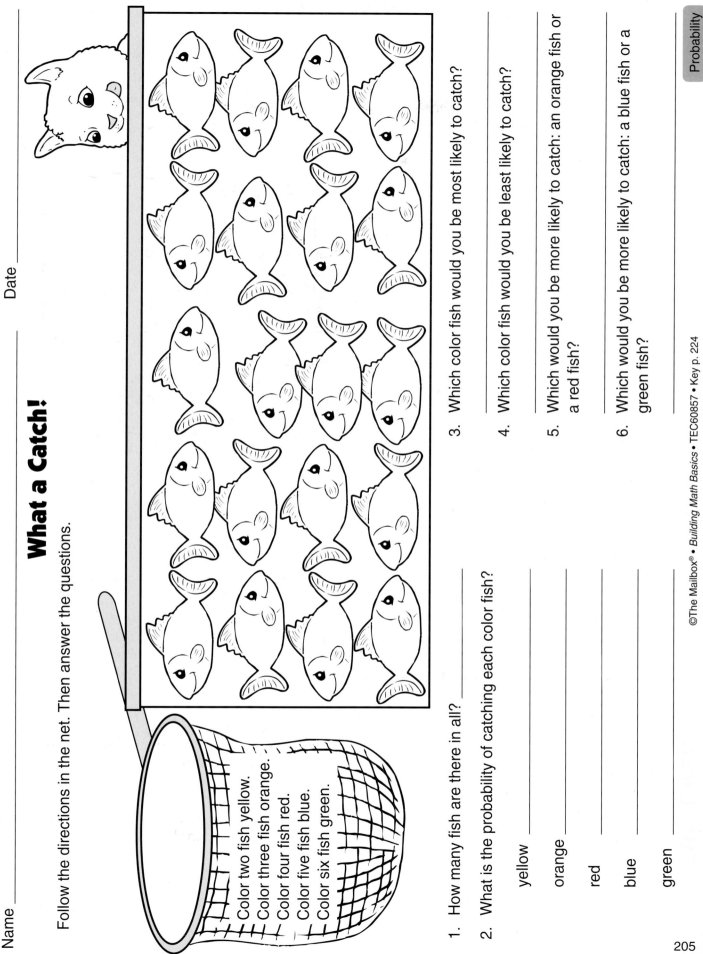

Color two fish yellow.
Color three fish orange.
Color four fish red.
Color five fish blue.
Color six fish green.

1. How many fish are there in all? _____

2. What is the probability of catching each color fish?

yellow _____

orange _____

red _____

blue _____

green _____

3. Which color fish would you be most likely to catch? _____

4. Which color fish would you be least likely to catch? _____

5. Which would you be more likely to catch: an orange fish or a red fish? _____

6. Which would you be more likely to catch: a blue fish or a green fish? _____

Probability

Name ___Ava Croce___    Date _____

# Cool Combinations

Gail wants to make 12 ice-cream feature flavors. Each feature flavor will have one ice-cream flavor, one mix-in, and one topping. Finish the tree diagram to figure out the possible combinations. Then write each new feature on the line. The first one has been done for you.

**Ice-Cream Flavors**

vanilla (V)
chocolate (C)
strawberry (S)

**Mix-Ins**

cookie dough (CD)
peanut butter (PB)

**Toppings**

sprinkles (S)
fudge (F)

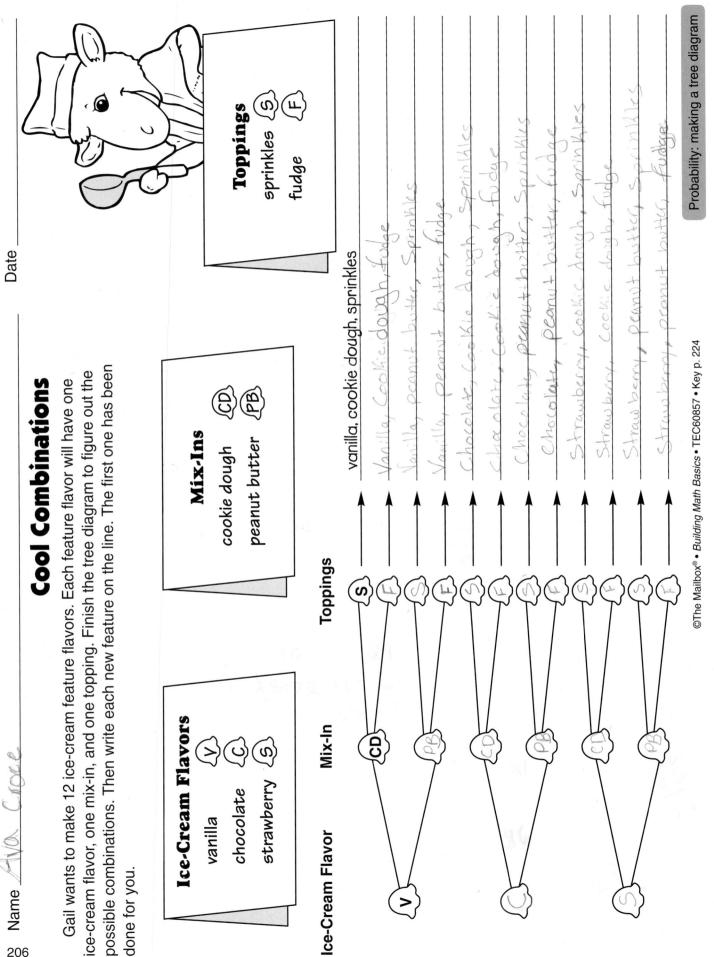

**Ice-Cream Flavor**    **Mix-In**    **Toppings**

vanilla, cookie dough, sprinkles
Vanilla, Cookie dough, fudge
Vanilla, Peanut butter, Sprinkles
Vanilla, Peanut butter, fudge
Chocolate, cookie dough, sprinkles
chocolate, cookie dough, fudge
Chocolate, peanut butter, Sprinkles
Chocolate, peanut butter, fudge
Strawberry, cookie dough, sprinkles
Strawberry, cookie dough, fudge
Strawberry, Peanut butter, sprinkles
Strawberry, peanut butter, fudge

Probability: making a tree diagram

# Input-Output Tables

## The Exit Game

Playing this simple game will provide plenty of practice with input-output tables! Pair students; then give each duo a deck of cards and a die. Instruct the partners to create a gameboard on paper, as shown (but without the numbers), and to stack their cards facedown in two piles: one for face cards and aces, one for number cards. Explain that each player will try to guess the rule of his partner's input-output table and that face cards or aces will determine the operation to use: ace—addition, jack—subtraction, queen—multiplication, king—division. Guide students through three rounds using the steps shown. Then declare the partner with more points the winner. For a greater challenge, have students draw two face cards or aces and roll the die twice to create a two-step rule!

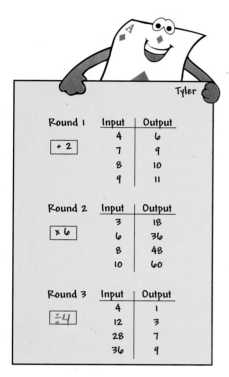

Tyler

| Round 1 | Input | Output |
|---|---|---|
| + 2 | 4 | 6 |
|  | 7 | 9 |
|  | 8 | 10 |
|  | 9 | 11 |

| Round 2 | Input | Output |
|---|---|---|
| x 6 | 3 | 18 |
|  | 6 | 36 |
|  | 8 | 48 |
|  | 10 | 60 |

| Round 3 | Input | Output |
|---|---|---|
| ÷ 4 | 4 | 1 |
|  | 12 | 3 |
|  | 28 | 7 |
|  | 36 | 9 |

**To play:**

1. Draw four number cards and one face card or ace. Record the four numbers in the output column for division or subtraction and the input column for multiplication or addition.
2. Take turns secretly rolling the die to determine the number by which to add, subtract, multiply, or divide.
3. Complete your table. Say, "Exit," when you are finished.
4. Trade papers with your partner. Guess the rule represented by the numbers in her table. Write the rule in the box and return the paper.
5. Award your partner five points if her guess is correct. If not, reveal the correct rule.

## Cereal Designs

Give your next lesson on input-output tables a "cereal-ously" new look! Give each child a 12" x 18" sheet of light-colored paper, a marker, glue, and a handful of same-shaped cereal pieces, such as Os or squares. Direct the student to start a pattern by gluing one cereal piece to the sheet and labeling the action "Step 1." Next, have her decide how many cereal pieces to add to the first piece to create a design. Instruct her to add the pieces, glue them, and label the design "Step 2." Have her continue adding that number of cereal pieces until she has completed five steps. Then direct her to draw a chart at the bottom of the sheet, as shown, fill in the information for Steps 1–5, and then do the math to complete Steps 6–10 on the chart. Have her also add to the paper a sentence that explains her design's pattern. While she shares her design with the class, have her ask the following questions: How many cereal pieces would I need to complete Step 25? Step 100? What fun!

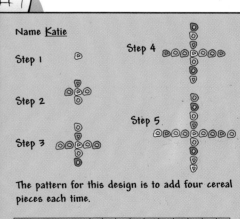

Name Katie

Step 1

Step 2

Step 3

Step 4

Step 5

The pattern for this design is to add four cereal pieces each time.

| Step Number | 1 | 2 | 3 | 4 | 5 | 6 | 7 | 8 | 9 | 10 |
|---|---|---|---|---|---|---|---|---|---|---|
| Cereal Pieces | 1 | 5 | 9 | 13 | 17 | 21 | 25 | 29 | 33 | 37 |

**Find more student practice on pages 208–209.**

Name __Ava Croce__    Date _____

# Unlock the Safes!

Help Callie and her friends win $100 from the Keep It Safe Company! Open each safe below by using the rules to find the missing numbers in each table. Then write the numbers in the blanks in order from least to greatest. Good luck!

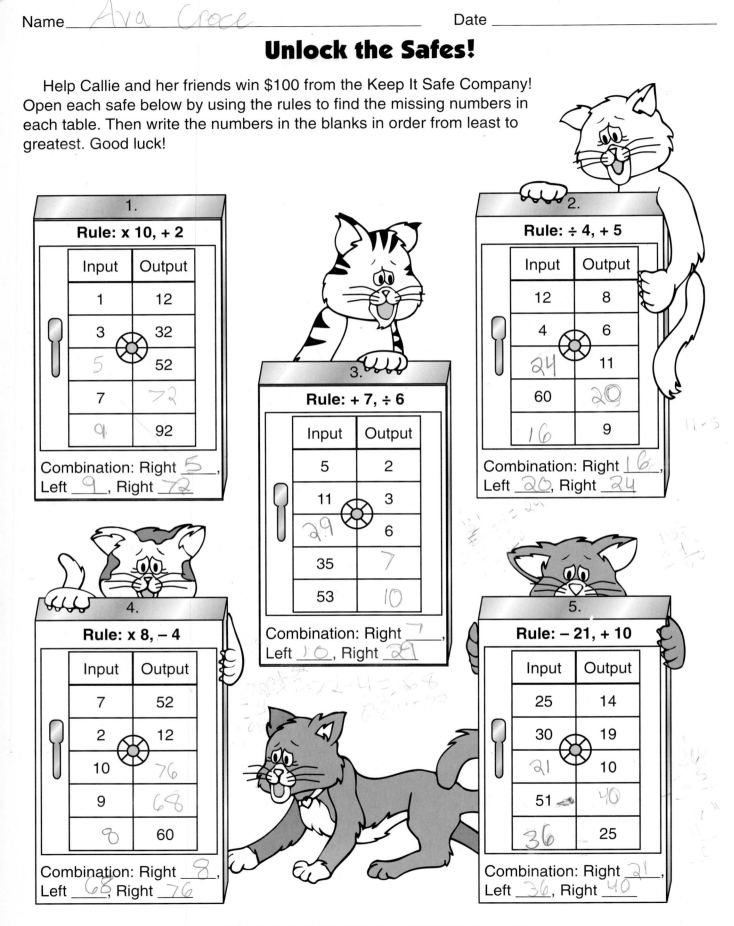

**1.**

**Rule: x 10, + 2**

| Input | Output |
|-------|--------|
| 1 | 12 |
| 3 | 32 |
| 5 | 52 |
| 7 | 72 |
| 9 | 92 |

Combination: Right _5_, Left _9_, Right _72_

**2.**

**Rule: ÷ 4, + 5**

| Input | Output |
|-------|--------|
| 12 | 8 |
| 4 | 6 |
| 24 | 11 |
| 60 | 20 |
| 16 | 9 |

Combination: Right _16_, Left _20_, Right _24_

**3.**

**Rule: + 7, ÷ 6**

| Input | Output |
|-------|--------|
| 5 | 2 |
| 11 | 3 |
| 29 | 6 |
| 35 | 7 |
| 53 | 10 |

Combination: Right _7_, Left _10_, Right _29_

**4.**

**Rule: x 8, − 4**

| Input | Output |
|-------|--------|
| 7 | 52 |
| 2 | 12 |
| 10 | 76 |
| 9 | 68 |
| 8 | 60 |

Combination: Right _8_, Left _68_, Right _76_

**5.**

**Rule: − 21, + 10**

| Input | Output |
|-------|--------|
| 25 | 14 |
| 30 | 19 |
| 21 | 10 |
| 51 | 40 |
| 36 | 25 |

Combination: Right _21_, Left _36_, Right _40_

Name **Ava Croce**　　　　　　　　　　　Date _____

# Keeping Out the Wolf

These smart piggies built houses that kept out that pesky wolf! What two-step rules did they use? Use their hints to help you write the missing numbers and the rule. Then answer the question.

**Add first. Then multiply!**

**1. Petey's House**

| Input | Output |
|-------|--------|
| 11 | 28 |
| 14 | 34 |
| 17 | a. 40 |
| 19 | b. 44 |

c. The rule is ___+3×2___

d. If the input is 100, the output will be __206__.

**Divide first. Then add!**

**2. Paulie's House**

| Input | Output |
|-------|--------|
| 100 | a. 15 |
| 200 | 25 |
| 300 | 35 |
| 400 | b. 45 |

c. The rule is ___÷10+5___

d. If the input is 10, the output will be __5__.

**Divide first. Then add!**

**3. Petunia's House**

| Input | Output |
|-------|--------|
| 33 | a. 4 |
| 55 | 6 |
| 66 | 7 |
| 132 | b. 13 |

c. The rule is ___÷11+1___

d. If the input is 77, the output will be __8__.

**Multiply first. Then subtract!**

**4. Patty's House**

| Input | Output |
|-------|--------|
| 7 | 82 |
| 8 | a. 94 |
| 9 | b. 106 |
| 10 | 118 |

c. The rule is ___×12−2___

d. If the input is 20, the output will be __238__.

20×12=240−2

# Geometric and Number Patterns

## The Daily Number

Follow this weekly plan to give students daily practice with number patterns.

**Day 1:** Display a number pattern that begins with the number 1 (see the box below for number pattern ideas). Direct students to continue the pattern and describe its rule.

**Day 2:** Divide students into groups. Have each group create a pattern that starts with the number 2 and uses the same rule as the pattern from day 1.

**Day 3:** Display a new number pattern that starts with the number 3 and uses a different rule.

**Day 4:** Direct each group of students to create a pattern that starts with the number 4 and uses the same rule as the pattern from day 3.

**Day 5:** Challenge each student to make up his own pattern that starts with the number 5 and uses a different rule than any other day. Have each student switch patterns with a classmate and then identify the rule and continue the pattern.

For ongoing practice, continue this plan each week, challenging students with increasingly complex patterns.

---

**Pattern Ideas**

Add a constant number.

Multiply by a constant number.

Add numbers following a pattern (for example, add 1, add 2, add 3…).

Add a number and then subtract a different number (for example, add 2, subtract 1).

---

# Challenge Boxes

This easy-to-set-up activity puts a new twist on working with number patterns. Create two number patterns and randomly write inside a box drawn on the board all the numbers making up each pattern. (See the example.) Challenge students to re-create both patterns using each number in the box one time. Encourage students who correctly re-create the patterns to prepare a challenge box to be featured on another day.

15     19     5

23     17

20

21     10

**Patterns**

5, 10, 15, 20 (add 5)

17, 19, 21, 23 (add 2)

# Paint Swatch Patterns

Set up this colorful center for students to practice number or geometric patterns. In advance, collect a supply of paint color swatches. Number each swatch and program its blocks with a pattern like the one shown. Record on an index card each swatch's number and its pattern solution. Place the index cards in an envelope at the center. Also stock the center with lined paper. As each student visits the center, he chooses a pattern swatch, analyzes the pattern, and continues it for four places on lined paper. The student checks his answers before choosing another swatch. If desired, stock the center with blank paint swatches and allow each student who correctly identifies and continues five pattern swatches to create a new pattern and its answer card to add to the center.

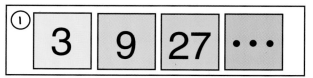

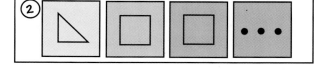

## Centered on Snakes!

These sneaky snakes will help squeeze in a bit more geometric patterning practice. Cut 12" x 18" sheets of light-colored construction paper into four equal 18-inch strips. Give each student one strip, scissors, and markers or crayons. Have each student trim her strip to resemble a snake. Then direct her to create a geometric pattern on her snake, stopping when half of the snake is decorated. Collect the completed snakes, laminate each one, and place them at a center along with wipe-off markers in the same colors as the patterns on the snakes. A student visiting the center selects a snake and uses the wipe-off markers to complete the pattern. "Sssimply" sensational!

# Bubbly Patterns

Complete each pattern on the bubbles. Then cut
out each fish and glue it under the matching bubbles.

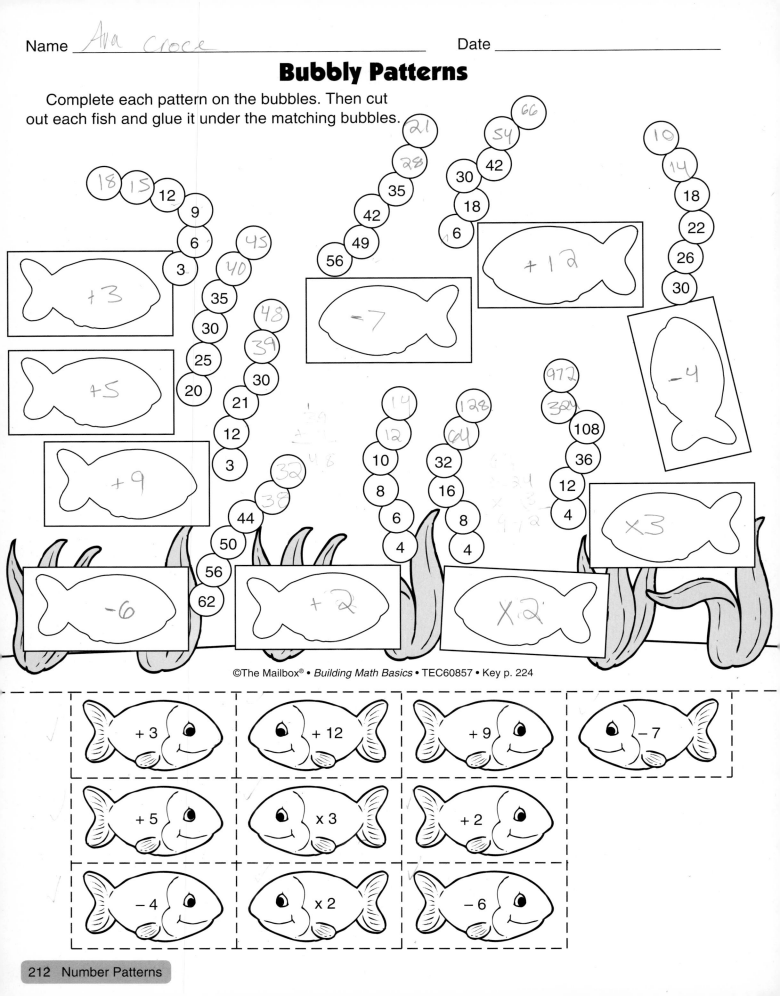

©The Mailbox® • *Building Math Basics* • TEC60857 • Key p. 224

# Leaping Patterns

Study each frog's pattern. Help each frog leap to its lily pad. Show the way by coloring the blocks that continue each pattern. Use the color given below each frog for its path.

**Color Green**    **Color Orange**    **Color Blue**

# Answer Keys

**Page 9**

15,500—Lily
33,486—Lisa
6,073,008—Laura
4,900,019—Lee
441,076—Leah
6,035,500—Libby
34,221—Lola
835,075—Lucy
4,002,707—Lynn
6,010,501—Lois
44,985—Lacy
18,970—Lori
33,333—Liz
836,014—Linda
18,059—LeAnn

**Page 10**

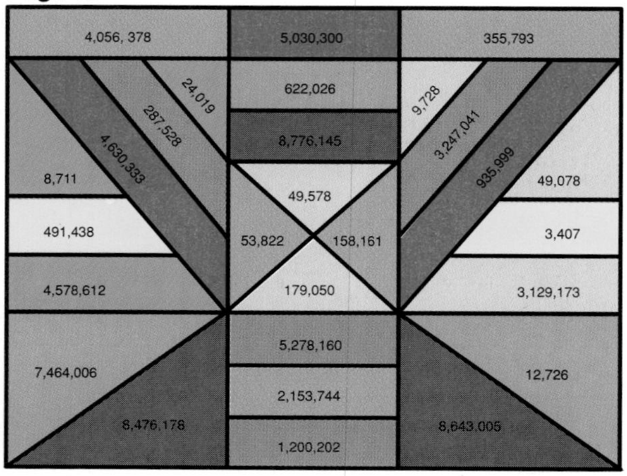

4,056, 378
5,030,300
355,793
622,026
8,776,145
24,019
287,528
4,630,333
9,728
3,247,041
935,999
8,711
49,578
49,078
491,438
53,822
158,161
3,407
4,578,612
179,050
3,129,173
5,278,160
7,464,006
12,726
2,153,744
8,476,178
8,643,005
1,200,202


**Page 11**

| | | | |
|---|---|---|---|
| 1. < | 6. < | 11. < | 16. < |
| 2. > | 7. > | 12. > | 17. < |
| 3. > | 8. > | 13. > | 18. > |
| 4. < | 9. > | 14. < | 19. < |
| 5. > | 10. < | 15. > | 20. > |

**Page 14**

1. $\frac{1}{2}$, 5
   $\frac{1}{2}$, 4
   $\frac{1}{2}$, 6
2. $\frac{2}{5}$, 4
   $\frac{3}{4}$, 6
   $\frac{3}{4}$, 9
3. $\frac{10}{10}$, 10
   $\frac{1}{4}$, 2
   $\frac{3}{4}$, 9
4. $\frac{1}{10}$, 1
   $\frac{8}{8}$, 8
   $\frac{1}{4}$, 3

**Page 15**

yellow, $\frac{1}{4}$ = 0.250, 25%, 0.25, $\frac{3}{12}$, $\frac{2}{8}$
blue, $\frac{3}{4}$ = 0.75, $\frac{6}{8}$, $\frac{15}{20}$, 75%, $\frac{12}{16}$
green, $\frac{1}{2}$ = 50%, $\frac{4}{8}$, $\frac{7}{14}$, $\frac{5}{10}$, 0.50, $\frac{3}{6}$, $\frac{6}{12}$
red, $\frac{1}{5}$ = $\frac{3}{15}$, 0.2, 20%, $\frac{4}{20}$

**Page 16**

$\frac{1}{5}$, 0.2, 20%
$\frac{1}{2}$, 0.5, 50%
$\frac{1}{4}$, 0.25, 25%
$\frac{3}{4}$, 0.75, 75%
E. 25%
O. 75%
T. $\frac{3}{4}$
K. 50%
A. 0.5
L. 20%
Y. $\frac{1}{4}$
They can't TAKE A "YOLK"!

**Page 17**

Some answers may be simplified.

1. $\frac{3}{4}$ 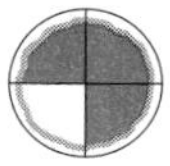
2. $\frac{3}{10}$ 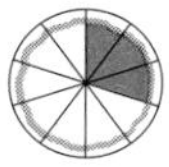
3. $\frac{9}{12}$ 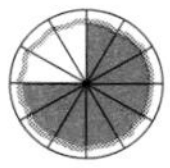
4. $\frac{4}{10}$ 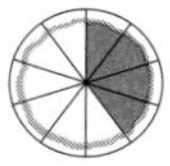
5. $\frac{2}{8}$ 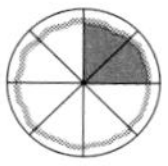
6. $\frac{1}{2}$ 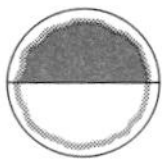
7. $\frac{5}{10}$ 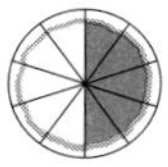
8. $\frac{8}{10}$ 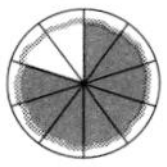
9. $\frac{1}{5}$ 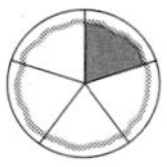
10. Pilar

**Page 20**

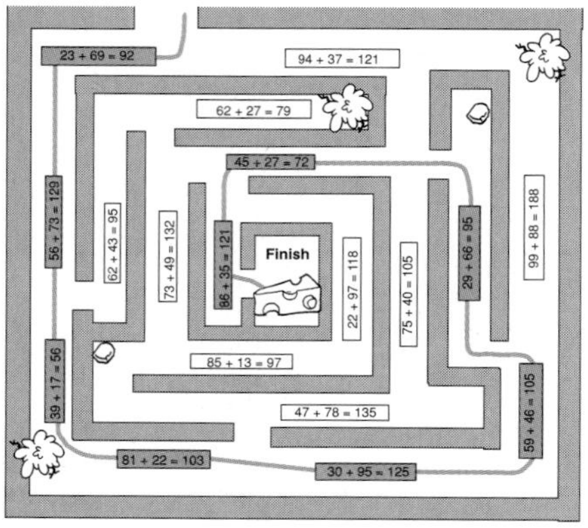

23 + 69 = 92
94 + 37 = 121
62 + 27 = 79
45 + 27 = 72
56 + 73 = 129
62 + 43 = 95
73 + 49 = 132
86 + 35 = 121
Finish
22 + 97 = 118
75 + 40 = 105
29 + 66 = 95
99 + 88 = 188
39 + 17 = 56
85 + 13 = 97
47 + 78 = 135
59 + 46 = 105
81 + 22 = 103
30 + 95 = 125


**Page 21**

1. 639 + 23**2** = 871
2. 1**5**7 + 951 = 1,108
3. 47**6** + 642 = **1,1**18
4. 532 + 18**7** = 719
5. 420 + **425** = 845
6. **7**04 + 3**0**6 = 1,01**0**
7. 3**7**5 + **5**4**3** = 918
8. 41**8** + 4**8**5 = 903
9. **8**88 + 5**1**6 = 1,40**4**
10. 5**5**7 + **6**6**0** = 1,217
11. 29**8** + **9**26 = 1,2**2**4
12. 876 + 5**4**3 = 1,**4**1**9**
13. 251 + **1**8**9** = 4**4**0
14. 17**6** + **7**27 = 9**0**3
15. 5**55** + **7**58 = 1,313

**Page 22**

E. 1,121
B. 3,190
M. 1,329
E. 2,873
Y. 1,335
F. 1,829
E. 1,410
A. 2,821
E. 2,998

I can't "BE-LEAF" MY EYES!

**Page 23**

1. 1,062
2. 2,103
3. 3,048
4. 876
5. 641
6. 1,182
7. 217
8. 7,911
9. 126
10. 6,177
11. 731
12. 1,291
13. 1,003
14. 3,034
15. 421

**Page 25**

1. yes
2. yes
3. $22
4. $46
5. $99

**Page 28**

T. 67
N. 42
J. 30
A. 81
H. 14
G. 20
O. 12
U. 6
I. 15
C. 11
R. 82
D. 10
S. 21
M. 23
W. 22
E. 2
P. 13
Q. 52
B. 16
L. 45

ONCE—BECAUSE THEN IT'S A WHOLE NEW EQUATION!

## Page 29
1. 50
2. 20
3. 40
4. 60
5. 10
6. 100
7. 300
8. 600
9. 200
10. 400
11. 500
12. 700
13. 7,000
14. 3,000
15. 1,000
16. 5,000

## Page 30
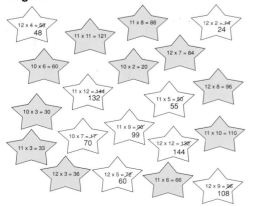

## Page 31

## Page 32
1. 8,741
2. 7,717
3. 7,717; 7,608
4. 6,673
5. 6,673; 4,192
6. 4,192; 3,685
7. 3,497
8. 3,497; 3,451
9. 3,451; 3,060
10. 2,386
11. 2,386; 1,852
12. 1,852; 935
13. 679
14. 679, 295
15. 295, 77

## Page 33
1. 776
2. 1,100
3. a. 135, b. 59, c. They picked up more bags in both June and August.
4. 172
5. 348

## Page 35
Giraffe: 7, 72, 20, 18
Elephant: 12, 12, 25, 10
Ostrich: 40, 70, 48
Koala: 32, 24
Lion: 30, 35
Gorilla: 20

## Page 36

## Page 37
1. 27
2. 77
3. 40
4. 66
5. 12
6. 24
7. 36
8. 80
9. 15
10. 60
11. 42
12. 56
13. 108
14. 32
15. 0
16. 20
17. 54
18. 64
19. 44
20. 48
21. 28
22. 25
23. 70
24. 45
25. 144

THEY JUST WING IT!

## Page 38
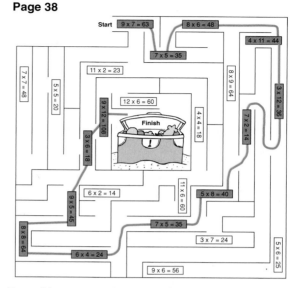

## Page 41
1. 160
2. 456
3. 192
4. 444
5. 69
6. 765
7. 184
8. 430
9. 1,124
10. 8,388
11. 2,700
12. 3.843
13. 5,936
14. 654
15. 1,950
16. 3,192
17. 2,505
18. 1,710
19. 2,948
20. 7,856

## Page 42
1. 2,989
2. 4,615
3. 6,336
4. 3,796
5. 6,460
6. 1,008
7. 3,276
8. 3,486
9. 3,599
10. 2,310
11. 1,323
12. 3,600
13. 3,337
14. 1,248
15. 3,120

## Page 43
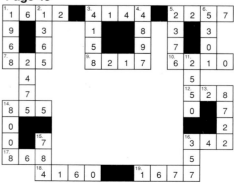

## Page 44

A. 7,112  E. 16,391  O. 72,270
Y. 17,800  T. 12,432  W. 29,412
N. 12,512  R. 54,675  C. 50,183
I. 19,133  B. 76,636  D. 22,572

IN "WEB–STER'S" DICTIONARY!

## Page 45

| | | | |
|---|---|---|---|
| 31,804 | 31,814 | 32,124 | **31,824** |
| 56,286 | 54,286 | **56,277** | 55,197 |
| 45,258 | 41,358 | **44,352** | 42,352 |
| 77,808 | **77,088** | 76,186 | 77,188 |
| **259,791** | 259,790 | 259,781 | 258,790 |
| 397,621 | **397,712** | 395,712 | 396,718 |
| 55,710 | 55,719 | **55,720** | 56,717 |
| 84,086 | 83,080 | 85,085 | **84,045** |
| 101,752 | 100,765 | **101,745** | 103,752 |
| 153,778 | **151,578** | 152,046 | 151,529 |
| **337,636** | 337,366 | 337,663 | 337,633 |
| 601,982 | **602,982** | 602,988 | 602,987 |

Moose on the Loose · Moose Magic · Alvin's Antlers · Canada Is the Coolest

## Page 46

1. 384
2. 10,088
3. 75,600
4. 336
5. 2.100
6. 916
7. 408
8. 690

## Page 48

E. 4  Y. 7  O. 8  H. 0
O. 8  D. 5  T. 6  I. 9
I. 9  Y. 7  R. 3  W. 1
Y. 7  R. 3  N. 2
T. 6  T. 6  D. 5

THEY'RE DOIN' THE TWIST

## Page 49

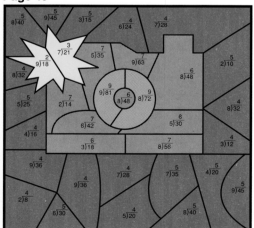

## Page 50

H. 1  C. 10  S. 12  H. 1
S. 12  I. 7  N. 8  O. 5
L. 6  N. 8  I. 7  B. 9
B. 9  U. 11  E. 2  I. 7
E. 2  D. 4  E. 2  C. 10
O. 5  A. 3  L. 6  A. 3

BECAUSE HE HAD A HOLE IN ONE!

## Page 51

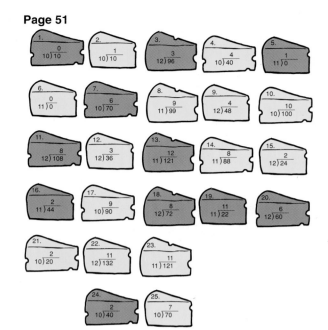

## Page 54

62 ÷ 14, 60 ÷ 10, 6
96 ÷ 9, 100 ÷ 10, 10
192 ÷ 8, 200 ÷ 10, 20
288 ÷ 22, 300 ÷ 20, 15
763 ÷ 18, 800 ÷ 20, 40

554 ÷ 263, 600 ÷ 300, 2
852 ÷ 27, 900 ÷ 30, 30
387 ÷ 53, 400 ÷ 50, 8
477 ÷ 16, 500 ÷ 20, 25
725 ÷ 97, 700 ÷ 100, 7

## Page 55

1. 43, D
2. 32, F
3. 30, S
4. 37, A
5. 28, N
6. 35, I
7. 29, Y
8. 18, B
9. 31, S
10. 34, X

SIX DAYS

## Page 56

1. 98 ÷ 7 = 14
2. 798 ÷ 19 = 42
3. 198 ÷ 9 = 22
4. 560 ÷ 16 = 35
5. 188 ÷ 4 = 47
6. 693 ÷ 21 = 33
7. 184 ÷ 8 = 23
8. 800 ÷ 20 = 40
9. 138 ÷ 3 = 46
10. 312 ÷ 12 = 26

Curly won first place.

## Page 57

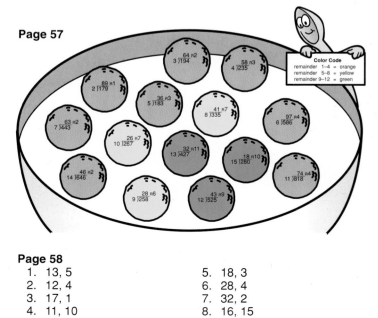

## Page 58

1. 13, 5
2. 12, 4
3. 17, 1
4. 11, 10
5. 18, 3
6. 28, 4
7. 32, 2
8. 16, 15

## Page 59

N. 52 R9
S. 60 R8
E. 24 R3
G. 32 R8
H. 41 R5
D. 53 R3
L. 494 R1
U. 29 R2
A. 152 R3
R. 141 R4

HER RED SUNGLASSES

## Page 64

E. $\frac{4}{9}$
Z. $\frac{4}{5}$
A. $\frac{2}{3}$
D. $\frac{5}{8}$
L. $\frac{3}{4}$
R. $\frac{3}{8}$
Y. $\frac{5}{12}$
N. $\frac{7}{10}$
S. $\frac{2}{5}$
O. $\frac{1}{2}$
B. $\frac{5}{6}$
M. $\frac{1}{4}$

ONE REALLY EMBARRASSED ZEBRA

## Page 65

B. $\frac{3}{5} < \frac{1}{3}$  >
A. $\frac{3}{5} > \frac{3}{10}$
E. $\frac{3}{16} = \frac{1}{8}$  >
N. $\frac{2}{3} < \frac{3}{4}$
E. $\frac{7}{20} < \frac{9}{10}$
S. $\frac{2}{3} > \frac{4}{6}$  =

R. $\frac{2}{4} = \frac{1}{2}$
P. $\frac{6}{7} > \frac{9}{10}$  <
V. $\frac{4}{5} = \frac{20}{25}$
A. $\frac{5}{6} = \frac{10}{18}$  >
O. $\frac{3}{8} < \frac{7}{10}$
U. $\frac{3}{4} > \frac{3}{5}$

S. $\frac{1}{5} < \frac{4}{10}$
T. $\frac{2}{3} > \frac{4}{5}$  <
R. $\frac{7}{9} > \frac{2}{5}$
K. $\frac{3}{4} < \frac{2}{5}$  >
E. $\frac{2}{5} = \frac{8}{20}$
X. $\frac{2}{9} < \frac{4}{5}$

A NERVOUS "REX"!

## Page 66

Duke's Bowls
$\frac{1}{2} = \frac{3}{6}, \frac{5}{10}$
$\frac{3}{4} = \frac{15}{20}, \frac{21}{28}$
$\frac{2}{3} = \frac{14}{21}, \frac{8}{12}$
$\frac{1}{4} = \frac{4}{16}, \frac{5}{20}$
$\frac{1}{5} = \frac{3}{15}, \frac{2}{10}$

Elfie's Bowls
$\frac{1}{9} = \frac{2}{18}, \frac{3}{27}$
$\frac{5}{8} = \frac{10}{16}, \frac{15}{24}$
$\frac{4}{5} = \frac{16}{20}, \frac{8}{10}$
$\frac{1}{3} = \frac{2}{6}, \frac{6}{18}$
$\frac{1}{8} = \frac{2}{16}, \frac{3}{24}$

## Page 67

1. $2\frac{3}{4}$
2. $3\frac{2}{7}$
3. $4\frac{1}{6}$
4. $3\frac{1}{3}$
5. $5\frac{3}{7}$
6. $1\frac{7}{8}$
7. $6\frac{4}{5}$
8. $4\frac{5}{6}$
9. $\frac{14}{3}$
10. $\frac{13}{2}$
11. $\frac{23}{10}$
12. $\frac{27}{8}$
13. $\frac{13}{9}$
14. $\frac{27}{5}$
15. $\frac{13}{8}$
16. $\frac{51}{8}$

## Page 70

1. $\frac{1}{2}$
2. $\frac{2}{3}$
3. $\frac{6}{7}$
4. $\frac{1}{4}$
5. $\frac{8}{9}$
6. $\frac{4}{5}$
7. $\frac{5}{6}$
8. $\frac{1}{3}$
9. $\frac{2}{9}$
10. $\frac{7}{10}$

"STABLE" TENNIS!

## Page 71

1. $\frac{1}{10} + \frac{3}{10}$
2. $\frac{4}{5} + \frac{1}{5}$
3. $\frac{7}{8} + \frac{2}{5}$
4. $\frac{1}{3} + \frac{1}{4}$
5. $\frac{1}{5} + \frac{7}{8}$
6. $\frac{8}{15} + \frac{8}{9}$
7. $\frac{1}{11} + \frac{5}{11}$
8. $\frac{6}{7} + \frac{1}{4}$
9. $\frac{3}{4} + \frac{1}{5}$
10. $\frac{5}{12} + \frac{1}{7}$
11. $\frac{5}{12} + \frac{7}{8}$
12. $\frac{13}{15} + \frac{5}{8}$

## Page 72

1. $1\frac{1}{4}$
2. $1\frac{1}{2}$
3. $1\frac{3}{8}$
4. $\frac{7}{12}$
5. $\frac{19}{20}$
6. $1\frac{1}{9}$
7. $\frac{9}{14}$
8. $\frac{11}{16}$
9. $\frac{1}{3}$
10. $\frac{13}{18}$
11. $\frac{3}{4}$
12. $\frac{13}{15}$

HIS BREATH

## Page 73

1. $4\frac{1}{2}$
2. $6\frac{2}{3}$
3. 8
4. $6\frac{2}{3}$
5. $2\frac{3}{4}$
6. 8
7. $4\frac{1}{2}$
8. $2\frac{3}{4}$
9. $6\frac{2}{3}$
10. $2\frac{3}{4}$
11. $4\frac{1}{2}$
12. 8
13. $6\frac{2}{3}$
14. $2\frac{3}{4}$
15. $4\frac{1}{2}$
16. 8
17. 8
18. $6\frac{2}{3}$
19. $2\frac{3}{4}$
20. $4\frac{1}{2}$

## Page 74

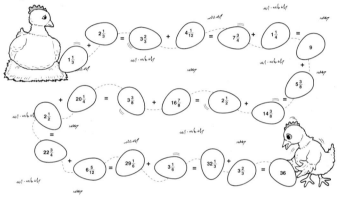

## Page 75

1. $5\frac{1}{2}$
2. $46\frac{1}{4}$
3. $5\frac{3}{8}$
4. $3\frac{1}{8}$
5. $7\frac{1}{4}$
6. $2\frac{1}{3}$

## Page 78

1. $\frac{1}{8}$
2. $\frac{1}{2}$
3. $\frac{1}{5}$
4. $\frac{5}{27}$
5. $\frac{1}{6}$
6. $\frac{1}{3}$
7. $\frac{7}{15}$
8. $\frac{3}{16}$
9. $\frac{1}{2}$
10. $\frac{1}{3}$
11. $\frac{6}{11}$
12. $\frac{9}{14}$
13. $\frac{1}{10}$
14. $\frac{5}{21}$
15. $\frac{3}{17}$

## Page 79

1. $\frac{1}{4}$
2. $\frac{1}{2}$
3. $\frac{1}{5}$
4. $\frac{1}{3}$
5. $\frac{1}{4}$
6. $\frac{1}{3}$
7. $\frac{1}{5}$
8. $\frac{1}{4}$
9. $\frac{1}{2}$
10. $\frac{1}{2}$
11. $\frac{1}{5}$
12. $\frac{1}{3}$

## Page 80

1. $\frac{1}{2}$
2. 0
3. 0
4. $\frac{1}{2}$
5. 0
6. 0
7. $\frac{1}{2}$
8. 0
9. $\frac{1}{2}$
10. $\frac{1}{2}$
11. 0
12. $\frac{1}{2}$

**Page 81**

**Page 82**

| | | | |
|---|---|---|---|
| $5\frac{2}{5}$ | $4\frac{9}{10}$ | $4\frac{1}{10}$ | $5\frac{1}{10}$ |
| $1\frac{2}{9}$ | $2\frac{5}{9}$ | $2\frac{2}{9}$ | $2\frac{3}{9}$ |
| $2\frac{4}{5}$ | $3\frac{5}{10}$ | $3\frac{1}{2}$ | $2\frac{8}{10}$ |
| $9\frac{6}{12}$ | $8\frac{5}{6}$ | $8\frac{1}{2}$ | $9\frac{5}{12}$ |
| $3\frac{3}{12}$ | $2\frac{1}{2}$ | $2\frac{11}{12}$ | $3\frac{11}{12}$ |
| $8\frac{2}{16}$ | $8\frac{13}{16}$ | $7\frac{3}{16}$ | $7\frac{13}{16}$ |
| $5\frac{1}{3}$ | $4\frac{4}{15}$ | $4\frac{1}{3}$ | $5\frac{1}{3}$ |
| $9\frac{2}{18}$ | $8\frac{5}{6}$ | $9\frac{1}{3}$ | $8\frac{2}{3}$ |
| $21\frac{14}{24}$ | $20\frac{7}{12}$ | $20\frac{17}{24}$ | $21\frac{7}{12}$ |
| $7\frac{4}{12}$ | $6\frac{11}{12}$ | $7\frac{1}{3}$ | $6\frac{3}{4}$ |
| $2\frac{1}{2}$ | $2\frac{13}{30}$ | $3\frac{1}{3}$ | $3\frac{17}{30}$ |
| $6\frac{1}{2}$ | $7\frac{5}{7}$ | $6\frac{3}{7}$ | $7\frac{1}{2}$ |

Seashell Beach

**Page 83**

1. $\frac{11}{21}$
2. $\frac{1}{12}$
3. $\frac{7}{20}$
4. $6\frac{5}{8}$
5. $3\frac{3}{5}$
6. $\frac{5}{12}$
7. $\frac{7}{10}$
8. $7\frac{2}{5}$

**Page 86**

1. $\frac{2}{12}$ or $\frac{1}{6}$, $\frac{2}{6}$ or $\frac{1}{3}$
   Cracker B is bigger.

2. $\frac{2}{6}$ or $\frac{1}{3}$, $\frac{1}{6}$
   Cracker C is bigger.

3. $\frac{1}{12}$, $\frac{1}{10}$
   Cracker F is bigger.

4. $\frac{2}{10}$ or $\frac{1}{5}$, $\frac{1}{16}$
   Cracker G is bigger.

**Page 87**

1. $\frac{1}{2} \times \frac{3}{4} = \frac{3}{8}$
2. $2\frac{2}{4} \times \frac{4}{9} = \frac{8}{36} = \frac{2}{9}$
3. $5\frac{3}{4} \times \frac{5}{6} = \frac{5}{24}$
4. $5\frac{5}{7} \times \frac{3}{4} = \frac{15}{21}$
5. $1\frac{1}{2} \times \frac{2}{5} = \frac{2}{10} = \frac{1}{5}$
6. $5\frac{3}{5} \times \frac{1}{6} = \frac{5}{30} = \frac{1}{6}$
7. $2\frac{3}{2} \times \frac{5}{3} = \frac{15}{4}$
8. $3\frac{5}{2} \times \frac{2}{3} = \frac{10}{18} = \frac{5}{9}$
9. $1\frac{1}{3} \times \frac{3}{7} = \frac{42}{3} = \frac{3}{2}$
10. $7\frac{4}{8} \times \frac{5}{7} = \frac{56}{3} = \frac{3}{9}$

Clyde is visiting **Clara**

$9 \times \frac{1}{3} = \underline{3}$   $\frac{2}{3} \times 6 = \underline{4}$

$8 \times \frac{3}{7} = \underline{3\frac{3}{7}}$   $15 \times \frac{2}{3} = \underline{10}$   $9 \times \frac{4}{7} = \underline{5\frac{1}{7}}$

$\frac{3}{4} \times 4 = \underline{3}$   $3 \times \frac{1}{2} = \underline{1\frac{1}{2}}$   $2 \times \frac{2}{3} = \underline{1\frac{1}{3}}$

$\frac{2}{3} \times 4 = \underline{2\frac{2}{3}}$   $5 \times \frac{2}{8} = \underline{1\frac{1}{4}}$   $6 \times \frac{3}{4} = \underline{4\frac{1}{2}}$   $\frac{4}{6} \times 4 = \underline{2\frac{2}{3}}$

**Color Code**
whole number answer = red
mixed number answer = green

**Page 89**

1. 18 lemons
2. 8 pictures
3. 12 butterfly eggs
4. 3 pieces of pizza
5. 25 envelopes
6. 14 parts
7. 30 inches
8. 16 tickets

**Page 90**

1. $\frac{2}{15}$
2. $1\frac{1}{9}$
3. 8
4. $\frac{63}{64}$
5. $\frac{1}{2}$
6. $\frac{1}{24}$
7. $\frac{9}{28}$
8. $\frac{1}{18}$
9. $\frac{3}{10}$
10. $\frac{26}{27}$
11. $1\frac{3}{10}$
12. $\frac{2}{9}$
13. $1\frac{1}{8}$
14. $3\frac{1}{4}$
15. $\frac{1}{6}$
16. $1\frac{1}{20}$

HE HAD JUST WASHED HIS HARE AND
COULDN'T DO A THING WITH IT!

**Page 91**

1. 9
2. $8\frac{1}{4}$
3. 2
4. $3\frac{1}{4}$
5. $4\frac{1}{2}$
6. $2\frac{5}{6}$
7. $7\frac{1}{2}$
8. 20
9. $7\frac{7}{8}$
10. $9\frac{3}{4}$
11. 55
12. $1\frac{1}{3}$
13. $23\frac{5}{6}$
14. $12\frac{2}{5}$
15. $6\frac{4}{5}$
16. $6\frac{2}{7}$
17. $6\frac{1}{2}$
18. $16\frac{7}{8}$
19. $4\frac{2}{5}$
20. $9\frac{3}{4}$

**Page 93**

1. $\frac{3}{4}$
2. $\frac{2}{3}$
3. $\frac{4}{5}$
4. $\frac{4}{5}$
5. $\frac{1}{2}$
6. $\frac{2}{3}$
7. $\frac{1}{2}$
8. $\frac{3}{4}$
9. $\frac{4}{5}$
10. $\frac{2}{3}$
11. $\frac{3}{4}$
12. $\frac{1}{2}$

Uncolored cars: 3, 4, and 9

**Page 94**

1. 18
2. 8
3. 15
4. $6\frac{2}{3}$
5. 4
6. 9
7. $19\frac{1}{4}$
8. $10\frac{4}{5}$
9. $7\frac{1}{2}$
10. $10\frac{2}{3}$
11. $11\frac{2}{3}$
12. 160

**Page 95**

1. 2, blue
2. $3\frac{3}{7}$, red
3. $3\frac{5}{9}$, red
4. $1\frac{1}{2}$, red
5. 3, blue
6. 4, blue
7. $2\frac{4}{7}$, red
8. 6, blue
9. $2\frac{2}{15}$, red
10. $1\frac{1}{4}$, red
11. $3\frac{11}{15}$, red
12. $1\frac{2}{25}$, red
13. $1\frac{4}{11}$, red
14. $1\frac{1}{34}$, red
15. 12, blue
16. $6\frac{3}{4}$, red
17. $3\frac{3}{5}$, red
18. $3\frac{7}{15}$, red

**Page 96**

1. $1\frac{1}{3}$
2. $1\frac{1}{2}$
3. $1\frac{9}{13}$
4. $1\frac{11}{15}$
5. $1\frac{11}{14}$
6. $3\frac{3}{4}$
7. $1\frac{13}{15}$
8. $1\frac{3}{7}$
9. $3\frac{3}{16}$
10. $3\frac{9}{20}$
11. $2\frac{17}{24}$
12. $1\frac{11}{27}$

She's a "CLOTHES-HOUND!"

**Page 97**

Estimated quotients will vary.

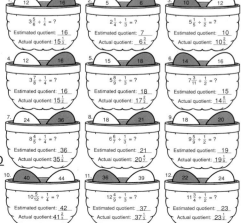

1. $3\frac{5}{6} \div \frac{1}{4} = ?$ Estimated quotient: 16   Actual quotient: $15\frac{1}{3}$
2. $2\frac{1}{4} \div \frac{1}{3} = ?$ Estimated quotient: 7   Actual quotient: $6\frac{3}{4}$
3. $5\frac{1}{5} \div \frac{1}{2} = ?$ Estimated quotient: 10   Actual quotient: $10\frac{2}{5}$
4. $3\frac{7}{11} \div \frac{1}{4} = ?$ Estimated quotient: 16   Actual quotient: $15\frac{1}{11}$
5. $5\frac{8}{9} \div \frac{1}{3} = ?$ Estimated quotient: 18   Actual quotient: $17\frac{2}{3}$
6. $7\frac{3}{11} \div \frac{1}{2} = ?$ Estimated quotient: 15   Actual quotient: $14\frac{6}{11}$
7. $8\frac{4}{5} \div \frac{1}{4} = ?$ Estimated quotient: 36   Actual quotient: $35\frac{1}{5}$
8. $6\frac{6}{7} \div \frac{1}{3} = ?$ Estimated quotient: 21   Actual quotient: $20\frac{4}{7}$
9. $9\frac{5}{9} \div \frac{1}{2} = ?$ Estimated quotient: 19   Actual quotient: $19\frac{1}{9}$
10. $10\frac{5}{12} \div \frac{1}{4} = ?$ Estimated quotient: 42   Actual quotient: $41\frac{2}{3}$
11. $12\frac{4}{9} \div \frac{1}{3} = ?$ Estimated quotient: 37   Actual quotient: $37\frac{1}{3}$
12. $11\frac{3}{4} \div \frac{1}{2} = ?$ Estimated quotient: 23   Actual quotient: $23\frac{1}{2}$

**Page 102**
1. E, J
2. A
3. A
4. E, H
5. I
6. C, E
7. H
8. A, I
9. G, J
10. None
11. B, D, J
12. D
13. C, F
14. None
15. B, D

**Page 104**
1. True
2. False
3. True
4. False
5. True
6. False
7. True
8. True
9. False
10. True

The new club member is
<u>BEN E. BEAVER</u>.

**Page 105**

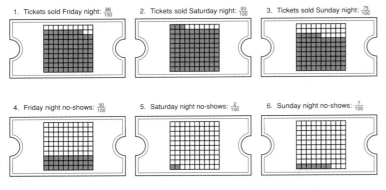

1. Tickets sold Friday night: $\frac{88}{100}$
2. Tickets sold Saturday night: $\frac{93}{100}$
3. Tickets sold Sunday night: $\frac{75}{100}$
4. Friday night no-shows: $\frac{30}{100}$
5. Saturday night no-shows: $\frac{2}{100}$
6. Sunday night no-shows: $\frac{7}{100}$

7. $\frac{33}{100}$  8. $\frac{61}{100}$  9. $\frac{1}{100}$  10. $1\frac{6}{100}$  11. $1\frac{43}{100}$  12. $1\frac{90}{100}$

**Page 108**

Color Code
0.1–5.0—blue
5.1–10.0—green
10.1–15.0—brown
15.1–20.0—yellow

**Page 103**
1. $1.00, red
2. $32.00, yellow
3. $8.00, red
4. $10.00, yellow
5. $5.00, red
6. $1.00, yellow
7. $50.00, red
8. $3.00, yellow
9. $25.00, red
10. $110.00, red
11. $60.00, yellow
12. $90.00, red
13. $78.00, yellow
14. $1,500.00, red

**Page 110**
Students should have colored M or P
for each problem.
1. $1.50
2. $1.40
3. B and C
4. less than $1.00
5. $4.06
6. $0.80
7. about $3.00
8. $3.93
9. D, E, G; A, C, E; or A, C, G
10. $7.70

**Page 109**
1. 24.6
2. 35.7
3. 13.3
4. 26.4
5. 28.4
6. 32.8
7. 9.7
8. 29.1
9. 27.6
10. 14.3
11. 32.2
12. 25.9
13. 19.4
14. 17.2
15. 44.8
16. 18.6

**Page 111**

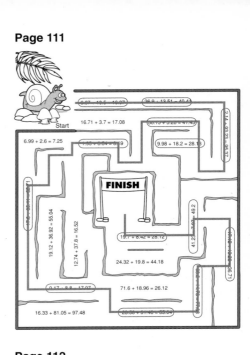

**Page 112**
A. 24.737
C. 15.298
D. 26.005
F. 16.737
I. 44.065
A. 15.780
N. 15.110
L. 54.908
R. 27.037
U. 34.488
T. 36.267
A. 65.061
S. 38.624

<u>A FRUIT SALAD</u>!

**Page 116**

## Page 117

| | | | | |
|---|---|---|---|---|
| $719.86 − 311.24 = $408.62 | $186.43 − 21.56 = $164.87 | $157.57 − 28.84 = $128.73 | $94.00 − 14.03 = $79.97 | $125.73 − 76.84 = $48.89 |
| $636.00 − 87.10 = $548.90 | $92.93 − 15.27 = $77.66 | $426.16 − 318.07 = $108.09 | $86.71 − 24.69 = $62.02 | $219.72 − 171.93 = $47.79 |
| $844.00 − 703.72 = $140.28 | $256.18 − 214.92 = $41.26 | $222.75 − 214.70 = $8.05 | $169.49 − 121.56 = $47.93 | $179.99 − 56.99 = $123.00 |
| $419.68 − 407.72 = $11.96 | $163.26 − 18.69 = $144.57 | $509.50 − 79.25 = $430.25 | | |
| $397.17 − 256.04 = $141.13 | $86.00 − 65.24 = $20.76 | $70.26 − 35.14 = $35.12 | | |

## Page 118

U. 2.078    O. 0.513    H. 0.474    M. 0.816
N. 1.489    C. 0.064    N. 0.078    T. 0.269
M. 0.949    O. 0.597    W. 1.019    W. 1.181

Let us MUNCH, and you WON'T MOW!

## Page 121

1. 3.6 oz.     6. 11.4 oz.
2. 5.6 oz.     7. 6.3 oz.
3. 14 oz.      8. 6.4 oz.
4. 7 oz.       9. 2.7 oz.
5. 16.5 oz.   10. 15.3 oz.

## Page 122

1. $13.44    4. $15.36    7. $9.60     10. $7.42
2. $18.50    5. $2.95     8. $14.85    11. $5.31
3. $7.92     6. $5.88     9. $23.10    12. $16.34

## Page 123

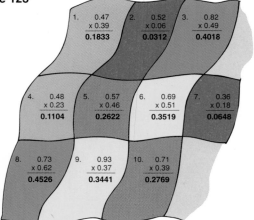

1. 0.47 × 0.39 = 0.1833
2. 0.52 × 0.06 = 0.0312
3. 0.82 × 0.49 = 0.4018
4. 0.48 × 0.23 = 0.1104
5. 0.57 × 0.46 = 0.2622
6. 0.69 × 0.51 = 0.3519
7. 0.36 × 0.18 = 0.0648
8. 0.73 × 0.62 = 0.4526
9. 0.93 × 0.37 = 0.3441
10. 0.71 × 0.39 = 0.2769

## Page 124

O. 1.02      L. 0.3421
I. 20.4      B. 8.32
C. 8.64      E. 0.255
T. 32.41     H. 0.14
E. 2.496     R. 1.92

THREE-BONE CHILI

## Page 127

1. 2.564     6. 2.314
2. 3.589     7. 1.358
3. 4.464     8. 5.263
4. 0.776     9. 4.215
5. 1.257    10. 5.214

| 5.263 | 6.014 | 1.358 | 13.581 | 0.776 |
|---|---|---|---|---|
| 3.589 | 4.464 | 4.215 | 1.135 | 2.564 |
| 2.314 | 2.440 | 5.214 | 52.141 | 1.257 |

## Page 128

1. 5        7. 3
2. 3        8. 0.6
3. 0.5      9. 0.6
4. 0.4     10. 0.7
5. 0.9     11. 0.4
6. 0.4     12. 0.3

The path ends at the super market.

## Page 129

A. 12       N. 200
B. 25       O. 700
E. 60       S. 4,700
H. 300      T. 4,500
I. 400      Z. 2,800
M. 600

THE AMAZON BASIN

## Page 130

1. $5.00     6. 2.39
2. 8         7. 1.75
3. 20        8. 8.25
4. 5         9. $3.39
5. 7        10. $31.00

UNDER THE BIRDHOUSE

## Page 133

1. P        7. N
2. L        8. E
3. A        9. V
4. Y       10. R
5. S       11. H
6. G       12. W

HE ALWAYS GAVE SNAPPY ANSWERS

## Page 134

Drawings may vary slightly. Possible answers include the following:

1.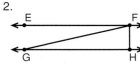
2.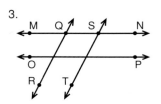
3.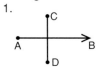
4.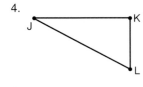
5.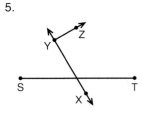

**Page 137**

acute angles: G, D H, K, E, L
obtuse angles: F, M, A, N, C
right angles: I, J, B, O

**Page 138**

1. 30°
2. 60°
3. 90°
4. 150°
5. 180°
6. 30°
7. 90°
8. 180°
9. 90°
10. 360°

**Page 141**

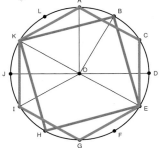

1. Gordie
2. Eddie and Connie
3. Annie and Freddie
4. Donnie
5. Eddie and Connie
6. Barnie
7. Annie
8. No one. Connie's and Eddie's diameters are the same length.
9. Drawings may vary.
10. Drawings may vary.

**Page 142**

1. thumbs-up
2. thumbs-down
3. thumbs-down
4. thumbs-up
5. thumbs-down
6. thumbs-up
7. thumbs-up
8. thumbs-down
9. thumbs-up
10. thumbs-down
11. 5.5 cm, square
12. 4 cm, hexagon

**Page 145**

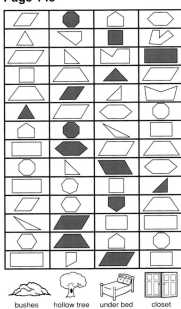

bushes    hollow tree    under bed    closet

**Page 146**

Rocky Rhombus Road
1. 4 sides
2. 2 sets of parallel sides
3. all sides are equal
4. 2 acute angles
5. 2 obtuse angles
6. parallelogram

Strawberry Square Sorbet
1. 4 sides
2. 2 sets of parallel sides
3. all sides are equal
4. 4 right angles
5. parallelogram

Toffee Trapezoid Crunch
1. 4 sides
2. 1 set of parallel sides
3. angles vary

Raspberry Rectangle
1. 4 sides
2. 2 sets of parallel sides
3. 4 right angles
4. 2 different sets of equal sides
5. parallelogram

**Page 149**

Cube: 6, 12, 8, $6.20
Square Pyramid: 5, 8, 5, $4.50
Octahedron: 8, 12, 6, $6.80
Triangular Pyramid: 4, 6, 4, $3.50
Rectangular Prism: 6, 12, 8, $6.20
Triangular Prism: 5, 9, 6, $4.85
Cylinder: 2, 0, 0, $0.80
Cone: 1, 0, 1, $0.50
Hexagonal Prism: 8, 18, 12, $8.90

**Page 150**

Cylinder: 2 circles, 1 rectangle
Cube: 6 squares
Rectangular Prism: 2 squares, 4 rectangles
Square Pyramid: 1 square, 4 triangles
Cone: 1 circle, 1 fan
Triangular Prism: 2 triangles, 3 rectangles
Octahedron: 8 triangles
Dodecahedron: 12 pentagons
The mystery shape is a <u>tetrahedron</u> (or triangular pyramid).

**Page 153**

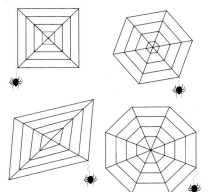

**Page 154**

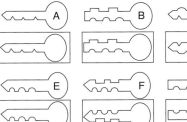

**Page 158**

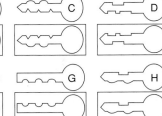
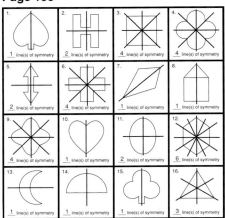

## Page 161

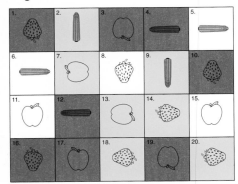

## Page 162

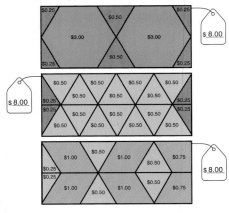

## Page 165

Designs and prices may vary. Possible designs include the following:

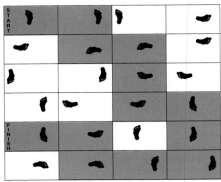

## Page 167

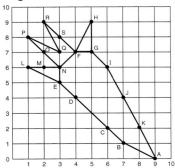

## Page 168

1. "HOPPY" DISCS!
2. PLAY HOPSCOTCH!
3. THEY HAVE "HARE" CONDITIONERS!

## Page 170

| Ribbon | Inches | Feet | Yards |
|---|---|---|---|
| Golden Goose | 36 | 3 | 1 |
| Robin Red | 72 | 6 | 2 |
| Bluebird Blue | 252 | 21 | 7 |
| Poodle Pink | 108 | 9 | 3 |
| Peacock Purple | 324 | 27 | 9 |
| Osprey Orange | 144 | 12 | 4 |

1. no
2. 24
3. 156
4. yellow: 4
   pink: 1
5. 27

## Page 171

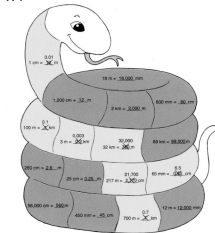

## Page 173

Problems 1, 3, 4, 6, 7, 10, and 12 should be colored.

2. 150
5. 256
8. 28
9. 140
11. 104

## Page 174

Room A: 7 inches
Room B: 10 inches
Room C: 8 inches
Room D: 8 inches
Room E: 7 inches
Room F: 5 inches
Room G: 10 inches
Room H: 8 inches
Room I: 5 inches
Room J: 8 inches

## Page 176

1. 14
2. 12
3. 14
4. 9
5. 14
6. 16
7. 16
8. 13
9. Answers will vary.

## Page 177

1. 77
2. 25
3. 108
4. 160
5. 56
6. 42
7. 96
8. 117

The total is 681 square yards.
Yes. Mel has 19 more square yards of carpet than he needs.

## Page 179

| Building | Radius | Diameter | Circumference |
|---|---|---|---|
| Library | 1.5 cm | 3 cm | 9.42 cm |
| Circle City Grille | 0.5 cm | 1 cm | 3.14 cm |
| Skate Park | 1 cm | 2 cm | 6.28 cm |
| Swim Center | 2 cm | 4 cm | 12.56 cm |
| Round About Market | 2.5 cm | 5 cm | 15.7 cm |

## Page 180
1. 81.64
2. 94.2
3. 37.68
4. 13
5. 7.5
6. 1.5

## Page 182
1. 0.525
2. 2.5
3. 7,800
4. 2,700
5. 0.45
6. 1,560
7. 7,000
8. 4,900
9. 0.685
10. 2,561
11. 6,500
12. 8.47

Number 8 should be colored red and number 9 should be colored blue.

## Page 183
1. 6 oz., 16
2. 8 oz., 1½
3. 20 oz., 64
4. 26 oz., 6
5. 42 oz., 80
6. 710 lb.; 2,000
7. 16 oz., 40
8. 14 oz., 3
9. 8 oz., 32
10. 1,000 lb.; 2

## Page 185
1. 594 cm³
2. 486 ft.³
3. 144 in.³
4. 105 cm³
5. 160 ft.³
6. 135 cm³
7. 216 cm³
8. 240 cm³
9. 100 in.³
10. 270 cm³

He wanted to <u>POP THE QUESTION</u>.

## Page 186
Boxes A, C, D, F, G, and J should be colored.
Box B: 495 in.³
Box E: 294 in.³
Box H: 660 in.³
Box I: 156 in.³

## Page 188
Numbers 1, 2, 5, 7, and 10 should be colored.
11. 350 mL
12. 100 mL
13. 2 L
14. 5 mL
15. 300 mL

## Page 189
1. 32
2. 2
3. 2
4. 64
5. 36
6. 16
7. 10
8. 10
9. 1
10. 208
11. 32
12. 6
13. 1
14. 2
15. 12

## Page 191
1. 72
2. 64, Down 8
3. 92, Up 28
4. 86, Down 6
5. 54, Down 32
6. 70, Up 16
7. 65, Down 5
8. 82, Up 17
9. 75, Down 7
10. 69, Down 6
11. 87, Up 18
12. 74, Down 13

## Page 192
1. 34, swimsuit
2. 22, shorts
3. 30, tank top
4. 8, jeans
5. -16, parka
6. -8, winter coat
7. 28, sandals
8. -8, sweater
9. 32, tank top
10. 4, long sleeves
11. 20, windbreaker
12. 12, jeans

## Page 195
1. 35 minutes
2. 3 hours and 5 minutes
3. 3 hours and 25 minutes
4. *Cow Capers*
5. 6 hours and 55 minutes
6. 1 hour and 30 minutes
7. 3:15 P.M.
8. 5 hours
9. *The Green, Green Grass*
10. 7 hours and 5 minutes

## Page 199

Answers may vary.

Pictograph title: **Customers**

| Day | Customers |
|-----|-----------|
| Monday | ♀ ♀ ♀ |
| Tuesday | ♀ ♀ ♀ ♀ |
| Wednesday | ♀ ♀ ♀ ♀ ♀ |
| Thursday | ♀ ♀ ♀ ♀ ♀ ♀ |
| Friday | ♀ ♀ ♀ ♀ ♀ ♀ ♀ |

Each ♀ = 2 customers

Bar graph title: **Sales**

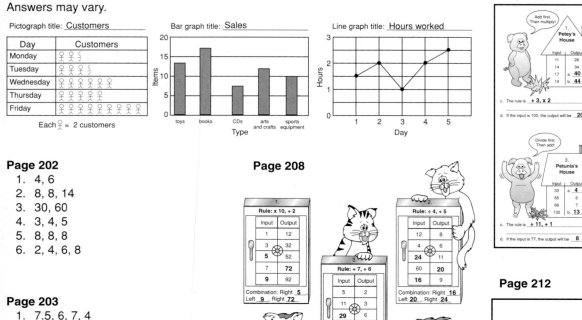

Line graph title: **Hours worked**

## Page 202

1. 4, 6
2. 8, 8, 14
3. 30, 60
4. 3, 4, 5
5. 8, 8, 8
6. 2, 4, 6, 8

## Page 203

1. 7.5, 6, 7, 4
2. 15, 13, 13, 18
3. 48.5, 44, 45, 22
4. 108, 104, 105, 15
5. 300, 316, 311, 41

## Page 205

1. 20
2. yellow: 2 out of 20
   orange: 3 out of 20
   red: 4 out of 20
   blue: 5 out of 20
   green: 6 out of 20
3. green
4. yellow
5. red
6. green

## Page 206

Order may vary.

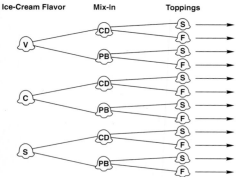

vanilla, cookie dough, sprinkles
vanilla, cookie dough, fudge
vanilla, peanut butter sprinkles
vanilla, peanut butter fudge
chocolate, cookie dough, sprinkles
chocolate, cookie dough, fudge
chocolate, peanut butter sprinkles
chocolate, peanut butter fudge
strawberry, cookie dough, sprinkles
strawberry, cookie dough, fudge
strawberry, peanut butter sprinkles
strawberry, peanut butter fudge

## Page 208

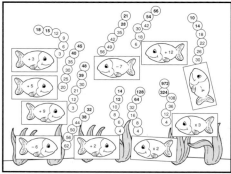

## Page 209

## Page 212

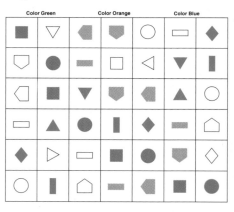

## Page 213

| Color Green | | Color Orange | | Color Blue | | |
|---|---|---|---|---|---|---|
| ■ | ▽ | ⬠ | ⬠ | ○ | ▭ | ◆ |
| ⬠ | ● | ▬ | □ | ◁ | ▼ | ▮ |
| ⬠ | ■ | ▼ | ⬠ | ◀ | ▲ | ○ |
| ▭ | ▲ | ● | ▮ | ◆ | ▬ | ⌂ |
| ◆ | ▷ | ▭ | ■ | ● | ⬠ | ◇ |
| ○ | ▮ | ⌂ | ▬ | ⬠ | ■ | ● |

224